Behind the Gates

Behind the Gates

Life, Security, and the Pursuit of Happiness in Fortress America

SETHA LOW

ROUTLEDGE NEW YORK AND LONDON

Published in 2004 by
Routledge
270 Madison Avenue
New York, NY 10016
www.routledge-ny.com

Published in Great Britain by
Routledge
2 Park Square
Milton Park, Abingdon,
Oxon OX14 4RN U.K.
www.routledge.co.uk

First Routlege hardback edition, 2003
First Routledge paperback edition, 2004

Library of Congress Cataloging-in-Publication Data

Low, Setha
    Behind the gates : Life, security, and the pursuit of happiness in fortress America / Setha Low.
        p. cm.
Includes bibliographical references and index.
ISBN 0–415–94438–4 (hbk) — ISBN 0-415-95041-4 (pbk)
    1. Gated communities—United States. 2. Community life—United States. I. Title.

HT169.59.U6 L69 2003
307'.0973—dc21   2002036620

FOR ALEXANDRA

CONTENTS

ACKNOWLEDGMENTS

Research depends on the contributions and cooperation of others. I am indebted to residents, builders, architects, sales managers, and real estate agents for their participation in this project. Even though I cannot thank them by name to maintain confidentiality, I am grateful for their willingness to share their stories and residential histories. As for my family, they have supported this endeavor from the beginning. My sister, Anna, my brother-in-law, Bob, and especially my niece, Alexandra, encouraged me every step of the way. Anna, also a college professor, even contributed a few lines of her own dialogue. My mother, Marilyn Rudley, clipped the *Los Angeles Times* diligently and found the article on the "fake" gated communities and many other newspaper references. And my husband, Joel Lefkowitz, was always there, as my companion in travel, photographer, editor, ideal reader, and friend *par excellence*.

Funding from the Wenner-Gren Foundation for Anthropological Research and from the Research Foundation of the City University of New York made this research project possible. I would like to thank Susan Malus, Maria Luisa Loeb, Maria Russo, Stephane Tonnelat, Kristin Koptiuch, Carole Browner, Ron Davidson, Ivelisse Rivera-

Bonilla, and Dana Taplin for their readings and discussions of the book. Peter Weiss suggested the title *Behind the Gates* in a spirited argument with friends, Gloria and Mike Levitas, while eating Mexican food in Watermill.

Colleagues also generously directed me to analyses that I might have missed. Gated community scholar Edward Blakely encouraged me to focus on the psychological aspects of living in gated communities, while Georgeanna Wilson-Doenges kept me up to date with her work in southern California. Catherine Silver offered social splitting as a way to understand residents' fear of others. Gabriella Modan pointed out ways to deepen my use of discourse analysis, and Kevin Birth asked me questions about the ethnic and gender composition of each community. John Van Sickle helped me write about Roman walls, and Richard Briffault and Evan McKenzie offered commentary and helpful suggestions on the legal aspects of private governance. Michael Newman and Katrina Van Valkenburgh brought the photographs of Kendell Geers, Cprints entitled "Suburbia," to my attention. Gary McDonogh sent me a copy of *Snow Crash*. And Dolores Hayden read the entire manuscript offering intellectual guidance, emotional support, and editorial clarification. I am grateful for their help.

I could not have completed this work without the contributions of my coresearchers—Elena Danaila, Andrew Kirby, Lynmari Benitez, and Mariana Diaz-Wionczek—who were graduate students at the time in the Ph.D. Program in Environmental Psychology at the Graduate Center of the City University of New York. Elena interviewed residents in Manor House, Long Island while Andrew completed the interviews in Pine Hills, Long Island and Waterview, New York. Mariana Diaz-Wionczek provided entry and interviewed residents in Mexico City, and joined Lynmari Benitez in translating and transcription. Suzanne Scheld, an anthropologist, and Laurel Wilson, a friend, also transcribed interviews and offered their counsel. Their participation at various times over the eight years I worked on this book added to the pleasure and excitement of discovery that are often difficult to sustain working alone on a long-term project.

Melissa Waitzman, Cindi Katz, and the members of the social theory seminar at the Graduate Center contributed insightful comments on the ideas presented in chapter 1. The gated community scholars who participated in the International Conference on Urban Governance, June 5 through 9, 2002 at the Institute of Geography, Johannes Gutenberg University in Mainz, Germany—Georg Glasz, Frantz Klaus, Chris Webster, Evan McKenzie, Richard Briffault, Dennis Judd, Renaud Le Goix, Tom Frazier, Stuart Robinson, David Parsons, Sarah Blandy, Jenny Dixon, and Michael Janoschka—contributed greatly to my thinking about the importance of private governance presented in chapters 1 and 9, and provided a global perspective on gating. Michael Janoschka also treated me to a tour of Berlin planned housing developments and expanded my knowledge of Latin American private cities. Jörg Plöger, a research assistant at University of Kiel in Germany, shared his data, photographs, and insights from his master thesis research on North Hills, Long Island gated communities.

Mary Jane Meeker and the Writer's Workshop in East Hampton, New York, offered suggestions that transformed the Prologue and many of the chapters and provided encouragement throughout the writing process; and with the help of Erica Duncan and the members of Herstory, I was able to integrate elements of memoir writing into the ethnography. Marjory Dressler came to the rescue with her computer graphics skills to create the illustrative house and street plans.

This book could not have been finished without the dedication of a great editor. Dave McBride offered the perfect balance of support and editing, asking the right questions, and finding solutions to countless problems. Nicole Ellis kept the book on schedule navigating the labyrinth of production. Liana Fredley provided meticulous copyediting, and Dutton and Sherman beautifully designed the book. My warmest thanks for all their hard work.

PROLOGUE

GROWING UP IN WEST LOS ANGELES

I don't know when I first became intrigued by gates and gated communities. Maybe it began because the only way to get to my childhood home was through two huge pillared arches onto a winding, fern-lined road that leads up and up to the top of the hill. Each twist and turn brings you closer to my house, but every fork in the road is a decision point. A random left or right brings you to another world, a different hill and a separate reality. Some hills are still rustic with crisscrossing fire roads and ranches, others are covered by suburban houses with ivy-carpeted front lawns and welcoming brick walkways, while most are graced by Mediterranean-style mansions where Hollywood movie stars live. My home was a two-story Georgian colonial on Somera Road, the last stop on the school bus—a dead-end street at the crest of a fifteen-hundred-foot rise where the ocean view is breathtaking on a smogless day.

If you turn right rather than left on Bellagio, you end up on Stradella Drive—a neighborhood of wealthy gated estates where my friend Dolly Smith lived. It is there, in front of the wrought-iron gates of Dolly's house that I lost my first friend. I am supposed to get off the bus with her to play until my mother comes to pick me up. I am quite young, six and in the second grade, so I barely understand. But her mother meets the bus outside the gate and says that I can't come in. I fiddle with the rick rack trim on my blue-and-white-checked uniform, knowing that everyone on the bus is watching. I ask Dolly what is going on. She says she doesn't understand either, but that I can't come in, and that her mother said we are not to play together anymore. I get back on the bus to go home.

My mother cannot make any sense of it. For a woman who knows everything, she has nothing to say. I always play with Dolly at school, but I have never been invited to her home.

At school the next day, I ask Dolly what happened, hidden so that no one can see us. All that she can tell me is that I am "low class."

"What does that mean?" I ask.

"I don't know," Dolly says, "my mother says that you're Jewish, and that I am not to play with you anymore."

I am puzzled and hurt. It is not clear what she is talking about. When I get home that evening, I tell my mother what Dolly said. I do not remember exactly what Mother tells me, but she makes light of it, and says not to pay any attention. She is relieved when I finally drop the subject.

I don't actually understand what transpired until many years later when my father takes us to Passover dinner after my parents' divorce. And it is not until I write this book that I become aware of how gates remain fixed in my memory. The gates of Dolly Smith's estate loom in my dreams.

Because of this early incident, gates for me became symbols of exclusion. Even though I did not understand at the time, I was rejected because I was "not like them," or "other." "Other" is always defined by historical period, geographical location, or social circumstances. When I was growing up, the Christian establishment that ruled Los Angeles was threatened by the increasing power and wealth of Jewish moguls in the motion picture industry.[1] During the 1950's, there was a war between the two groups for control of the best country clubs, neighborhoods, and other elite institutions. My story is a tiny offshoot of that political struggle. Its impact, however, was to teach me what it feels like to be excluded and feared. This experience contributed to my becoming a cultural anthropologist, someone who studies "others" in order to understand and bridge the differences between groups. And later it sparked my interest in the gated community phenomenon.

VISITING MY SISTER IN SAN ANTONIO

On our first visit to my sister's new home in San Antonio, Texas, my husband, Joel, and I are amazed to find two corral gates blocking the entrance to her development. I push an intercom button on the visitors' side. Getting no response, I hit the button repeatedly, finally rousing a disembodied voice that asks who we want to see. I shout Anna and Bob's last name. The entrance gate swings open, and we accelerate through onto a divided drive enclosed by a six-foot wall covered with bougainvillea and heavenly bamboo.

Once inside, large homes loom beside small vacant lots with "for sale" signs. The houses are mostly Southwestern stucco painted Santa Fe colors with terra-cotta tile roofs and a sprinkling of brick colonials with slate shingles and wood trim. Uniformly attractive, with neat lawns and matching foundation plantings, the street looks like a set from the movie *Pleasantville*. It is not just peaceful, wealthy, and secure, but unreal, like a doll's house or a planned development in Sim City.[2] Everything looks perfect.

Even before we see men playing golf, we are jolted by speed bumps announcing a right-of-way, and stop as two twelve-year-old kids cross in their shiny red golf cart. We drive up and park in front of an enormous Scottsdale-style house, seafoam green with a dark tile roof and a two-story glass entrance hall. Anna and my niece, Alexandra, stand dwarfed by the scale of the building. Tall and willowy with long straight hair, my twin in coloring, weight, and stature, but sexier, and with a wicked sense of humor, Anna looks like a country-western star in her favorite cowboy boots, blue jeans, and DKNY T-shirt. She rearranges Alexandra's hair as they wait to greet us.

"I am so glad you are finally here," Alexandra says, pulling away from her mother and throwing her small arms around my neck.

Wriggling out of her strong grasp, I stand back and look at her. She has grown since I last saw her, and now, as a six-year-old, she resembles us both, with her dark brown hair and eyes, long limbs, and athletic body. She takes my hand and starts dragging me toward the door. "Come and see my room."

Joel stands patiently, his face tilted upward, trying to catch a few rays, sun-starved by winter in New York. He fits right in, six foot two and lanky, in a polo shirt and black jeans, ready to enjoy the sunshine and tennis of Anna and Bob's new home. Only his hair is different, thick and curly, and his New York accent, which he exaggerates to tease Alexandra.

Anna turns to greet me. "I wanted to pick you up at the airport, but I had too much to do. How was the flight?" She risks a brief glance to see if I'm miffed about not being picked up. There is always some tension between us—a hypersensitivity to a tone of voice or manner of delivery that might signal disapproval or even rejection. I flash a reassuring smile. I know that she is pleased to see us, simply over-whelmed by having house guests.

"It's fine, we rented a car," Joel answers, hugging Anna for a moment. "Where's Bob?"

"He'll be home after tennis," Anna says. She starts to lift one of the suitcases, but Joel steps in and heaves both bags inside.

Inside, the bright sunshine filters through the closed shutters. My boot heels clatter on the marble floors and echo down the long hall-way. As I walk up the white carpeted stairs from the landing to the guest room, I see the green slate kitchen floor Anna had told me about. Everything is huge and out of scale, giving the impression that you have stepped into a five-star hotel complete with a guest suite, master bath, and walk-in closet. Each room is more spacious than the next, with tall windows, ten-foot ceilings, wide hallways, and long vistas from one part of the house to the other; on the second floor there's a view of the golf course and cottonwoods beyond. A stucco wall encircles the house, blocking views from the first floor.

The next morning I get up early to have a cup of tea. I go down-stairs to the kitchen and start water on a glowing glass-covered burner. Shimmering sunshine draws me to the window, through which I can see a brick patio with a wrought-iron table and chairs surrounded by a high wall. Imagining how pleasant it would be to sit outside, I unlock the French doors and slowly push them open. With no warning, a harsh wailing disrupts my tranquility. For a moment I panic, wondering what I have done, and then I realize it's the burglar alarm.

Anna comes running from her bedroom. "What are you trying to do?" She shuts off the alarm. "Trying to wake the neighbors and call the cops?"

"I wanted to enjoy the morning air," I protest. "It never occurred to me that you leave the alarm on when you're home. Why do you need it living in a gated community?"

"You don't understand," she says.

"You're right, I don't," I reply.

Bob, followed by Alexandra in her Snoopy nightgown and socks, comes running down the hallway.

"What happened? Did you get the alarm turned off? Did you call the company to tell them it's a false alarm?" Then turning and looking straight at me, his face serious, "What were you doing opening the door? What could you have been thinking?"

My niece takes hold of my hand, pulling me down so that she can whisper in my ear. "Don't worry," she confides. "They'll get over it. Just wait until they calm down to explain." I look into her wise, little face, and wonder if she has had a similar experience when opening a door to go out to play.

"I promise to be more careful," I say. As I walk back into the kitchen to finish making tea, I wonder about Bob's level of concern. He is uncomfortable when visiting us in Brooklyn, and didn't want to move from Washington, D.C., to another large city with a high crime rate. He lives in a gated development and sets the burglar alarm at night and when he leaves in the morning to protect his wife and child. But are the northern suburbs of San Antonio dangerous? Joel raised two children in Brooklyn, giving them free rein in New York City. He believes that children have to learn to be independent and defend themselves.

Later that day there is another incident. I cannot open the front door. Every door leading outside has a metal plate with a large keyhole and oval knob. When you turn the knob, nothing happens unless the lock is opened with a key. We have a similar lock on our glass-paneled front door in Brooklyn. It is to prevent someone from break-ing the glass, reaching in, and opening the door from inside. We keep a key hidden nearby in case of an emergency.

"Where is the key to the front door?" I ask, walking down the long hall to the bedroom where Anna is getting dressed. "I want to join Alex rollerblading," I add.

"I'll let you out, but you can't get in by yourself. I'm not sure when I'll be back." She looks harried. I know it is hard raising a child and working full time and I don't like disturbing her.

"Don't you have an extra key?" I ask.

"No, we don't want Alexandra to go out on her own," she explains.

"What are we supposed to do?" I say, trying to hide my frustration.

"I'll lend you my keys or be here to let you in," she answers.

I'm stunned. I feel trapped, claustrophobic, and uneasy, as if something dangerous is just outside the door. With a flash of insight, I realize I had these same feelings while working on an archaeologi-cal dig in El Salvador. The hacienda house and yard was surrounded by high walls capped with jagged broken bottles and barbed wire. Through my bedroom window, the glass fragments glittered like dag-gers in the tropical sun.

Ever since that visit I have been fascinated by why Anna wants to live behind gates and walls. She is the brash and adventuresome one: an outlaw, a rebel, and fiercely nonconformist. What is she doing liv-ing behind gates, with a guard who watches her coming and going on a video camera, regulated by a thick book of rules dictating everything from the color of her Christmas tree lights to the size of her trash can? Her reasons are complex, like those of most gated community resi-dents. The answer to this question is the subject of this book.

CHAPTER 1

Unlocking the Gated Community

FELICIA—"FEAR FLIGHT": SAFETY, COMMUNITY, AND FEAR OF OTHERS

I climb into Felicia's Volvo station wagon, carefully setting my tape recorder on the dashboard. Outside, the twisted junipers and gray-green cottonwoods of San Antonio flash by. The six-lane highway posts a seventy-mile-per-hour speed limit, but we are doing eighty. New gated developments with partially constructed houses and bulldozers leveling wild grass fields stretching as far as I can see suddenly disappear, leaving countryside that looks like it's been untouched for the past hundred years. The contrast between the small-town past and suburban present is demarcated as we speed north.

Felicia is a tall, thin woman in her mid-forties who sits straight upright in the driver's seat. Her long fingers clutch the steering wheel as she drives; she is telling me about her college and graduate degrees. Even with the amount of education she has accumulated, she decided to stay home to take care of her seven-year-old daughter. They moved from California because of her husband's job and the opportunity to have a more comfortable life with a bigger house. They now live on an attractive cul-de-sac in a two-story, four-thousand-square-foot Scottsdale model located within a gated subdivision on the northern edge of the city.

7

She is articulate and gets right to the point. When they were shopping for a house, school district and aesthetics were important considerations. In fact, she had some reservations about living in a gated community, including the fact that it only has one exit if there is a fire. But they were concerned for their child's safety, and now feel that it was a good choice because it allows her to go outside and play. As Felicia puts it, "We're in San Antonio, and I believe the whole country knows how many child-kidnappings we've had. . . . My husband would not ever allow her outside to play without direct adult supervision unless we were gated." It allows them the freedom to walk around the neighborhood at night, and their daughter and her friends from nongated neighborhoods are able to ride their bicycles safely.

Felicia, however, thinks it has a flip side in that it produces a false sense of safety. The guards aren't "Johnny-on-the-spot," and anybody who wants to could jump the gate. There's a perception of safety among residents that may not be real and could potentially leave one more vulnerable "if there was ever an attack." For instance, when she walks in the neighborhood, she does not look to see who is coming out of a driveway as she would on an open city street or in another suburban area. "You don't rely on your own resources so much," she explains.

Their development is made up of people who are retired and don't want to maintain large yards, or people who want to raise families in a more protected environment. There is a lot "fear flight," people who have moved in the last couple of years as the crime rate, or the reporting of the crime rate, has become such a prominent part of the news. She knows people who are building because they want to get out of their exclusive subdivisions that don't have gates; she mentions one family that was shopping for a house in the gated community because they had been robbed many times.

Their neighbors are upper middle and middle class, white, Christian, and, apart from one Jewish family, quite homogeneous—businessmen and doctors, with stay-at-home wives, many without college educations. On their street, they know everyone by sight and visit with neighbors who have children; but they no longer have a party when new people move in. The houses are "very nice," architecturally designed and custom built, and she worries that the new ones will not be as tasteful or beautiful.

Felicia feels safe inside the community, but expresses considerable anxiety about living in San Antonio:

When I leave the area entirely and go downtown [little laugh], I feel quite threatened just being out in normal urban areas, unrestricted urban areas. . . . Please let me explain. The north central part of this city [San Antonio], by and large, is middle class to upper-middle class. Period. There are very few pockets of poverty. Very few. And therefore if you go to any store, you will look around and most of the clientele will be middle class as you are yourself. So you're somewhat insulated. But if you go downtown, which is much more mixed, where everybody goes, I feel much more threatened.

Her daughter was four years old when they first moved, and I wonder about the psychological impact of moving from a rambling, unfenced Californian suburb to a gated community. Felicia says her daughter feels threatened when she sees poor people, because she hasn't had enough exposure:

We were driving next to a truck with some day laborers and equipment in the back, and we were stopped beside them at the light. She wanted to move because she was afraid those people were going to come and get her. They looked scary to her. I explained that they were workmen, they're the "backbone of our country," they're coming from work, you know, but . . .

So living in a secured enclave may heighten a child's fear of others. It's unclear, though, whether Felicia's observation reflects many children's experience of growing up in a gated community, or simply her daughter's idiosyncrasy and modeling of her mother's anxiety.

Felicia and her husband wanted to buy the nicest house in the best school district, while providing a safe environment for their daughter, one where they can be cloistered from any class differences. They consider the neighborhood "a real community" where you know your neighbors, although it is not as friendly as where they used to live. For them, the gated community provides a haven in a socially and culturally diverse world, offering a protected setting for their upper-middle-class lifestyle.

Desire for safety, security, community, and "niceness," as well as wanting to live near people like themselves because of a fear of "others" and of crime, is not unique to this family, but expressed by most residents living in gated communities. How they make sense of their new lives behind gates and walls, as well as the social consequences of their residential choices, are the subjects of this book. The emergence of a fortress mentality and its phenomenal success is surprising in the United States, where the majority of people live in open and unguarded neighborhoods. Thus, the rapid increase in the numbers of Americans moving to secured residential enclaves invites a more complex account of their motives and values. Like other middle-class Americans, residents of gated communities are looking for a place where they feel comfortable and secure, but this seemingly self-evident explanation reflects different underlying meanings and intentions. And collectively, their individual decisions are transforming the American dream of owning a suburban home in a close-knit community with easy access to nature into a vision that includes gates, walls, and guards.[1]

Based on eight years of ethnographic research in gated communities in New York City, suburban Long Island, New York, and San Antonio, Texas, I present the stories of residents' search for security, safety, and community in a globalizing world. Parents with children, young married couples, empty-nesters, singles, widows, and retirees recount the details of living in recently constructed gated developments. Their residential histories and daily experiences highlight the significance of this growing middle- and upper-middle-class lifestyle and the conflicting values embodied in its architecture.

One explanation for the gated community's popularity is that it materially and metaphorically incorporates otherwise conflicting, and in some cases polarized, social values that make up the moral terrain of middle-class life. For example, it reflects urban and suburban tensions in the United States regarding social class, race, and ethnicity and at the same time represents the perennial concern with creating community. The gated community's symbolic power rests on its ability to order personal and social experience.

Architectural symbols such as gates and walls also provide a rationale for the moral inconsistencies of everyday life. For instance, many residents want to feel safe in their homes and argue that walls and gates help keep out criminals; but gated communities are not safe than nongated suburban neighborhoods, where crime rates are already low.[2] Instead, the logic of the symbolism satisfies conventional middle-class understandings of the nature of criminal activity—"it makes it harder for them to get in"—and justifies the choice to live in a gated community in terms of its moral and physical consequences—"look at my friends who were randomly robbed living in a nongated development."

Living in a gated community represents a new version of the middle-class American dream precisely because it temporarily suppresses and masks, even denies and fuses, the inherent anxieties and conflicting social values of modern urban and suburban life. It transforms Americans' dilemma of how to protect themselves and their children from danger, crime, and unknown others while still perpetuating open, friendly neighborhoods and comfortable, safe homes. It reinforces the norms of a middle-class lifestyle in a historical period in which everyday events and news media exacerbate fears of violence and terrorism. Thus, residents cite their "need" for gated communities to provide a safe and secure home in the face of a lack of other societal alternatives.

Gated residential communities, however, intensify social segregation, racism, and exclusionary land use practices already in place in most of the United States, and raise a number of values conflicts for residents. For instance, residents acknowledge their misgivings about the possible false security provided by the gates and guards, but at the same time, even that false security satisfies their desire for emotional security associated with childhood and the neighborhoods where they grew up. Living in a gated development contributes to residents' sense of well-being, but comes at the price of maintaining private guards and gates as well as conforming to extensive homeowners association rules and regulations. Individual freedom and ease of access for residents must be limited in order to achieve greater privacy and social control for the community as a whole. These contradictions—which residents are aware of and talk about—provide an opportunity to understand the psychological and social meaning-making processes Americans use to order their lives.

DEFINING THE GATED COMMUNITY

A gated community is a residential development surrounded by walls, fences, or earth banks covered with bushes and shrubs, with a secured entrance. In some cases, protection is provided by inaccessible land such as a nature reserve and, in a few cases, by a guarded bridge.[3] The houses, streets, sidewalks, and other amenities are physically enclosed by these barriers, and entrance gates are operated by a guard or opened with a key or electronic identity card. Inside the development there is often a neighborhood watch organization or professional security personnel who patrol on foot or by automobile.

Gated communities restrict access not just to residents' homes, but also to the use of public spaces and services—roads, parks, facilities, and open space—contained within the enclosure. Communities vary in size from a few homes in very wealthy areas to as many as 21,000 homes in Leisure World in Orange County, California—with the number of residents indexed to the level of amenities and services. Many include golf courses, tennis courts, fitness centers, swimming pools, lakes, or unspoiled landscape as part of their appeal; commercial and public facilities are rare.

Gated communities are different from other exclusive suburban developments, condominiums, cooperatives, and doorman apartment buildings found throughout the United States. At the level of the built environment, the walls and gates are visible barriers that have social and psychological as well as physical effects. In practical terms, gated communities restrict access to streets and thoroughfares that would otherwise be available for public as well as for private transportation. And in some cases, gated communities limit access to open space and park land donated by the developer to the municipality or town in exchange for building higher-density housing than allowed by local zoning. Such land is designated as in the public domain, but is available only to people who live within the development.

HISTORY OF THE GATED COMMUNITY

Gated communities have been traced to the first permanent structures built by humans. Ancient walled towns were designed to protect inhabitants and their property, and the demands of defense required walls.[4] Legend has it that Rome's founder, Romulus, defined his new city with a wall, indeed killed his brother Remus for insulting its height. Surviving courses of gray volcanic stone in today's city testify that Rome certainly built massive fortifications not many decades into its life. Roman armies at the end of each day's march secured their new camp (*castrum*) with a palisade of wooden stakes called *vallum*, from which the early English took the word *wall*. Settled Roman camps (*castra*) gave rise to many British towns—for example, Chester, Worcester, and Lancaster. But the founding legend of both Romans and Greeks, Homer's narrative of the war at Troy, turns on the interplay between the inexpugnable city wall and the self-destructive pride of defenders and attackers alike.[5]

Walls, however, were costly to construct. Citizens living in towns that were not military command posts or imperial cities had to raise money to enclose the largest area with the least amount of brick or stone and thus built the smallest possible perimeter, a compact circular wall.[6] Walls were used to protect against theft or destruction, but also to control entry and exit during peaceful times. Medieval town walls followed Roman tradition and included a wall, one to two meters thick and up to twenty meters high, a tower with openings for a maximum field of crossfire, and a gate, where you waited for the guards to inspect goods and collect a toll.[7]

Lewis Mumford writes that the medieval wall made the town seem like an island, and held deep symbolic value, not just military utility, representing the "wall of custom" that bound classes and "kept them in their place."[8] He adds that the psychological importance of the wall was also important, creating a feeling of unity and security when the gates were locked at sundown, shutting out the rest of the world.[9]

Systems of walls, spatial segregation, and class division are also deeply ingrained in Europe as a means for wealthy people to protect themselves from the local population. During the "long" sixteenth century, from 1450 to 1600, there was a rise in poverty documented by a drop in real wages and an increase in the percentage of people too poor to be taxed. The resulting polarization of rich and poor increased restrictions placed on poor people and vagabonds, partly because of a fear of social disorder, but also because of the risk of communicable diseases. Enforcing spatial segregation therefore became more important.[10]

In the United States, early colonists walled the settlements of Roanoke and Jamestown and Spanish fort towns to protect them from attack. But with the virtual elimination of the indigenous population, the need for defensive walls ceased to exist.[11]

Gated communities in the United States first originated for year-round living on family estates and in wealthy communities, such as Llewellyn Park in Eagle Ridge, New Jersey, built during the 1850s, and as resorts, exemplified by New York's Tuxedo Park, developed in 1886 as a hunting and fishing retreat with a barbed-wire fence eight feet high and twenty-four miles long.[12] Another early resort was Sea Gate in Brooklyn, established with its own private police force in 1899. The architect and real estate developer Julius Pitman designed the majority of St. Louis's private streets between 1867 and 1905, borrowing from the English private square to create exclusive residential enclaves for the business elite.[13]

Planned retirement communities such as Leisure World, which emerged in the 1960s and 1970s, however, were the first places where middle-class Americans walled themselves off. Gates then spread to resort and country club developments, and finally to suburban developments. In the 1980s, real estate speculation accelerated the building of gated communities around golf courses designed for exclusivity, prestige, and leisure. This emerging social phenomenon was reported in magazine articles in *Harper's*, on National Public Radio, on the Phil Donahue television show, and in feature articles in the *New York Times*.[14] The science fiction television series *X-Files* even ran an episode, "Arcadia," about a gated community where residents who didn't follow the homeowners association rules disappeared and were eaten by a monster, and the best seller *Snow Crash* by Neal

Stephenson portrays futuristic suburbs as entirely gated, where the only escape is through the Internet.[15]

Gated communities first appeared in California, Texas, and Arizona, drawing retirees attracted to the weather. Currently, one-third of all new communities in southern California are gated, and the percentage is similar around Phoenix, Arizona, the suburbs of Washington, D.C., and parts of Florida. In areas such as Tampa, Florida, gated communities account for four out of five home sales of $300,000 or more. Since the late 1980s, gates have become ubiquitous, and by the 1990s they were common even in the northeastern United States. Gated communities on Long Island, New York, were rare in the 1980s, but by the early 1990s almost every condominium development of more than fifty units had a guardhouse.[16]

The number of people estimated to be living in gated communities in the United States increased from four million in 1995, to eight million in 1997 and to sixteen million in 1998. By 1997, it was estimated that there were in excess of twenty thousand gated communities with more than three million housing units. A recently released census note by Tom Sanchez and Robert E. Lang, however, provides more accurate demographic statistics based on two new questions on gating and controlled access that were added to the 2001 American Housing Survey.[17] They found that 7,058,427, or 5.9 percent of households reporting that they live in communities, live in those surrounded by walls or fences, and 4,013,665 households or 3.4 percent, live in communities where the access is controlled by some means such as entry codes, key cards, or security guard approval. The percentages varied by region with the West having the highest number of households living in walled or gated communities (11.1 percent), followed by the South (6.8 percent), the Northeast (3.1 percent), and the Midwest (2.1 percent). The metropolitan areas of Los Angeles, Houston, and Dallas have over one million walled residential units.[18] These figures correspond to the original estimates that approximately 16 million people live in gated communities, (16,234,384 based on the census, assuming 2.3 persons per average household) and that most are located in the Sunbelt.[19] Sanchez and Lang also found two distinct kinds of gated communities: those comprised of mostly white, affluent homeowners, and those comprised of minority renters with moderate incomes. They also found that African Americans were less likely to live in a gated community than Hispanics or whites.

But it is not just a U.S. phenomenon—gated communities are proliferating in Latin America, China, the Philippines, New Zealand, Australia, postapartheid South Africa, Indonesia, Germany, France, the former communist countries of Eastern Europe, urbanizing nations of the Arab world such as Egypt, Lebanon, and Saudi Arabia, and tourist centers along the Spanish coastline and the Côte d'Azur. In each context, gated communities serve different purposes and express distinct cultural meanings. For example, they house expatriate workers in Saudi Arabia, replicate socialist *datcha* housing in Moscow, provide a secure lifestyle in the face of extreme poverty in Southeast Asia, protect residents from urban violence in South Africa, create exclusive compounds for emerging elites in Bulgaria and China, and offer exclusive second homes or industry-sponsored housing in Western Europe. Gated communities are found at every income level throughout Latin America and take various forms, including upgraded housing complexes, retrofitted older neighborhoods, upscale center-city condominiums, small suburban developments and large-scale master planned communities. Gating is a global trend drawing upon U.S. models but also evolving from local architecture and sociohistorical circumstances, and is always embedded within specific cultural traditions.[20]

THEORIES OF GATING

There is extensive debate as to why gated communities have become so popular. Arguments range from supply-side claims that the financial benefits to developers, builders, and municipalities drive gating's success, to demand-side proposals that home buyers preferences are the principal motivating factor.[21] Broader processes of social and political inequality also contribute to this recent trend, and many consider gating a logical outcome of residential patterns already in place. This public debate is heightened by media attention and political commentaries. It influences what residents say about their decision to move and offers a backdrop for further discussion.

The gated community is a response to transformations in the political economy of late-twentieth-century urban America.[22] The increasing mobility of capital, marginalization of the labor force, and dismantling of the welfare state began with the change in labor practices and deindustrialization of the 1970s, and accelerated with the "Reaganomics" of the 1980s. This economic restructuring and relocation of global capital produced political changes with far-reaching social consequences.

The political shift to the right during the Reagan years, and the mixture of conservatism and populism in U.S. politics, intensified an ideological focus on free-market capitalism. Power, wealth, and income all tilted toward the richest portions of the population during this regime. While the income share of the upper twenty percent of Americans rose from 41.6 to 44 percent from 1980 to 1988, the average after-tax income of the lowest ten percent dropped 10.5 percent from 1977 to 1987, producing an increasingly bifurcated class system.[23] These economic and political changes intensified already existing inequalities of neighborhood resources and services, and escalating housing prices left more families homeless and without health care.

Globalization and economic restructuring also weaken existing social relations and contributed to the breakdown of traditional ways of maintaining social order. Social control mechanisms and their associated institutions, such as the police and schools, are no longer seen as effective.[24] This breakdown in local control threatens some neighborhood residents, and the gated residential community becomes a viable and socially acceptable option.

The creation of gated communities (and the addition of guardhouses, walls, and entrance gates to established neighborhoods) is an integral part of the building of the fortress city, a social control technique based on the so-called militarization of the city.[25] In America it is a strategy for regulating and patrolling an urban poor comprised predominantly of Latino and black minorities living in ghettos and other deteriorating residential areas. Gating, however, is only one example of this new form of social ordering that conceals, displaces, and regulates people or activities rather than eliminating them.[26] In this scheme of "spatial governmentality," policing and enclosures create areas where a

protected group—for example, the very wealthy—is shielded from others' behavior.[27] A safe environment excludes all those who are considered dangerous. But while this strategy may work for the privileged few
living within the protected area, it has the drawback of diminishing collective responsibility for the safety of society as a whole.

Racism is another major contributor to patterns of urban and suburban separation and exclusion in the United States. Cities continue
to experience high levels of residential segregation based on discriminatory real estate practices and mortgage structures designed to insu-
late whites from blacks. Blacks are less likely to move to the suburbs
in the first place, and then more likely to return to the city.[28]
Residential proximity to blacks intensifies whites' fear of crime, and
whites who are racially prejudiced are even more fearful.

Whiteness in the context of the suburban United States, however,
is not only about race, but is a class position and normative concept.
Whiteness is defined by a person's "cultural capital"—that is, the ability to have access to and make use of things like higher education and
social graces, vocabulary, and demeanor that allow one to prosper or
at least compete within the dominant culture. It is also a sense of enti-
tlement to certain privileges that are out of the reach of others. Thus
middle-class whiteness is defined as much by mainstream acceptance
of norms, values, and life expectations as by race or ethnicity.[29]

Residents of middle-class and upper-middle-class neighborhoods
often cordon themselves off as a class by building fences, cutting off
relationships with neighbors, and moving out in response to problems and conflicts. At the same time, governments have expanded
their regulatory role through zoning laws, local police patrols, restrictive ordinances for dogs, quiet laws, and laws against domestic and
interpersonal violence that narrow the range of accepted behavioral
norms. Indirect economic strategies that limit the minimum lot or
house size, policing policies that target nonconforming uses of the
environment, and social ordinances that enforce middle-class rules of
civility further segregate family and neighborhood life.[30] The gated
community is an extension of these practices.

The suburb historically was an exclusionary enclave peopled by
the upper and middle classes searching for an ideal "new town" or

"green oasis" that reinforced race and class separation. In the nineteenth century, longstanding anti-urban sentiment in combination
with land speculation and new transportation technology produced
the "streetcar suburbs." Appearing first in Philadelphia, the new
middle-class enclaves spread across the country. The suburban
expansion intensified in the decades after World War II, this time gen-
erated in part by "white flight" from densely populated, heterogeneous cities. Enclave developments with districts segregated by race,
class, and social status define the contemporary United States, and
exclusion is a fundamental organizing principle buttressed by elaborate legal institutions.[31]

The creation of "common interest developments" (CIDs) provided
a legal framework for the consolidation of suburban residential segregation. A common interest development is "a community in which
the residents own or control common areas or shared amenities," and
that "carries with it reciprocal rights and obligations enforced by a
private governing body."[32] Specialized "covenants, contracts, and
deed restrictions (CC&Rs) that extend forms of collective private land
tenure and the notion of private government were adapted by the
lawyer and planner Charles Stern Ascher to create the modern insti-
tution of the homeowners association in 1928.[33]

The evolution of "pod," "enclave," and cul-de-sac suburban
designs further refined the ability of land use planners and designers
to develop suburban subdivisions where people of different income
groups would have little to no contact with one another. Regulated
resident behavior, house type, and "taste culture" are more subtle
means of control. Even landscape aesthetics function as a suburban
politics of exclusion, often referred to as making everything "nice."[34]
The number of legal proceedings in California courts has grown as
some residents attempt to deregulate their rigidly controlled environments,[35] but litigants have not been successful—CIDs and their restrictions are too important as selling features. CIDs guarantee a " bundle
of goods," including security, exclusiveness, and an extraordinary
level of amenities, and this promise is "nestled at the center of all
advertisements for the new walled cities."[36]

Private land use controls are not new, but there is a trend away from governmental control over land use toward increased reliance on privately created controls. The shift in the zoning process from a publicly debated and voter-enacted system to a privately imposed system may be far more restrictive than any state statute or local ordinance. Gated communities and their use of CID legal restrictions are both redefining and privatizing the political, social, and aesthetic dimensions of the suburban home.[37]

Another question about privatization is whether municipal governments or proprietary developments—shopping malls and industrial parks, as well as gated communities—are the most efficient institutions for the provision of basic goods and services. In these discussions, modern gated communities are evaluated as "spatially defined markets in which innovative neighborhood products are supplied by a new style of service producer."[38] For the people living inside gated communities it is an efficient solution because of the legal requirement to pay fees, homogeneity of community needs and desires, and because residents can choose their package of communal goods according to their personal preferences. Rather than being taxpayers who pay for public goods and services that are not always available, they become club members who pay fees for private services shared only by members of the community. Thus, for some, the gated community is seen as an opportunity to experiment with new solutions for the provision of goods and services that distribute those goods more efficiently and equitably—albeit more restrictively—than do current governmental strategies.

Supply-side economic factors also figure prominently in understanding the widespread expansion of gated, private communities. Developers want to maximize their profits by building more houses on less land. Incentive zoning packages for common interest development housing allows them to cluster units and achieve this higher density within otherwise low-density residential zoning areas. California and other states that have experienced a property tax revolt find common interest development housing particularly attractive because it transfers the debt liability, building of infrastructure, and provision of services to private corporations, while at the same time the municipality collects property taxes from residents.[39]

The economic restructuring of the 1970s not only stimulated many of these neoliberal practices, but also transformed the U.S. city in three major ways: (1) racial ghettos became abandoned spaces; (2) "edge cities"—suburban communities with combined residential, business, social, and cultural areas—expanded; and (3) luxury housing with separate facilities and services became concentrated in the city center. Peter Marcuse argues that these spatial changes have produced a social hierarchy of built forms based on walls and partitions. Skyscraper apartment buildings create the walls of the dominating city, "walls of aggression" defend the pioneers of gentrification, stucco walls shelter gated and exclusive suburban communities, concrete barricades and chain-link fences protect public housing, and walls of deserted buildings and deteriorating landscapes surround the abandoned city.[40]

Walls can provide a refuge from people who are deviant or unusual and perceived as dangerous, but the borders require patrolling to be sure that no one gets in. The resulting vigilance necessary to maintain these "purified communities" actually heightens residents' anxiety and sense of isolation rather than making them feel safer.[41]

In some cases, the micropolitics of exclusion is about distinguishing oneself from the family who used to live next door. Status anxiety about downward mobility due to declining male wages and family incomes, shrinking job markets, and periodic economic recessions has increased concern that children will not be able to sustain a middle-class lifestyle.[42] Middle-class status anxiety also takes the form of symbolic separation from other families who have fallen on hard times, families who share many of the same values and aspirations but who for some reason "did not make it." The exclusivity and status advertised by new gated communities are being marketed to an already anxious audience created by the economic turbulence of the 1980s. Assurances that walls and gates maintain home values and provide some kind of class status or distinction are heard by prospective buyers as a partial solution to upholding their middle- or upper-middle-class position.

And the psychological lure of defended space and "purified

communities" becomes even more enticing with increased media coverage and national hysteria about urban crime. News stories chronicle daily murders, rapes, drive-by shootings, drug busts, and kidnappings—often with excessive and extended media coverage. An ever-growing proportion of people fear that they will be victimized. Not surprisingly, then, fear of crime has increased since the mid-1960s, even though there has been a decline in all violent crime since 1990.[43]

Crime and fear of crime also have been connected to the design of the built environment. Jane Jacobs first pointed out that keeping "eyes on the street" is an important solution for creating safer streets and neighborhoods. Oscar Newman, who uses the term *defensible space* for this idea, argues that high-rise buildings are dangerous because the people who live in them cannot defend—see, own, or identify—their territory. He proposes that gating city streets can promote greater safety and higher home values as long as the percentage of minority residents is kept within strict limits. Timothy Crowe, a criminologist, runs a crime prevention program that involvs all local agencies—police, fire, public works, traffic, and administration—as well as planners in formulating neighborhood plans and designs implementing Newman's defensible space concepts.[44]

These diverse approaches depict a world that increasingly relies on urban fortification, policing, and segregation to maintain social order. A number of legal strategies, such as common interest developments, CC&Rs, and homeowners associations, as well as suburban design and planning, laid the groundwork for the development of gated communities. Architectural solutions such as defensible space contributed to an understanding of how the environment plays a role in crime prevention. And evaluating gated communities based on their economic efficiency and supply-side incentives helps explain why proprietary communities are growing in popularity.

OBSERVING GATED COMMUNITIES

Theories, however, are not always borne out in real life, particularly in communities facing the intricacies of individual actions and fluctuating social relations. Observers of gated communities in the United

States have provided details on the types of gated communities that exist and their importance for residents.

Based on a national survey, Edward Blakely and Mary Gail Synder identify three kinds of gated communities—lifestyle, elite, and security zone—each categorized by income level, amenities, aesthetic control, and location in the region.[45] Lifestyle gated communities include retirement communities and golf and country club developments, while elite communities, emphasizing status and prestige, include enclaves for the wealthy and "executive community" developments. The security zone gated communities are most often retrofitted with gates or barricades and include the "city perch"—the defensive fencing (often chain-link) of a threatened neighborhood in the center of the city; the "suburban perch"—the fencing of an existing inner suburban neighborhood surrounded by deteriorating conditions; and the "barricade perch"—where concrete barricades are used to partially close off the streets. All security zone strategies are used to block street access to reduce crime.[46]

These categories reflect differences in social values and motivation. For example, the lifestyle community is primarily about privatization and the provision of services. The elite community, on the other hand, is primarily about stability and a need for homogeneity. For security zone communities, exclusion and separation from the rest of society is most important.[47]

Blakely and Synder also found that residents identified security as an important reason for them to buy there. And only 8 percent of the residents surveyed characterized their community as "neighborly and tight-knit," and 28 percent indicated that their developments were "distant or private" in feeling.

In a regional survey of 641 gated communities in the Phoenix, Arizona, area, Klaus Frantz found that residents also say they moved to a gated community to feel safer and because of their fear of crime. They take advantage of gating to stabilize their housing values and to guarantee provision of services. Residents believed that they had the power to control the physical and social quality of their neighborhood: "They feel that this is a way to guarantee that the community that they have bought . . . will not change drastically in the course of time."[48] He also reported a range a community types: 13 percent were upper-class enclaves, 49 percent were middle class, and 2 percent were lower middle class.

Unfortunately, there is no evidence that homes in gated communities maintain their value any better than those in nongated neighborhoods in comparable suburban areas.[49] Nor is there evidence that gated communities are safer, although in southern California they are associated with perceptions of greater safety among the upper middle class.[50] What these and other studies do identify, though, is a desire for security and safety even in the face of low crime rates in suburban areas in the United States.[51]

BEHIND THE GATES: INTEGRATING THE SOCIAL AND PSYCHOLOGICAL

Understanding how residents make sense of living inside gated communities requires connecting the experiential and psychological levels of explanation with a critical analysis of society. Interviews and participant observation provide data on individuals, families, and neighborhoods, while comparative studies, theoretical treatises, and reviews of advertisements, television and radio transcripts, and newspaper reports generate a broader view of the societal impact. Bringing these levels together without losing the complex reality of individual experience can be accomplished by examining how social and political forces—through ideology and practice—are manifest in everyday behavior and conversations.

Another difficulty is how to portray myself as an active participant in the creation of this work. Often, the author is presented as an uninvolved, placeless observer without gender, class, tastes, or preferences. In critical analysis as well as in ethnography the author is sometimes obscured, as if she were not the narrative's producer, interpreter, or guide.

I address these concerns by using three narrative voices—a personal voice, the voices of the interviewees, and a professional voice—to present residents' lives, motivations and concerns.[52] Through my eyes, thoughts, academic musings, and interpretations, the reader learns about gated communities and my own residential history. By interposing memoir and interviews, I elucidate the interconnection between the experience of the author and her subject.

I begin each chapter with a personal vignette followed by a story (such as Felicia's). I then examine the evidence and explore the conflicts—conscious and unconscious—in what is said, as well as in what is left unsaid. I am interested particularly in how political and economic perspectives illuminate the psychological, and how personal experience sheds light on the social. I conclude by discussing how these interpretations and forms of discourse intersect, diverge, and disagree.

The book is organized around the psychological and social explanations given by residents for their move. Chapter 2, "Arriving at the Gates," begins with the difficulty of gaining entrée into the New York gated communities and describes the setting, housing style, and design of each development. Each subsequent chapter focuses on a different aspect of how residents make sense of their new lives. Chapter 3, "Searching for Community," discusses the role of social nostalgia and memory in finding the right place to live. Chapter 4, "Re-creating the Past," explores residents' desire to recreate the neighborhoods of their youth. In chapter 5, "Protecting the Children and Safety for All," mothers worry about creating a safe environment to protect their children in an increasingly impersonal, socially diverse world. Chapter 6, "Fear of Crime," analyses the discourse of urban fear and explores what it means. Chapter 7, "Fear of Others," probes residents' fear of people who work in their communities or who live nearby. Chapter 8, "Niceness and Property Values," sums up residents' visions of an ideal neighborhood and examines the trade-offs residents make by moving into gated developments. Chapter 9, "Private Governance, Taxes, and Moral Minimalism," explores the importance of service provision and private government. Chapter 10, "Easing the Way to Retirement," examines retirees reasons for living in a gated community, and chapter 11, "Don't Fence Me In," concludes by exploring the social, cultural, and political implications of gating and gated residential developments for the contemporary United States.

In many ways, buying a home in a gated residential community is a microcosm of the contemporary American dream. It reflects the social concerns and conflicts as well as the pleasures and desires of modern middle-class life. But it is the American dream with a twist, one that intentionally restricts access and emphasizes social control and security over other community values. Thus, by exploring the lives of gated community residents, we learn about ourselves, and at the same time we glimpse an increasingly secured and segregated world—a fortress America.

We need to know more about the quality of life of gated community residents to decide what we want as a society and for our children. What are the costs, benefits, and consequences—personally and socially—of living in secured residential environments? Unlocking the gated community allows us to examine the social, political, and cultural implications of gating for the future.

CHAPTER 2

Arriving at the Gates

GAINING ENTRÉE TO MANOR HOUSE ON LONG ISLAND, NEW YORK

I drive up and down Cove Hollow Road in suburban Long Island at least three times. Nothing along the winding thoroughfare looks like a residential development, much less a guardhouse. Flowering trees obscure hidden driveways and make it difficult to read road signs. I stop and get out to look at a map, and then climb back into my rust-stained Volkswagen, retracing my way down the treacherous roadway. At the last curve I turn left onto a narrow drive with a gold-leaf painted sign announcing "Manor House."

Two electronically controlled gates block the entrance: one marked "residents" next to the guardhouse, and the other "visitors." On the visitors side is a sign instructing drivers that the gates close automatically to allow the passage of only one car at a time. A young African American man in a security guard uniform comes out and asks who I want to see, then raises the arm of the barricade.

At the end of a curving road defined by period lamp posts is a white Victorian house perched on a hill overlooking houses and vacant lots. The unsold property, dense with scrub oaks and wild grass, evokes the overgrown lots of my childhood where I would make a fort and hide for an entire day. Those empty lots finally filled up, just as these will, turning the woods into a suburban, pastoral landscape.

It has taken almost two years since I visited my sister's home to find this gated residential development on the edge of New York City. Starting a new project is demanding, but this research is particularly fraught because I am working in my own culture. It is harder to explain to your peers why you want to interview them than it is to interview Costa Ricans, who assume that you know nothing about their lives. I climb the steep stairs to the verandah of the manor house, turn the ornate brass knob, and open the front door.

I am ushered into a marble entry hall with a crystal chandelier and a Chippendale rosewood secretary. A slight woman, dressed in a black silk suit with her hair pulled back in a chignon, extends her hand.

"Hello, I am the sales manager for Manor House, can I help you? Are you considering a new home?"

"I called last week to inquire whether I can interview residents in your development. I'm studying gated communities," I say, returning her handshake.

Her face lights up. "Oh, you're the professor from the City University of New York. How nice to meet you. My daughter's completing her degree in sociology at Hunter College, and I know what problems she's had. I'll do whatever I can." She leads me into a light-filled rotunda with what looks like a miniature village in a Plexiglas case.

"Here's a model of the original design. It's been modified since it was purchased by the current owner, but the roadways, lot lines, and community spaces are the same. We're the Rolls-Royce of gated communities, so you've come to the right place. We're still selling lots and building houses, and residents are just beginning to move in." She says that when the development is complete there will be 141 houses, but that only about half of the houses have been purchased to date.

"Let me show you some of our decorated rooms that give our buyers ideas about style and design," she says, as I follow her into the adjoining room. The large parlor is decorated like a Versailles palace, complete with copies of French tapestries and landscape paintings.

"Do residents plan to decorate their homes in this style?" I ask.

"Our clients want the best," she replies. "The land was formerly owned by a wealthy family. The estate and manor house were bought to design a community of luxury homes. But the original developer went bankrupt. We purchased the land, modifying the initial design concept. Now the houses are being sold for between $745,000 and $845,000, depending on size." She stops to catch her breath. "Let me show you what I mean."

She gestures to a series of architectural drawings rendered in plan and perspective. "Here are the six model houses that we offer: the Hampton and Newport are two-story with four to five bedrooms, the Lexington and Nantucket are ranches with three to four bedrooms, while the Madison and Vineyard have a master suite on the first floor and three to four bedrooms upstairs. We can go see a model home if you like."

"That would be great," I say. "Maybe I can meet some of the new residents as well?"

"I'm not sure," she replies. My face shows my disappointment. She adds, "The people who live here guard their privacy. But I'll speak to some residents that I'm friendly with, and ask if I can give you their telephone numbers. You'll have to contact them to make an appointment." She hesitates and then continues, "And you must talk to the owner, who is also the builder and architect. He must approve the project before you can start."

She points to the sales desk piled with ceramic tiles, rug samples, marble chips, granite slabs, Formica chips, and squares of colorful fabrics. "Buyers are encouraged to customize their houses by upgrading the finishing materials. Most residents add granite kitchen counters and marble floors in the master bathroom."

I follow her black Mercedes down the hill lined with model houses and vacant lots. We stop in front of a two-story shingled cottage, painted pale yellow with white wood trim.

She motions for me to get out: "This is the Hampton model. It is a two-story Colonial with four bedrooms upstairs; about four thousand square feet. The garage is tucked away on the side so the car will not be in front of the house. The Vineyard over there," she gestures across the street, "is a smaller version of a home the architect built in Brookline. This design, however, was created just for this development. Shall we go inside?"

She takes out a heavy ring of keys. "I've had trouble keeping track of keys and alarm codes. I set off the alarm almost every day. The local police know me by now, and pay no attention." I give her a knowing look. She laughs, finds the right key, and opens the door.

An insistent beeping accompanies us inside. In one motion she punches in the alarm code and turns on the light. The beeping stops, and I turn around to admire the entry hall.

"We try to make each model distinctive. The Hampton is for a large family."

There is a small living room and formal dining room on one side of the entry hall, and on the other side, a large family room off a country kitchen. Each room is painted a pale earth tone, trimmed with stenciling in the dining and living rooms. The family room contains a built-in tiger maple cabinet for a large television set with surround sound, and a stone fireplace opens through to the kitchen. The windows sparkle with reflected light from outside, broken by the trim of the window-panes. I can see other houses, and the beginnings of foundation planting for additional privacy.

"All light and space," I observe.

"Even though I'm selling real estate," she says, "I think of myself as a specialist in people. Part of my job is to learn what they want in a house, which requires asking questions and observing their behavior. I'm most successful when I have a sense of their unstated concerns and fears, and find the lot and house that suits them." She suggests that we go upstairs.

It's quite cozy by comparison. The bedrooms are decorated in soft pastels with floral chintz covering comfortable lounge chairs and matching drapes. The beds are piled high with pillows of all colors and sizes, with matching coverlets, dust ruffles, and sheets.

"The idea is to make the house seem lived-in and homey," she says. The tour continues as she touches upon important selling points. "The baths are white and green tile with a shower stall and bathtub. The master bath has his and hers sections with separate sinks, dressing areas, walk-in closets, and commodes. It is a new luxury for our working couples. Husbands and wives can get dressed at the same time without getting in each other's way." I recall bumping into my husband this morning in our five-by-eight-foot Victorian bathroom. "I can certainly see the advantage," I say.

"What do you think about the design?" she asks. "Do you like the rooms? Mary Ellen of Bayshore is the decorator. I worry the bedrooms are too frilly for men, but women love the pillows. I think Mary does a wonderful job. She's been working with the architect for a number of years, and everyone on the island knows her work. She was written up in *Style* and *Town and Country*."

Do people who decide to live here also use Mary Ellen, I wonder. Wouldn't that mean that both their interiors and exteriors would look like their neighbors'? Do residents choose to have their homes conform in terms of style and design? It reminds me of William H. Whyte's "organization man" of the 1950s, when middle- and working-class families moved to suburbs like Levittown, purchasing identical houses and lots in the search for a better life. Is this a similar residential shift, but with the addition of walls, gates, and guards?

"Are couples with children buying these houses?" I ask.

"At the moment it seems to be mostly empty-nesters, couples with grown children or even grandchildren. I think it's because houses are relatively expensive. These couples are close to retirement, travel a lot, and want more space and security. We're beginning to attract younger families, though. A young couple with a small baby just bought this model, and we have three or four families with small children who have already moved in."

I wonder what it would be like to grow up here. There are not many houses yet, but I can see children riding bicycles on the quiet streets and playing ball on the grass. Maybe the clubhouse has a children's playroom where mothers meet.

"We designed houses for families and others for retirees. For instance, we have two ranch models, one with two master suites so that both grandparents and parents can live in the house. It offers great flexibility."

We walk back downstairs and out onto the covered porch. "What do you think?" she asks. "Would you like to live here?"

Not sure how to answer, I change the subject. "When can I call you about contacting residents?" I ask.

"As soon as you meet the builder," she replies.

▥

AN INTERVIEW WITH THE ARCHITECT AND BUILDER OF MANOR HOUSE

In the *Town and Country* photograph, Edward Gaines stands in front of one of his luxury homes in Southampton, New York. Dressed in khaki slacks and Oxford blue shirt, he looks youthful, with the tan of someone who plays a lot of golf and tennis. According to the article, he is trained as an architect and builds custom houses for the very wealthy. Manor House is his first large development.

When I reach Gaines by telephone, his voice is reserved, even cool. I explain my project as quickly as possible.

"I'm currently building three-million-dollar homes in my newest community out on Long Island," he begins. "There are not many upscale developments in Long Island. Until recently there haven't been major builders in the Northeast. The industry is dominated by mom-and-pop companies who are not very sophisticated. What's going to happen is there will be hundred-thousand-dollar homes in gated communities as well as places like Manor House."

"Why do you think people are moving into Manor House?" I ask.

"Some people move for the gates. Some people would move anyway. We're surrounded by other gated communities, and security is an issue."

According to Gaines, early industrialists and wealthy entrepreneurs such as J. P. Morgan, Henry Ford, and William Vanderbilt moved their families out of the city and commuted to Manhattan by rail and ferry. By 1920, more than six hundred mansions on large estates dotted the North Shore of Long Island.[1] The Manor House mansion was built in 1916. It was purchased by a famous singer in 1958, and one of his daughters lived there for thirty years. The first developer bought the estate in 1988, but by 1990 had lost his stake to the bank during the real estate recession.

The process of producing an acceptable plan was relatively complex.[2] The village had to approve the homeowners association, and there was a great deal of concern about the application of the "cluster zoning" open space ordinance. Cluster zoning means increasing the density of buildings on one part of a site, while the remainder of the parcel is retained in its natural state. It is used to preserve forest and farmland as well as historic structures and landscapes. The developer calculates the maximum density allowed by local zoning standards, but distributes it differentially. For example, two-acre residential zoning allows a developer to build ten houses on twenty acres, each house on a two-acre lot. With cluster zoning, a developer can build ten houses on quarter-acre lots, leaving the remaining seventeen and a half acres as open fields, woods, or setting for a historic structure.

Gaines proposed small lot sizes, close together, but with detached houses. This kind of clustering had previously only been used with townhouses. He wanted to keep most of the land open with no fencing, owned communally through the homeowners association. It was an innovative plan that finally got approval in 1994.

"What were you trying to achieve?" I ask.

"I wanted to design homes on narrow lots with driveways on the side. I think it creates more sociability. I also wanted a textured environment with different colors, shapes, and styles. I compromised by designing six house types—the ones that you saw."

He worked with the village to create a governance structure that separates ownership of common areas from ownership of individual lots. Buyers purchase "fee simple" lots; that is, they own their land and house. But they also purchase the right to be a member of the homeowners association that owns and oversees the mansion, tennis courts, pool, and common grounds, so that each member collectively owns these spaces.

The homeowners association at Manor House is not yet functioning. As long as Gaines owns the majority of the lots, he retains the decision-making power. It will be activated when most of the residents have moved in, and all the lots are sold. In the interim, a corporation manages the community.

There are often problems in community interest developments when the developer retains a major financial interest. Residents want to make their own decisions about maintaining the landscape, hiring pool lifeguards, refurbishing tennis courts, or adding other amenities. Some developers hire management firms for the day-to-day operation of the development. Outside contractors are known to ignore resident requests in order to maximize profit.

I hear his sales manager's voice in the background. "I have to go," he says. "I have a prospective buyer waiting. You can call again at any time."

"Do I have your permission to start?" I ask.

"My sales manager feels it's useful to know what people think once they move in, and I want to learn more about what buyers want in their homes and their community."

"Thanks," I say. "It was great having a chance to talk." Hesitating a moment, I add, "Can I begin immediately?"

"The sales manager will let you know how to proceed. Good luck with your interviews."

SETTING

I began my study by gaining entrée into upper-middle- and middle-income gated subdivisions in 1994 and 1995: one in Nassau County on Long Island on the edge of New York City, and three in the northern suburbs of San Antonio, Texas. These two places—one located in the Northeast, and the other in the Southwest and Sunbelt region, are great complements, and when paired together illuminate broader trends. Both have large, culturally diverse, urban populations and publicized incidents of urban crime. Each suffers from increasing socioeconomic disparities, a history of residential segregation, and middle-class residents moving to an ever widening outer ring of exclusive suburbs. But there are also profound differences in their local population demographics, economic growth, land use patterns and density, governmental and legal structures, crime rates, and cultural contexts and norms of behavior. The historically liberal political attitudes of the Northeast and the more conservative leanings of the Sunbelt permeate residents' discussions of why they moved and their attitudes about private and public governance. Further, the history of gated community development and the scale and design of gated communities in the regions are quite distinct; there are very few subdivisions in or around New York City, while almost all new housing in the northen suburbs of San Antonio is being built inside gates. These comparisons help to elucidate what role regional and cultural variation, as well as individual preferences, play in determining gating trends. From 1998 through 2002, I added middle-income and middle- to lower-middle-income communities in the New York City area—and a gated community in Mexico City—to answer other questions about regional and cultural differences that had arisen in the course of my conversations.

Gated communities are predominantly new settlements built as part of large-scale housing developments or "master-planned communities."[3] They are located mostly at the edge of or just outside the city on rural or otherwise undeveloped land. Within any one master-planned community there are various kinds of subdivisions built for buyers of different income levels. Each has its own architecture, amenities, and facilities, but they are often connected by shared parks, golf courses, artificial lakes, or shopping centers.

Developers acquire the land, come up with a master plan submitted for approval to the local planning board, and, once approved, set up the infrastructure, including laying the electric wiring and network of roads as well as constructing some part of the leisure-oriented facilities.[4] The financial risk is considerable because large amounts of capital borrowed will not be recovered for many years, and many original developers went bankrupt during the real estate recession in 1990 through 1993. It is the second or even third developer who realizes the profit of the initial investors. In Phoenix, for instance, some developers covered their risk by taking on sponsoring investors such as branches of big oil companies like Exxon.[5]

Once the roads and lights are in, developers divide up an area into subdivisions, survey the individual house lots, and then sell the rights to builders who function as general managers. The builder constructs a few model homes to attract buyers and provides detailed architectural models and drawings, much like the display model in Manor House. There is considerable variation in the degree to which the style of the houses is controlled by the developer and builder. For example, Manor House offers only six models, while in San Antonio a number of different companies introduced a wider range of house types and finishing materials.

The developer also sets up the legal framework, the common interest development agreement, and the covenants, conditions, and restrictions for each private community. These rules and regulations stipulate how the houses and gardens will be maintained, and establishes the homeowners association that will ultimately govern the community. A management company is usually hired to organize the necessary services until the lots are completely sold and the developer relinquishes his financial and administrative control.[6]

THE GATED COMMUNITIES

For this study I identified new suburban housing developments located approximately thirty to forty minutes' drive from their respective downtown city halls. Gaining entrée was not always a simple matter, as the field vignettes suggest, although contacting developers, builders, designers, sales managers, and homeowners association presidents to obtain permission to interview offered rich material on the history and design of the community. Each has its own regional style and distinctive design features, but all are enclosed by a five- to six-foot masonry wall (photograph 1) or an iron fence (photograph 2),

Photograph 1. "Masonry walls." Joel Lefkowitz. Used with permission.

Photograph 2. "Iron fencing." Joel Lefkowitz. Used with permission.

broken only by entry gates and monitored by a guard or video camera from a central station. All the gated communities I studied had additional amenities, including swimming pools (photograph 3), clubhouses, health spas, golf courses, and walking trails, and all were landscaped with indigenous trees, grasses, flowers, and shrubs maintained by an army of gardeners and automatic sprinkler systems (photograph 4).

Queens, New York City and Nassau County, Long Island, New York

New York City is a global city of more than eight million inhabitants. Queens, the easternmost borough, is incredibly diverse; over 138 languages are spoken.[7] New York City annexed Queens in 1897. The Long Island Railroad and electric trolleys linked it to Brooklyn, while ferries in Long Island City provided access to Manhattan. With a population of 1,966,685 in 1997, Queens is the section of the city closest to suburban Nassau County.

There are few gated developments in New York City, with the exception of Seagate in Brooklyn, built over a hundred years ago. Doorman buildings in Manhattan, however, have guarded entrances. In Queens, there are three gated complexes of townhouses and apartments, and a new one currently being built with one hundred two-family houses.[8] The loss of manufacturing jobs—ten million square feet of industrial space has been converted to retail, residential, or office space—as well as lower salaries and lack of available land may account for the limited development of new—much less gated—housing. Although Queens is the most economically diverse of the New York City boroughs, with manufacturing, transportation, trade, and service, each accounting for at least 10 percent of private-sector jobs in 1998, it has not experienced the same accelerated growth in the service sector as the rest of New York City has.[9]

Nassau County, Long Island, on the other hand, has experienced a resurgence of residential development, much of it gated, following the decline in the real estate market in the early 1990s. With a population of 1,298,842 in 1997, Nassau County abuts the eastern boundary of Queens. Although complete statistics for the number of gated commu-

Photograph 3. "Swimming pool and other amenities." Joel Lefkowitz. Used with permission.

Photograph 4. "Landscaping." Jörg Plöger. Used with permission.

nities in Nassau County have not been compiled, a 2001 survey of the Manor House neighborhood identified seven gated developments along the main road,[10] and in the Pine Hills area farther to the east, there were least three gated communities located in the vicinity.[11]

Nassau County is politically organized as a series of towns and villages. Incentive zoning regulations allowing gated communities and permitting clustering of houses have been added to the original zoning and building codes of only a few of these governmental entities. These changes give the developer considerable economic concessions and freedom to develop housing with fewer zoning constraints, but require that some form of financial compensation or public amenity be donated to the town or village for this privilege. For example, in North Hills a developer paid $510,000 as a condition of complying with the village's new zoning code regarding the provision of public amenities. Most developers in the area have paid this fee.[12]

Manor House. Located in Nassau County on Long Island, this mostly white and wealthy development of single, detached houses is situated on an old estate with the original manor house retained as a community center. There is a security guard who controls the entrance gate (photograph 5). The individual houses are large (3,250 to 4,500 square feet), generally two-story structures, built in a variety of traditional styles, and sell for anywhere between $745,000 and $1,000,000.[13] The floor plans include three-, four- and five-bedroom homes with a variety of luxury details, including a great room with a fireplace and terrace, atrium foyer, and large walk-in closets.

Houses are situated along a winding thoroughfare with dead-end streets branching off, leading to groups of houses clustered quite close together on small lots, fifteen feet wide, on a quarter to a third of an acre. The remaining property near the housing is landscaped to create a parklike atmosphere, and the original site plan left most of the surrounding forested areas unchanged as an amenity for the residents. Since Manor House was developed as a community interest development, all of the twenty-six forested acres are maintained by the homeowners association. The built-out community will contain 141 houses, tennis courts, and an outdoor swimming pool. The mansion

Photograph 5. "Entrance guardhouse." Jörg Plöger. Used with permission.

has also been renovated to accommodate an indoor pool, billiards saloon, library, conference rooms, sauna, and cigar smoking rooms. There are a few lots remaining, and some houses are still being built.

Pine Hills. Pine Hills is a gated development of eighty units completed in 1997. There is a gatehouse, and residents use electronic identity cards to raise the arm blocking the entrance (photograph 6). Located on eighteen acres near the Long Island Expressway in Nassau County, Pine Hills is a middle-income, mostly white community made up of long rows of similar-looking houses in three basic styles— attached townhouses, duplexes, and a few detached single-houses. All the houses are two-story, white and beige clapboard, single-family structures with wood or stone trim (photograph 7). There are few amenities except for the streets, sidewalks, and jogging paths. The undulating terrain with curving roads and extensive landscaping creates a number of hidden cul-de-sacs (photograph 8), and the contours

Photograph 6. "Entrance guardhouse with electric arm." Setha Low. Author's own.

Photograph 7. "Townhouses in a gated community." Andrew Kirby. Used with permission.

Photograph 8. "Residential cul-de-sac in a townhouse gated community." Andrew Kirby. Used with permission.

make the site feel smaller than it really is. The location and quality of the houses have kept the prices in the $300,000 to $600,000 range even though it is located in a prestigious suburban neighborhood.

Waterview. Waterview is a gated condominium complex of 238 townhouses on over twenty-six acres in the middle-class neighborhood of Bayside, Queens. There is both a guarded entrance and a pedestrian entryway that can be opened with a key (photograph 9). Organized as a series of three-story townhouses, each with three apartments arranged around a swimming pool with health club facilities and sauna, Waterview has been successful in maintaining its prices in the $350,000 to $450,000 range. Many of the apartments are rented by their owners, so there is a broad spectrum of residents of various income and job levels and a relatively culturally diverse population including African nationals, African Americans, Korean Americans, and whites.

Photograph 9. "Guardhouse in a townhouse/apartment complex." Andrew Kirby. Used with permission.

The apartments are small (1,200 square feet) in comparison to the houses in the other communities, although some residents purchase all three levels and reconfigure the space as a single-family town-house (photograph 10). The normal configuration, however, is a one-bedroom apartment with a small garden enclosure and garage on the first floor, a two-bedroom apartment with a bay window and rights to park on the street on the second floor, and a third-floor apartment with two or three bedrooms and a balcony with rights to park on the cement driveway in front of the house.

San Antonio, Texas

San Antonio is a relatively large city, with a population of 1,464,356 in 1995. The settlement began in the eighteenth century with a series of Spanish missions and has retained much of its Mexican-Spanish heritage. Since 1990, Texas has accounted for 14 percent of all new

Photograph 10. "Apartment/townhouse complex with access to the street from the second floor." Andrew Kirby. Used with permission.

jobs created in the United States, including rapid growth in high-tech manufacturing. Population growth in the metropolitan statistical area of San Antonio grew 21.5 percent from 1980 to 1990, and another 10.1 percent from 1990 to 1994. The increases in skilled jobs and population stimulated construction of new middle-class suburbs, many of them gated communities, and a downtown renovation project, with tourist shops and restaurants, known as Riverwalk.

San Antonio is divided by Loop 410, a highway that circles the city, creating an inner and outer loop, each with distinct demographics, quality of life, schools, housing development, and municipal services. Inside the loop, 96 percent of the residents are non-Anglo and poor, and house prices average $20,000; beyond Loop 410, residents are mostly Anglo and wealthy, and homes in newly constructed gated communities average $200,000. Inside Loop 410, 43.5 percent of people mention crime as a neighborhood problem, contrasted with 26 percent of residents outside the loop. The area north of Loop 410, originally five ranches in 1983, now is one of the fastest-growing residential areas in the country.[14]

Like Nassau County, many of the incorporated towns north of Loop 410 have amended their zoning ordinance to allow private subdivisions. But erecting gates around neighborhoods can be costly for residents, because they must pay for street maintenance and other expenses. Nevertheless, the demand for gating is increasing. In 1996 one in three new single-family homes in the city was built in a gated community.[15]

Gaining entrée into gated communities in San Antonio was much easier than in the New York area. New residential developments in the northern suburbs are almost all gated and built by a number of different architects and investment groups. Access is not concentrated in the hands of one owner, builder, or real estate agent. An introduction to a resident who agreed to be interviewed was all that was necessary, and she then suggested other people to contact.

While being passed from one interviewee to another, I met Wayne Trestle, an urban planner who currently works for private developers and knows the history of the northern suburbs. According to Trestle, the early 1980s was a boom period in Texas, a time when savings and loan banks became partners with developers. Because it was so easy to get financing, mistakes were made in terms of the scale and extent of development. Instead of starting with a hundred houses or a few hundred acres, subdividing took place all at one time. Everybody thought that the economy was good, and that it was going to stay that way forever.

This development spurt was the beginning of single-family gated communities in the San Antonio area. Prior to the early 1980s there were only small, attached townhouse developments. The subdivisions that Sun Meadow and the Links are a part of (along with one other that was built at that time) were designed as "country club gated communities" around golf and tennis facilities. "Those were the first major gated communities in San Antonio. From there, you began to see people stepping back. A few years passed, and the gated community seemed to be what a lot of people wanted. I've worked with one developer for the past six years, and all seven projects have been gated," Trestle says.

Some developers tried to create smaller communities with a wider price range of houses or types of residential environments, but a smaller number of people or a more diverse group did not have the ability to pay for the security portion of the amenity package. As Trestle puts it:

> It's been termed by a lot of critics of the new suburban belt as being economic segregation. But you gotta look at the reality [of] the market. You have to look at where your supply and demand is. And particularly what people want. I know more traditional theories of city planning would say it's better to have nice mixes of things that seem to work well socially within a community. But the hard facts are that unless you're talking about a more sophisticated market like the Northeast, [where] they have a long history of high-priced housing intermixed with moderate-priced housing well set within the social fabric of the community, you just can't duplicate the same thing in suburban America.

Sun Meadow. Sun Meadow is part of the master-planned suburban development described above—it is centered around a private golf and tennis club, with swimming pools, a restaurant, and a clubhouse. The subdivision includes 120 lots, a few fronting the golf course, and is surrounded by a six-foot masonry wall (photograph 11). The main entrance is controlled by a grid design gate that swings open electronically by a hand transmitter or by a guard who is contacted by an intercom and video camera connection (photograph 12).

The broad entrance road divides into two sections leading to a series of short streets ending in cul-de-sacs. The single-family detached houses are large (3,000 to 6,000 square feet) two-story brick or stone colonials or stucco Scottsdale designs, with a few one-story brick ranch-style houses, and they sell for between $275,000 and $650,00 (Photograph 13). A wide variety of house plans are offered from the three different builders, including a two-story, four-bedroom family model with the master bedroom on the first floor, a two-story model with a game room, and a single-level four-bedroom house with a "morning" room, family room, and "owner's retreat" (figure 1.) These

Photograph 11. "Walls." Joel Lefkowitz. Used with permission.

Photograph 12. "Electronically operated entrance gate." Joel Lefkowitz. Used with permission.

Photograph 13. "Stucco Scottsdale-style house." Joel Lefkowitz. Used with permission.

Figure 1. "House plan for four-bedroom ranch." Marjory Dressler. Used with permission.

Photograph 14. "Stone detailing on house." Joel Lefkowitz. Used with permission.

different models accommodate predominantly white upper-middle- and middle-income families. There are a few Hispanic families and a small number of upper-class Mexican nationals who live here part of the year. More than two-thirds of the houses have been built and occupied; all the remaining lots are currently under construction.

The Links. The Links is a mostly white and upper-income luxury gated community with a twenty-four-hour guard and an elaborate entranceway landscaped with ponds and lush vegetation. All of the twenty-two lots face the golf course. The single-family houses are large (4,000 to 6,000 square feet), designed by individual architects to look like small mansions with French, Italian, or Southwestern architectural details, similar to those found in wealthy areas of Beverly Hills or Palm Springs, California, and other upper-income resorts (photograph 14). They sell for between $500,000 and $750,000. These houses have large gardens as well as common landscape spaces that abut the clubhouse and tennis courts of the master-planned development.

The Lakes. The Lakes is a white and Hispanic middle-income gated community in a northwestern suburb of San Antonio. The forty-two lots are organized along a series of curving roads, with four prized cul-del-sac neighborhoods (figure 2). Located on a hill that looks out at the city, these lots are smaller and include three blocks of attached townhouses among the single-family detached homes (photograph 15). The mixture of house types is unusual, and lowers the overall house prices to the $150,000 to $300,000 level. Three house styles are available: brick colonial, modern ranch, and Southwestern.

GATED COMMUNITIES AND THE SUBURB

Five of these six communities are located in the suburbs or at the edge of the central city. In San Antonio, the gated communities have been recently annexed and are now part of San Antonio, while in New York, except for Waterview in Queens, the developments are located in townships within Nassau County. Gated communities also share a number of suburban demographic characteristics, including lower population density, lower crime rates, higher percentages of middle-class and upper-middle-class professionals, and better schools and services, and are disproportionately white when compared to adjoining urban areas. Many of the reasons people and businesses leave the city for the suburbs—to avoid negative factors such as crime, to benefit from lower tax burdens, to have a better standard of living and a wider range of amenities—are similar to those people give for choosing gating. In myriad ways, then, gated communities are a special kind of suburb with many of the same features and benefits as those found in nongated suburban areas.[16]

While the number of gated communities is increasing, the rush to the suburbs that transformed the United States during the past fifty years slowed modestly in the 1990s, with the nation's population becoming 15 percent more suburban in the 1990s, down from 21 percent in the 1980s. Various factors are contributing to this deceleration in suburban growth. Constrained by commuting distances, air and water pollution, and geographical barriers, suburbs in the western and southern United States are being forced to fill in (and in the

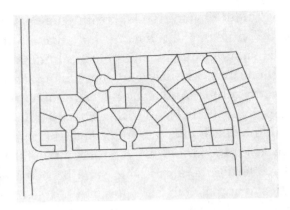

Figure 2. "Street and lot plan with forty-two house sites and four cul-de-sacs." Marjory Dressler. Used with permission.

Photograph 15. "Townhouse/apartment complex." Joel Lefkowitz. Used with permission.

South, leapfrog) older developments, creating new islands of suburban housing in contiguous but distant rural areas. In the North and Northeast, older suburbs are near their physical limits and beginning to decline.[17] Young professionals and immigrants, as well as some retirees, prefer urban life.[18] And a counter-trend of accelerating population growth and density in small towns, so-called hot towns, also is competing with the development of traditional suburbs.[19] In response, developers are searching for new ways to accommodate these shifting preferences by offering more desirable suburban communities with added amenities to attract young couples and retirees. Gated communities are just one product being currently marketed.

But something else is happening when people move to gated communities rather than to traditional suburbs. This is truly a new phase of residential development: architectural and planning parameters are redefining neighborhoods physically and socially by using walls and guards—not just distance, street patterns, and middle-class norms and mores. Even though the gated community evolved from suburban designs and development practices and responds to middle-class values and desires, this housing solution is distinctive in its political significance and potentially disruptive consequences, and must be understood in terms of how it changes the social organization of the neighborhood and a sense of community and security for individuals. By looking at gated communities in the suburbs and on the edge of the city, we can tease out the differences between gated communities and traditional suburbs in order to understand another aspect of why gating is increasing.

CHAPTER 3

Searching for Community

There was once a place where neighbours greeted neighbours in the quiet of summer twilight. Where children chased fireflies. And porch swings provided easy refuge from the care of the day. The movie house showed cartoons on Saturday. The grocery store delivered. And there was one teacher who always knew you had that "special something." Remember that place? Perhaps from your childhood. Or maybe just from stories. . . . There is a place that takes you back to that time of innocence. A place where the biggest decision is whether to play Kick the Can or King of the Hill. A place of caramel apples and cotton candy, secret forts, and hopscotch on the streets. That place is here again, in a new town called Celebration.

—From promotional materials for Disney
Corporation's town, Celebration

I grew up during the 1950s, when Westwood Village was a two–movie theater town, with Ralph's grocery, Bullock's department store, Wil Wright's ice cream shop, and a seedy bowling alley. Bordered by the University of California, Los Angeles, campus, Wilshire and Sunset boulevards, and the veterans' cemetery, Westwood was a small, pro-

53

Photograph 16. "Fox movie theater in Westwood Village." Joel Lefkowitz. Used with permission.

tected enclave tucked inside a culturally diverse, expanding city. It was physically compact and safe enough for me to be allowed to go to the movies alone on Saturday afternoons. I kissed a boy for the first time in the Fox Theater (photograph 16), met my high-school boyfriend while he scooped ice cream, and smoked my first cigarette upstairs at the bowling alley. Today, the "village" has become an extension of the Wilshire high-rise corridor, full of restaurants and boutiques. It no longer feels like an oasis in the city, and is undifferentiated in density and urban design from the rest of west Los Angeles.

I try to recapture the environment and ambiance of this idyllic place by visiting Long Island's East Hampton Village, an old colonial settlement defined by a town pond with resident swans, a Dutch windmill, and the Atlantic Ocean. East Hampton retains its townlike atmosphere and the sociability of earlier times characterized by the Bonackers (descendants of local families who lived by subsistence farming and fishing), and Baymen (commercial fishermen who fish for striped bass), amid Hollywood celebrities and hordes of summer visitors. But the village is now struggling to hold on to its social and physical intimacy in the face of intense development pressure. Two and a half hours' drive from New York City, it suffers the same problems that have transformed other Long Island beach towns into suburban sprawl.

An alternative solution is Disney's Celebration, a new town built in the late 1990s within commuting distance of Orlando, Florida. Celebration was planned by the neotraditionalists Robert Stern and Jacquelin Robertson based on "new urbanist" principles—high-density housing with small back gardens and porches, communal parks and plazas, and shopping, schools, and services within walking distance. This urban re-creation within a suburban setting has attracted considerable media attention. Thousands of potential buyers, drawn by the Disney name and promotional materials that evoke images of an idealized American town improved by the technology of the future, stood in line to participate in a lottery for the right to purchase houses.

So what are we looking for in these small towns and neighborhoods? Part of this search is a yearning for the intimacy and predictability small-town life represents, a nostalgia for a mythic, uncomplicated past, one that probably never existed. But it is also about Americans' perennial desire for community, that undefinable something—the relationships, social networks, and localities—that bind people together. We associate community with images of small-town life because the scale of social relations allows for overlapping networks, enhancing familiarity and contact between neighbors, institutions, service providers, and businesses. Further, the physical scale ensures propinquity, and the probability that you will bump into your doctor, teacher, local farmer, or grocer because you are living in the same environment. These encounters lead to ongoing relationships and shared local meanings. By contrasting the small town and the city, community stands for the way individuals are able to secure a sense of belonging and identity that counteracts the size and potential alienation of the city and globalizing world.

Defending community is not recent; the creation of suburbs and their incorporation as separate legal entities in the nineteenth century were established practices of how community was created and safe-guarded.[1] The "decline of community" is a historical concern of social scientists worried that needs once met by the local group are now more easily resolved by modern technology.[2] Robert Putnam, in *Bowling Alone,* warns Americans that civic engagement such as that found through neighborhood friendships, dinner parties, group discussions, club memberships, church committees, and political participation has diminished over the past thirty years. He is concerned that a lack of social connectedness, trust, and reciprocity is eroding community ties. And a recent study found that the more hours people use the Internet, the less time they spend with real human beings, creating even greater social isolation.[3]

The sense of community in the United States has seemingly deteriorated to the point where improving it, saving it, and nurturing it are slogans for a variety of movements, including gated communities.[4] One gated subdivision uses the small-town analogy to market itself as "a nineteenth century town for the late twentieth century, harking back to a time when lemonade stands, not crime were on every corner. A new American town of Fourth of July parades and school bake sales."[5] A newspaper advertisement announces "a community that you can come home to," accompanied by a photograph of children playing on narrow streets watched by attractive mothers.

In Calabas, California, thirty miles northwest of downtown Los Angeles, a heavily gated community celebrated its success in creating a shared ideal of what community life should be. This overcrowded suburb voted to become a city and grew to 25,000 residents, 45 percent of them living behind gates, each community with its own covenants, conditions, and restrictions. Places like Calabasas, Rolling Hills, Palos Verdes Peninsula, and the recent Coto de Caza—all in southern California—are cities that lie behind security gates. They argue that seeking cityhood is part of a quest for community that's been lost. At a time when government can't spend any dollars, community is being created privately."[6]

Developers, public officials, and residents all raise the ideal of community when talking about gating. They refer to safety, reduced traffic and noise, and children playing as examples of what they mean, but they also talk about a "feeling of community," a friendly place where neighbors are like themselves, "where they feel at home."[7] The important elements of community—shared territory, shared values, shared public realm, shared support structures, and shared destiny—are all part of the gated community package. But gated communities and homeowners associations often fall short of residents' expectations for a rich and varied community life.

The observation that developers market gated communities by offering a "sense of community" intrigued environmental psychologist Georgeanna Wilson-Doenges so much that she decided to examine perceptions of community in suburban Orange County and urban Los Angeles. Using a mail survey of two hundred residents, she looked at differences between gated and nongated communities in both poor and wealthy housing developments. She found that high-income gated community residents report significantly less sense of community compared to nongated residents, while in low-income housing projects there were no significant differences between those living with and without gates.[8] Wilson-Doenges worries that high-income, suburban residents are not getting the "community" that is being advertised, even though they feel marginally safer, while public housing residents receive no benefit—in the sense of community, at least—from the expense of building gates and maintaining guards.

Many of the residents I spoke with are also searching for community. Families with young children capitalize on neighborhood ties and form play groups and car pools, and residents organize Christmas parties that bring neighbors together. Tara, a resident of Sun Meadow, Texas, for example, is looking for a "community" where people share her preferred style of social interaction, creating what she calls "an old-fashioned neighborhood."

TARA—SEEKING AN OLD-FASHIONED COMMUNITY

Tara's husband, Danny, greets me at the door of their two-story Santa Fe–style house, holding their eight-month-old baby. He is a handsome man in his late thirties, dressed in jeans, running shoes, and a polo shirt. Behind him, Lilly, aged four and a half, timidly peeks around his legs and says hello. Lilly and I have met a number of times on the street. Lilly, accompanied by her Spanish-speaking babysitter, and I have spoken at length in both English and Spanish. I am surprised to see Danny home at ten o'clock in the morning, but he quickly explains that he has the morning off to take care of the children so Tara and I can talk.

"Oh, please join us," I say. "I would like to have your point of view."

Danny shrugs his shoulders. "No, really Tara is the one to talk to, and I promised to take the kids for a walk. Thanks anyway. I'll pop back in when I return to see if you have any questions."

Danny's response to my invitation is typical of many of the husbands I encounter. In some cases it's a scheduling problem; many of the women are stay-at-home⁹ moms and are thus more available. But that's not the only reason. I wonder if the husbands feel uncomfortable or think that interviewing, like talking, is women's work.

Danny shows me into the living room, where Tara, a thirty-year-old blonde in black leggings and an oversized shirt, sits on a brown tweed couch behind a glass-and-metal coffee table with a large Bible on it. He quickly exits, dragging Lilly, who is waving good-bye. I wave back, and then turn to Tara, who offers me coffee. Tara and I chat about how hard it is to keep up with two young children, and how she misses the free time she had when she was working.

Tara and Danny have lived in Sun Meadow for eight years. Right after they were married, they first lived in the nongated suburb of Canyon Village, but did not like it there because it was not the kind of community they were looking for. It was a brand-new area, and Danny had lived there, so he decided to have the home built. Tara thinks that one of the reasons they didn't like it is that there were so many people moving in, and the new people were not friendly. "I don't know if that had to do with [the fact that] a lot of people are so transient. We would be looking for people to talk to, but they would just go into their garage, press the button, and that was it," Tara says.

They were looking for a gated community because Tara had lived in one in Dallas when she met Danny. Tara is originally from Albuquerque, and Danny is from a small town in Wisconsin. Moving to Dallas was a shock because there was so much crime, and Tara felt she had to have gates. At first, not having gating in Canyon Village didn't seem to matter, but then they had so many door-to-door solicitors they felt gates would give them a sense of protection. Her husband was traveling a lot then, and she was still working. So when they decide to move, they looked for a gated development.

They both like where they live and like their street:

I was talking to Danny about that this morning when I told him that you were coming. People seem to take pride in their homes, they are concerned about their yards. It's like an old-fashioned neighborhood where everyone knew everyone, but it's not to the point where everyone is a busybody and into everyone else's business. We had many opportunities to move, and I'm just so frightened that I could never find something like this because Lilly knows everybody in the neighborhood, and I know that if anyone saw her, if, you know, a construction worker or somebody was talking with her, I know that in a heartbeat they would call me or ask Lilly what she was up to. It is just like the old-fashioned neighborhoods we grew up in, where people know everyone. Granted, there are so many new homes being built. [But] I feel confident with the people that are on my street, that Lilly could run to, or any of us could run to and they would help instead of just pull into their garage and press a button, that's it.

I ask her if she would prefer to stay in a gated community, and when she says that she would, I ask her why. "The sense of community. I don't know . . . growing up with our parents back then, people weren't so transient. People grew up with the same neighbors that were always there. I think with this neighborhood, people take pride in their neighborhood." She thinks that gated communities are less transient because the people who live there have had their house built. Several of her neighbors have built their own homes, have plans of staying a long time, and know that their jobs are stable. She feels that the people who move to Canyon Village and into other nongated neighborhoods know that they are not going to be around very long.

For Tara, her first, nongated development was too transient to evoke the feel-

ing of community she was searching for, while her new gated subdivision satisfies her desire for neighborhood stability and continuity. San Antonio is a rapidly
growing city with many transient neighborhoods. Tara even mentions that San
Antonio is now the eighth—not the ninth—largest city in the United States. And
while many of the older neighborhoods are known for their stability and depth of
family and communal ties, these neighborhoods are located inside Loop 410, a
less desirable part of the city.

I end the interview by asking her if there is anything else she would like to
tell me. She says, "I know in a lot of neighborhoods, there's a lot of busybodies.
. . . Here if you want to be overly friendly with people, that's fine, and if you
don't, that's fine too. People don't see you as being unfriendly [just because] you
are into yourselves. I like that because people aren't just ringing your doorbell all
of the time, bugging you. But I think that a lot of [other] neighborhoods are not
friendly at all."

Tara has found her old-fashioned neighborhood at Sun Meadow. She admits
that it might be just luck that her neighbors are so friendly and considerate. But
she found what she and her husband consider a community, a place to bring up
their children, where they know everyone, and their neighbors are there to stay.

Constance Perin, a cultural anthropologist who writes about
Americans' need to keep "everything in its place," argues that all land
use practices—planning, zoning, and development practices—are
value-laden. They act as moral codes for unstated rules governing
what are widely regarded as correct social categories and relationships. By examining these codes, she uncovers Americans' ideas of
how society is and ought to be organized.[10]

Perin makes two points that help us to understand the underlying
meanings of Tara's concern with "transients." The first is that these
land use practices are based on the economic impact of the social
meaning of owning a home. For example, along the expanding suburban frontier the distinction between newcomers and old-timers, as
well as between those people who stay and those who leave, dominates. Within this ostensibly moral scheme, newcomers and transients are suspect because of their lack of commitment to the neigh-

borhood, their instability, and other associated characterizations. Newcomers and transients also can lower property values and the quality of life; they pose an economic as well as a social threat. Regulations in the form of zoning codes and the covenants and restrictions of gated communities work to legitimize, even "sanctify," homeowners' rights to a protected investment. Couched in moral terms are very real economic concerns. Tara's concern with transients and their disruption of her sense of community should also be understood as defending her underlying economic well-being, with the stability of her home—and community—as an investment.[11]

Perin's second point is that transients, like renters, are also culturally problematic because they are symbolically liminal. That is, they fall in between accepted suburban categories of stable, long-term homeowner and nonresident or stranger. They are the tricksters or changelings of the suburban myth, marginalized and unqualified to be members of the valued categories. Transients are never desirable, because it is not clear what their status is, and they therefore become targets for negative feelings and scapegoats for any problems that arise.

Community, though, can be defined in other ways. Georgette was searching for a sense of community that she originally found living in military compounds, and the gated community offers both the physical and social aspects of her idealized conception.

GEORGETTE—REPLICATING A MILITARY LIFESTYLE

Georgette is a grandmother married for forty-six years to a husband with an active military career; they have two children, and four grandchildren. She is an outgoing, buxom woman in her late sixties who knows what she wants and makes it happen. As we talk, I learn as much about her as about her neighbors; she is deeply involved in community life and church activities, and her husband is a board member of the homeowners association. She says that she knows at least 75 percent of the seventy households living in Sun Meadow either through neighborhood organizations, church activities, Christmas parties—where her husband dresses up as Santa Claus and gives out presents—or her own version of a welcome wagon.

I first met Georgette walking her dog near a grove of cottonwoods at the edge of the development. I was making a quick circuit to see what people were doing on a sunny winter morning. We greeted each other, and she proceeded to ask me who I was; she said that she knew everyone and did not recognize me. I introduced myself, and as we walked together along the street, she pointed out new houses, commented on who had been divorced or remarried, and gossiped about neighborhood life. I was delighted to run into such a knowledgeable person, and asked if I could interview her when I returned in the spring. She agreed, and now I'm seated in her homey family room, surrounded by mementos and photographs.

Georgette has moved many times and lived in many countries and places in the United States. She has lived in the community for four years; she moved to San Antonio because it would provide things needed in a city without being as big as Chicago or San Francisco. They decided to move to San Antonio because they were not living in a gated community in Florida, and had people's dogs all over their yard. People parked their boats and trucks in the driveway. "I don't want to live in that kind of environment. I like an orderly style of living," she says.

She is a very social person and lived on military posts for thirty years of her life. When you moved in, all of your neighbors came and said who they were and offered to help in any way possible. Some brought a casserole and others brought cookies or cake. So she has always done that where she has lived. She takes the newcomers a "little whatever" and gives them her card, saying, "If you need us, this is our name and number, please call us."

They decided to move into this neighborhood because they knew everybody was going to keep their garage door pulled down. Neighbors weren't going to put their trash out until it was Friday, trash day, and they weren't going to let their children play in their yard. She wasn't going to let her "business spill over into theirs," and they would do the same.

We looked at everything available to buy in San Antonio.

When I first interviewed the real estate person, and we talked about what my feelings were, I said that there are certain limitations. I must live in a gated community, and it must be an upscale community. I'm not a racist and I'm not a bigot. So that's not a factor in where I live. We looked at everything that was gated, and there are some lovely places that aren't gated that I really liked, but I couldn't allow myself to live there. I'd been living in a closed community all of my adult life, and when I went out in my yard and on my porch in the military, I knew that there was going to be no harm coming my way. I know that same thing here.

She also could rely on her neighbors, and initiated neighborhood activities and visits to make it more like the military community she had enjoyed. But they still put the alarm system on when they go to bed at night, and they are very aware of who they let in their house:

> I have had the same maid since I've been here, for four years. I trust her, but I put away my jewelry on the days that she's here. I put my jewelry in the safe. I see no point in challenging her; it's not fair. She's poor and never has any hope of any-thing except social security. I think I'm safe with her, but I wouldn't give her the keys to my house. Not that kind of safe. And when we travel, and a man comes in to check the house, we put our alarm system on another number for him so that when we are here nobody can get in our house. I just think that's just smart. But when I was growing up in Virginia, I don't ever remember the front door of our home being locked. The back door either. Probably wasn't.

They enjoy living in San Antonio and think the people who live in Sun Meadow would say they live here because it is the kind of community they want first and foremost, and secure. Second, the community has the quality of individ-ual they have been accustomed to socializing with, "without appearing to be a snob. . . . And we can avail ourselves of what the club at Sun Meadow has to offer, and that provides us with all the outlet that we need in life."

As I walk down Georgette's Mexican-tile front path, I glance back at her styl-ish Southwestern home—all on one floor, painted pale peach with a reddish tile roof. This is a comfortable place to live, and in many ways fulfills her ideal of an orderly, friendly, and socially familiar community, similar to her life on a military base. She contributes her time and energy to making it what she wants it to be, welcoming newcomers, planning neighborhood parties, and helping out when-ever she can. I am sure that her efforts are appreciated by the many young fam-ilies who are busy working and caring for young children. But Sun Meadow is not quite like her childhood home in Virginia, where her family never locked the doors. Even though she feels that San Antonio has no more crime than any other city, she still uses her house alarm to feel safe at night. She also talks about the importance of living a cosmopolitan life. They had tried living in Florida on the water, but found it too provincial, with too little to do and to talk about. So they decided to live near a large city, and the trade-off seems to be that she feels that she can not leave her doors unlocked all of the time.

Living in a military compound is like living in a gated community, and it seems that once someone has spent some time in one, they prefer it. One couple who spent a year in a Latin American gated apartment complex with a guard now prefers to live the same way in the United States. Tara, who lived in a gated condominium in Dallas, decided to live in one San Antonio.

But families and individuals who have spent their lives in the military prefer gated communities not just because they provide a protected environment. It is also that these subdivisions, with their higher prices and extensive rules and regulations, preselect a ready-made community of socially and economically similar people, "the quality of individual" Georgette wants to socialize with. In both of these interviews, community is defined by the kind of people who live there, how they behave, and who they are socioeconomically. The gates, restrictive covenants, prices, and homeowners associations do create this limited sense of community, one based mainly on social, cultural, and behavioral uniformity.

The urban sociologist Richard Sennett worries about this desire to limit the boundaries and quality of public life. He bemoans the loss of a public realm where strangers come into contact and observe an accepted code of tolerance for difference and eccentricity. This "fall of public man" occurs with the expansion of the family domain to the public sphere, with the private superimposed on the public, altering public behavior in fundamental ways. He traces the withdrawal of individuals into private family life with the emergence of the nineteenth-century bourgeois and cosmopolitan classes, which resulted in a fear of exposing one's personal life in public. This expansion of private morality to the public realm, he argues, destroyed any possibility of a true public sphere. And private morality, when applied to groups of people, often results in prejudice and intolerance.[12]

Sennett provides the example of a middle-class Jewish neighborhood in Forest Hills, Queens, that was threatened by a plan to build a housing project in the area. He traces how a "sense of community" developed that was seen as contingent on a shared outlook and perception, a feeling of being solidly and emotionally together against this attack from outside. The community formed by this sharing of impulses and feelings had "the special role of reinforcing the fear of the unknown, converting claustrophobia into an ethical principle." If people had contrary feelings or did not share the same impulses, there was a sense that the "community" would shatter, and anyone who did not share this singular attitude was seen as betraying the entire neighborhood.[13]

A sense of community, therefore, has both positive and negative attributes. While it provides a feeling of stability and comfort for "insiders," in an extreme form it reinforces perceptions that those who are not in the community are "outsiders" or marginal, and unworthy of being included. Further, the motives for attaining a strong sense of community can be economic as well as political, and may be used in a fight to keep others out and to resist changes that would benefit the wider public realm.

Other consequences of closed community feelings include the rise in NIMBY (not in my backyard) attitudes that are creating new tensions in American neighborhoods. The environmental justice movement documents how poor and disenfranchised neighborhoods have borne a disproportionate burden of environmental hazards, public housing, and mental health or drug rehabilitation facilities. To compensate for this inequity, the federal government now requires affluent urban and suburban neighborhoods to carry their "fair share" of these "undesirable" land uses. Some middle- and upper-middle-income areas refuse to comply, capitalizing on the overburdened court system to forestall any changes that might economically or socially damage their communities. Paramount in their legal arguments is how disruptive these land use intrusions would be to their sense of community.

There is a tension in a liberal democracy between the state and the citizen in terms of individual rights and the right to private property versus the rights of all, or the common good. This dichotomy is most apparent in NIMBY protests that set individual property rights against governmental policy implementation that could restrict private property or alter its value. The gated community, in a way, obviates this tension for the residents by creating a private government, the homeowners association, to deal with internal differences and reinforces community through physical boundaries that identify residents from those outside. But at the same time, gated communities exacerbate the deterioration of public life in general and pose a threat to democratic practices that uphold the common good for all.[14]

Not all gated community residents, however, actually find the sense of community that they are looking for. Eileen Aiello, who lives in Pine Hills on Long Island, New York, is clearly disappointed with the lack of community life there.

EILEEN—LOOKING FOR COMMUNITY BUT NOT FINDING IT

Eileen Aiello is in her early fifties, and married to Herman, a machine operator. She works part-time as a secretary. They have three grown children who live nearby, but visit infrequently. She is a short, slightly overweight blonde who comes to the door wiping her hands, wearing a plaid apron over her beige shorts and shirt. Their Pine Hills townhouse is decorated with button-backed velour sofas and tub chairs, a brass-edged circular coffeetable, poster art on the walls, and beige carpet throughout. Vertical blinds cover the picture windows at the back of the house to keep the bright sunlight out.

Eileen and Herman moved in ten years ago because they wanted to live in a condominium or co-op type of development. At the time, the gate was guarded only during the day, but after they moved Herman joined the board of the co-op and extended the coverage to twenty-four hours. They had previously lived in a similar-sized, but detached house.

> My husband didn't want to do any work. So the idea was to live in something like this rather than living in an apartment building, [where] he doesn't have to do anything outside. He's not here that much, so he doesn't have a lot of worries. He feels it's safe. I'm here a lot by myself. You don't have to do anything outside, you just

have to worry about the inside. So we really don't do anything. I mean, I plant some flowers, but I don't have much space. All the ground is considered common ground, so anybody can really do anything anywhere.

When you have to get up at four o'clock in the morning to go to work and you are worrying that you have to shovel yourself out. You don't have to do anything. . . . And as we get older, we want to do less. But meanwhile, he's on the board, and they spent $25,000 on snow removal for the winter, to have them available in case, and we had no snow. They still have to get paid. So it's kind of crazy. And everything just keeps going up. But everything would go up in a private house as well.

When I ask her if she knows people in the community, she laughs and says "no" quite emphatically.

It's the craziest thing. I just know the people next door. People come in and out through their garages, so you don't really see anyone. And this community has a lot of snowbirds, so just now the people are starting to come back from Florida. You see very few people. . . . [Our other neighbor] has probably had eight different renters in the time that we have been here, and it was just sold. And the people bought it and went to Florida, and we haven't seen them since. . . . [Actually] I don't have one friend in this development.

Her previous community was much more social; she knew many more people. She attributes this difference to Pine Hills being "older."

There's only the two streets, and for whatever reason, on the one street there seems to be some younger people, but right here in this little circle it's much older and most of them have second homes. They are not here. And you don't see anybody. Did you see anyone when you were walking up? I mean, it's very strange. Even in the back, [where] the decks are all attached, I rarely see anybody. It makes me crazy actually. [Because of this] I am looking to move.

She is hoping, though, that it will change soon because of the increase in maintenance fees and taxes. Some of the older people who are on fixed incomes have left, so younger people with children, attracted by the local schools, can move in.

It's quite isolated living here. For whatever reason, [in] this cul-de-sac here there's never been new families with small children. Whereas over there it has turned over a few times. It's the strangest thing. Like right now, in the cluster across from me there's maybe six houses. Five of those people are not back from Florida yet. So, I mean, people buy them as a second home. You know, they just come back and forth. You don't get to know them. You don't even see the people at the meetings.

She attends the board meetings because her husband is on it. She goes to give him moral support.

And it's the same few people. I have friends who live in New York, in co-ops and condos, and they tell me it's the same, but more people are involved. So for whatever reason, I don't know about other co-ops on Long Island, but this is like the same few people get involved, the same few people try to make it a better community, but the rest, they just want to come and go.

The board meets once a month. I mean, somebody needs work done outside, and they have to okay everything. There's all kinds of projects, roofs need to be done. Some of the units need to be painted. I don't know if you noticed walking up, but some of the units look terrible. And you know they are constantly looking to improve things here. But they only tell us [residents] like twice a year at the other meeting. Those meetings are to let everyone know what is going on in the development. The last big thing was about the North Shore taxes going up, and how that would affect everyone's shares. But you know all this when you purchase one of these. There's a book that's about this thick with rules and regulations of the co-op. Many of them are just rules and regulations by the state, you know, for co-ops. . . . And you get it all before you decide to move in.

Eileen talks about the conflicts that have emerged—and that the board had to solve. I would have thought that these conflicts might bring people together, but it seems they only work to push people further apart.

There was a woman who had some dogs. They were breaking a house rule. The people worked all day, and they tied them up to a tree, in the back, and they barked all day. So there was always the rule, but now they put a sign up [saying no animals allowed]. But if you were here with a broker they would let you know that. And there have been sales that didn't happen because the people had dogs.

The biggest problem . . . is the common grounds. There are people that get crazy when they see kids playing right in front of their place, when they live around on the other side. But they come over here to go around on their skateboards or . . . That doesn't really bother me, but some of the older people really get crazy. But it's common area. . . . I think a lot of people, they think that what's behind them is theirs, or what's in front of them is theirs. And it's not. It's like living in an apartment.

She finds the lack of social life very isolating and would like to move.

I said to my husband, if you want to live in an apartment, I'd rather live in an apartment in New York. He drives to New York every day. I don't need to be sitting out here with all this space, not knowing anybody, and my friends live in New York. We don't have a backyard now, so what's the difference? If I am going to live in an apartment with all kinds of rules I could live in an apartment in New York and have a pet, right? Maybe I could have a little dog [laughs]. I mean it does seem a little crazy. It's really nice [here], I can't complain, but I like the city. I like this, but it's too quiet.

My little sister lives on Park Avenue South and Twentieth Street, in a one-bedroom on the first floor. It's really a dump, with no doorman, and it's two thousand a month, and she thinks she's got a bargain. She has a roommate. And it's fine. I could be there, rather than being here. This is very isolated. I can go around in the evening and take a walk, and I won't see a person.

"So if you were in charge, you would change things?" I ask her. She replies affirmatively:

The one thing that is lacking and that probably would help create more of a sense of community is some sort of meeting place, like a clubhouse. And this is probably one of the few developments of its kind that doesn't have that. There's no pool, there's no tennis, there's no clubhouse per se. But the maintenance is considerably lower than those places that have all those services. And we don't have any more property. So there's no place to even put that up. And in the initial prospectus there wasn't any space for that. So, you know, people knew that buying in. But I don't know how many original people are still here. It would be interesting to know why those people left. Because you moved into this kind of development for one reason or another, and then to pack up and leave. A few people have died. They were just older, and they died. But that's the only thing I can see, if there's a place, like a clubhouse, that kind of thing.

As I leave, she steps outside with me to retrieve her trash can. She walks over to pick up the neighbor's can lid that the wind had blown across the grass, saying, "See, here I am doing a good deed for my neighbor. Not that they will ever know." It's a little vignette, a small demonstration of how she sees her life there.

Demographics and social needs vary on any block or cul-de-sac in a neighborhood, but in gated communities there are often amenities or meetings that bring people together. At Pine Hills, though, homeowners association and board meetings and the negotiation of internal conflicts have not created the kind of community Eileen wants, and without a clubhouse or swimming pool she does not expect that to change. Instead, she plans to move to the city, where she hopes to find more age diversity and friends.

The jury is still out as to whether gated communities actually provide a greater sense of community than nongated neighborhoods. The majority of residents surveyed in California and nationally do not feel that their gated community is particularly friendly or that it provides a sense of community.[15] Yet more than half of the people I spoke to mentioned community as a reason for choosing a gated community. Many, like Eileen, may be disappointed with what they find. Gates and guards do not necessarily make a group of people conform to your idea of what a community should be.

A few of the New York residents actually say that they do not expect to find community at Manor House, Pine Hills, or Waterview, and are not actively looking for it. They have friends from their previous neighborhoods and do not plan to make more. But again, it depends on how you define "community." In the same breath that a New York resident may say she is not interested in making friends or being part of a community, she also mentions that she attends all the community parties, organizes impromptu barbeques, plays ball with the neighbors, watches neighbors' children, and carpools to work. By most standards, these behaviors make up the daily interconnections of what I would call "community" life. Some of the contradictions, then, are in the differences between what people say and what they do. *Community* is a slippery term that can be used to market housing, stabilize resale values, and defend neighborhood boundaries, as well as bring people together. But gating does not necessarily create community; it only selects for a certain type of person and level of income.

CHAPTER 4

Re-creating the Past

I grew up in one of the most beautiful places in America, but did not know it at the time. Only now, spending a few days working on cultural conservation at the Getty Center, just two hills away from where I grew up, do I appreciate this landscape of endless sky and water framed by bare mountains (photograph 17). The entire day is spent sitting inside architect Richard Meier's stone-and-glass monument arguing about economics and culture. At least I am sitting on the side of the room facing the windows. The sunlight is so piercing I have to put on dark glasses.

We discuss endlessly, going round and around the issue of whether we can measure the value of cultural heritage.

"Value to whom?" I ask. "We can't define cultural heritage for others. Whose heritage are we talking about? Who decides what is valuable?" Some care about how a place feels, whether it is cozy and comfortable, while others worry about how it looks and whether natural features are protected.

"We should ask them what is important, and use their answers to inform our decisions," I say.

A conservation foundation executive I know replies "But don't

Photograph 17. "The Getty Center in Los Angeles." Setha Low. Author's own.

professionals know what's historically significant?" ending the discussion.

At five in the afternoon I sneak out the door to the bathroom. I need a break. The glare of the day is just beginning to fade to jewel colors. A soft breeze tickles my cheek. I pull my suit jacket tight around my neck and shiver. I should go back in; they are waiting for me, wondering where I am. I linger on a sandstone ledge gazing at the pale, layer-cake sunset framed by an inky, blue-velvet sky. Below, the expanse of twinkling lights flicker until the Pacific Ocean absorbs them.

The smell of sagebrush and scrub pine mixed with honeysuckle from the garden below is overpowering. A shudder travels down my body, and I experience a sense of deep longing. How did I miss it? I have returned to reconnect with my past: the view, the smells, the texture of the air. Like so many gated community residents, I miss my childhood home and respond, unaware, to its seductive familiarity.

Tara and Georgette, who we met in the last chapter, are seeking community—a community of people like themselves—and find it in their gated subdivisions. But Kerry and Andrea, in the vignettes below, give up close-knit communities to recapture fondly remembered childhood neighborhoods. Using the language of "security," they lament changes in places where they have lived for years, and purchase new homes in gated developments in the hopes of reclaiming the emotional sense of security they experienced growing up.

KERRY—REMEMBERING A CHILDHOOD HOME

"It's a mess and not finished," Kerry says, moving cloth samples to make room on the couch. An antique Chinese chest and carved ebony cocktail table are neatly arranged on an otherwise empty, beautifully waxed, parquet floor. The four-thousand-square-foot Hampton colonial is perched on a hill with windows looking out on freshly planted dogwoods, mowed grass, and azaleas lining the streets. From the couch in the living room I glimpse an open stone hearth in the adjoining family room, and cherry cabinets with granite counters in the kitchen, located across the two-story-high entrance hall. Beyond the sliding glass doors, climbing roses are beginning to make their way up the wooden trellis that covers the brick patio separating it from the garden of the house next door.

Kerry is an attractive woman, in her mid-thirties, wearing navy slacks and a starched white blouse. Her curly red hair, inherited from her Irish Catholic mother, cascades down her back, held in place by a velvet headband. George, her husband, works at a well-known financial center in Manhattan and just left for the day. She offers me ginger muffins and tea from a silver teapot, while describing their decision to move to Manor House from their first home.

> We lived in Sunnyside Gardens, Queens, which was a planned community built in 1928. It was designed to imitate English garden communities with two- and three-family attached and semiattached brick houses. Everyone has a private front and back yard with a communal garden behind. We paid a yearly maintenance fee and sometimes volunteered to help with the garden.
>
> The garden and volunteers made it a community. There's a street fair once or twice a year, and there's a local [neighborhood] organization. We were involved and had a great sense of a community.

So why did we leave? First of all, it's like what's happening to New York City. Things change, neighborhoods change, the makeup of the population changes. I was raised on Long Island, and missed the security of living there. And my husband was born in Portugal and was used to the openness of the land outside of Lisbon where he used to go climbing with his friends.

So we rented a house for a year, and then we moved to Sunnyside. We liked it very much. It's big old trees and gardens, very pretty, but you're close to your neighbor. There's a sense of a small community where everybody knows everyone; you walk up and down the street and you have ten people say good morning or good evening. [But] George just wanted to have more property like in Portugal, and I wanted [it] more like [Long Island] where I grew up.

She knew that she would never find another community where she could walk down the block and say hi to most of the people she passed. Other friends have moved, one to Manhattan and one to Westchester County on an acre across from a lake.

"But here," she says, "I'm free and clear." She doesn't have to worry about raking leaves, watering the garden, or plowing the driveway. But she does miss walking into the shops and seeing her friends.

The most important thing, though, is that it is a gated community, "and there is a guard. I can't believe I'm leaving this till the end, that I feel safe and secure. I mean, I walk around the house sometimes and the door is open. It feels like when I was growing up on the south shore [of Long Island]. . . . [And] it fulfills my husband's desire to have open space like when he was a child." The fact that Manor House is gated, has open space, and does the outside maintenance seems to make all the difference.

Florence Ladd, an environmental psychologist, says we re-create aspects of our childhood in distant communities wherever we resettle. We unconsciously remember places from our early childhood, when attachment to the mother diminishes and new relationships to objects and environments form, and these place memories reappear in our homes and landscapes. We turn to this window on the past to perpetuate settings where we were happy as children, and by discovering characteristics of remembered places we replicate them for ourselves and our children.[1]

Clare Cooper Marcus elicits memories of childhood places as a technique to help people create a home or adjust to new surroundings. She asks them to speak to their house as if it were alive, and then to become the house speaking back to themselves. Through this conversation, residents recognize the influence of significant childhood settings on their current home, garden design, and interior decoration. Conscious recognition of childhood emotions allows them to feel more comfortable and connected.[2]

How could it be otherwise? Our earliest spatial and environmental relationships are to our homes and local communities. These places are imprinted in our imaginations as given, even natural, and taken for granted until we grow up and begin to question them. Is it so surprising, then, that when we search for a home, community, or design concept we return time and again to this resource?

But why are these residents moving to a type of community that did not exist when they were young? The answer lies in how gated community residents infuse their desire to re-create a childhood place with the feelings of emotional security and protection of childhood. Gated community residents want to recapture physical elements of their childhood landscapes, just like other people, but this desire is entangled with an unconscious longing for security they identify with living behind gates and walls. The search for a childhood home, among other things, then, becomes a search for this unconscious sense of childhood security.

I was struck by Kerry's use of the term *security* and reminded that most gated community residents say they want to feel secure. A child riding a bicycle, walking alone at night, and feeling taken care of are the examples residents give. Like the concept of community, security evokes nostalgia for childhood, when they did not have to confront the complexities of adult life.

So what exactly do residents mean when they say "I feel secure in my community"? At an emotional level, it means feeling protected and that everything is right with the world; unconsciously it is associated with a sense of childhood trust and protection by parents.

Socially it means "I feel comfortable with my friends and neighbors." "I feel secure in my community" also means feeling physically safe, not just psychologically or socially comfortable. These meanings—and many others—are evoked whenever they talk about security. This simultaneity and ambiguity of meaning gives the concept the power to evoke a complex and ever-shifting set of feelings, feelings that become encoded in a variety of symbolic forms, including the built environment.

ANDREA—FINDING SECURITY IN THE FAMILIAR

The guard at Manor House calls Andrea, and then gives me directions to a Newport model located on the winding road near the mansion. There are no house numbers, so I stop in front of the first Newport I find, but the man who opens the door has not heard of my interviewee. After trying another house, I arrive later than expected.

Andrea glances at her watch as she guides me around two men putting up brass sconces in the hallway. The house is decorated with burgundy silk wallpaper, chair rails and wainscoting in the dining room, and hunting scenes hung over matching green-and-beige-striped settees. She is in her early sixties, trim with short gray hair, wearing a white T-shirt and khaki shorts. Her husband, Al, sold his business recently, but still consults a few days a week. She enjoys it when he goes to the city and, laughing, says she hasn't adjusted to his retirement yet. She is used to running everything on her own.

They moved in two months ago from an eastern section of Queens on the edge of New York City, where they had lived for most of their lives:

> The nice part about it was having stores on the corner, and if you needed to buy
> more milk or an extra bottle of soda, or if the kids or grandchildren came, an extra
> bottle of apple juice. I had my doctor on the corner, I had my eye doctor across the
> street. It was more of a community kind of living. Friends on the block, that was
> nice, and I had an express bus on my corner to get to the city. The synagogue was
> just two blocks away.

"So why did you move?" I ask.

"It was now or never. The lovely stores that were there had become fast-food places. . . . It's just not the place that it was when we moved in twenty-eight years ago."

Al walks in to join us, and nods in agreement. The politicians who had lived in their Queens neighborhood used to make sure that the garbage was picked up and the snow removed. He adds: "The stores were kept right, everything. But when they left, the neighborhood was not kept up as well, and stores kept closing. When Bloomingdale's moved out and K-Mart came in, the area changed. And it wasn't the place that it was."

"How do you feel now, living in Manor House?" I ask. Andrea glances at her husband as she speaks.

> At first it was traumatic and scary to leave, but you have to give up something to get what you want. There is no community life in Manor House yet. I finally met a neighbor who is going to move in about a month or so; he introduced himself. But I am not looking for it. I have a social life outside of here. And whether I wind up meeting friends, it's okay, and if I don't, it's also okay.

Instead, she says, the guard house makes her feel very secure. "This is where I want to be. It really is. I think it's better having a gated community."

Andrea was active in her old community, fighting the changes she felt were pushing her out. She went to meetings and got involved. Initially she and her husband had been reluctant to move, but eventually became attached to their new house through the process of building it.

Manor House reminds Andrea of growing up in Parkchester, a planned development with gardens and walkways built in the late 1930s in the east Bronx of New York City. I ask what makes it so similar, since Parkchester is a high-rise apartment development and Manor House is made up of single-family houses. She says that it is the feeling of security that comes with having gates. I comment that they sound like a commercial for living in a gated community, and they both laugh, agreeing with me.

Even though people grow up in the same place and time, they live in their own psychological worlds and perceptual environments. Different aspects of a place become emotionally salient. The same is true for re-creating the past—only fragments of a childhood landscape survive for each person—but these memories are powerful and influence preferences about where to live and how.

For instance, my husband, Joel, also grew up in Parkchester. He remembers his mother sitting on the curved benches that line the pathways dividing grassy areas with flowering trees and shrubs. But his overriding image of childhood is one of children as young as five and six playing on these quiet walkways—jumping rope, catching balls, and racing around without the presence of adults. Andrea also remembers the foliage at Parkchester, but not the children, noise, and boisterous activity. As a girl she did not run around as freely. She selects a protected gated community with lush landscaping as fulfilling her sense of childhood bliss, while Joel lives on a tree-lined street in Park Slope, Brooklyn, where children play street hockey and use the light post in front of our house as a basketball hoop.

The connection between a place and a person also resides in symbolic meanings of the landscape. When these symbols are threatened, such as by the deteriorating conditions Andrea and Al describe, place-protective behaviors (such as fighting to combat those changes) occur.[3] Place-protective behavior also defends a person's sense of attachment and location in the social world. Thus, Andrea's concern about trash and snow removal, the kind of stores available, and increased crime is about both preserving her neighborhood and establishing who she is to herself and to others. Andrea focuses on the changing neighborhood and her feelings about it as much as on her desire to re-create her childhood home, but both are important dimensions of her decision to move.

For some gated community residents re-creating a childhood home is a conscious, rather than unconscious, desire. Buffy Goldberg and her husband wanted to return to Long Island and find a place that reminded them of where they grew up after living in California.

BUFFY—RECREATING THE FAMILIAR

Buffy is surprised to see me when she opens the door at our agreed-upon time. The guard had called to ask whether I could come up, but she thought the interview would be by telephone. Her children are taking naps, however, so she invites me in. Buffy lives in Pine Hills, New York, with her husband and two small children. She is an attractive blonde in her early thirties, well groomed with long, manicured nails. The house is modern, decorated in all white with colorful accent pillows on the sofa and chairs. We set up at the kitchen table after clearing off toys, coloring books, and crayons to make room for the tape recorder.

Buffy and her husband moved in 1994. They chose Pine Hills after driving around looking for places when they decided to move back to New York:

> Well, I grew up on Long Island and so did my husband, but just before we moved here we lived in California. So we didn't live here beforehand, but we are from here. . . . We kind of picked the area, and then driving around we stumbled on it. It was a fluke, but, we found it.
>
> We just liked the community. It wasn't really near work when we first moved here. It is now, for my husband. But it wasn't really then. But we wanted to live here anyway. It reminded us of where we grew up.

In California they lived in an apartment building that was part of a very large complex that had private homes, townhouses, and garden apartments. It was a gated community, but not exactly like Pine Hills. They chose gating because that is what was available.

> They are very popular. That's pretty much the way they do it now. Especially the newer developments, they all seem pretty much self-contained. I guess it's for security, or the appearances of security. But the way the developers do it, they want their communities to have their own identity, and they start with a gate.
>
> In this particular community, there's no other facilities. There's no park, there's no pool, there's no tennis. A lot of the gated communities in California, and gated communities in general, have to provide things. We don't have anything, not a

clubhouse, nothing. And until recently, there wasn't security at the gate for twenty-four hours. That's like a relatively new thing. It was just, I think it used to be from four until midnight there was somebody.

Buffy says it was not the security that drew them to Pine Hills, but that it reminded them of the suburban Long Island communities of their childhood, and it was affordable. Most of the homes in the area were out of their price range, but the attached townhouses were more modestly priced.

I lived in Dix Hills. You know, it was close enough [to what we found]. And my husband went to school at the college down the road, so he was very familiar with this particular area. So he knew that he would love to live here. And of course, there was no security while we were driving around the streets, and we could say, oh, this is nice and we liked it here. And there were some homes that were under construction at the time. There was a number [of them], for the developers. So we called and made some inquiries that way. Now all the homes are owned by someone and you can't go through the developer to get something. People are individually selling or renting.

We wanted to live in the community, community being north shore, Nassau County, and we weren't living here at the time. We were in California. We were just looking around, saying, "What if we decided, where could we live." It was fairly new construction, which is not that common, it was more affordable, it just sort of worked out, like click, click, click. As soon as we saw this my husband got a job, and we just kind of fell into it.

I don't know how much you know [about] Nassau County, but there's not that much empty land that you are going to be able to get a parcel that will hold a hundred homes. . . . And especially around here, if they find it, I think people think they would be better off building seven multimillion-dollar homes on the same amount of land as they would putting this up. I think that's what usually happens when they find a few acres. That's what they end up doing. But, I mean, there are a couple. I'm sure I don't have to tell you.

Buffy explains that because of the limited amount of moderately priced housing in the area ($300,000 to $600,000 for a townhouse) the people in Pine Hills stay.

If you want to stay in the area, and you want to move, it's going to cost you a million dollars. You have to love it, you have to be really committed. But I know one of the girls who rents for longer than I have lived here, she had another kid, and a couple of times she decided that she was going to look. And that's kind of what they found. It was going to cost a lot of money to. And these are nice homes. If you want to like something else better it's not a lateral move. It's a way big step up.

The rental rules are quite liberal, so people who own them can go ahead and rent them out. A lot of people find that it works out for them. There are a lot of people who have rented for a longer time than I have lived here. Two or three people I know. People come and go, I guess, but it doesn't feel transient to me. A lot of people around us have been here for a long time.

They know "a handful" of people in the community, and have made a few friends. They like it, and don't have any intention of leaving.

I wouldn't say those are my closest friends, but I've certainly had barbecues with my next-door neighbor at times. You know, on a Sunday we are both out on a lovely day: Oh, by the way, we are going to barbecue, do you want to it too, and we'll get some extra packages of hot dogs or chicken or something and we'll do it together. They are lovely. The people on the other side of me, we haven't socialized, but we talk too. The people one house over there, we have socialized with, we have gone out to dinner and we have done things. And they have teenage children and one of the girls babysits for my kids.

It also works for their children, who enjoy playing outside.

Some of the kids are a little older. They play outside by themselves, without Mom. But I'm not that kind of a mother, so I'm sort of, you know, I'm on top of it. So if we happen to be outside and there's other kids, you know, we'll play together. But, you know, they [the children] have played outside all day by themselves.

They have had some rules that have been targeted at specific families. It's pretty obvious. Some kid had a scooter that he would ride around, that made a lot of noise. And now there's a rule that you are not allowed to ride a scooter or a motorcycle. But, you know, most people are glad when that one family had to deal with it. I know the kids write with chalk on the driveway, in the streets. And recently we got a thing, you can only write on your own driveway. I don't know what happened, whose kid wrote on someone else's drive. But it's only chalk. . . .

I think that the privacy of the road is the thing. Because there's very little traffic, and my five-year-old, I'm having a really hard time getting her to look both ways before she crosses the street. There's never a reason to here. When she goes to a normal road, no, you have to look, you know. So that really helps the kids be able to play outside. Even if I am looking away for a second, I'm secure that there's nothing . . . the only people that drive around here are people that live here. And it's not a through street to anywhere, and nobody is going to come here unless they are . . . and more than the security guard screening the people, it's the feeling of security.

But I didn't come here just for the security. Some people do. It was more important for them. I mean, there are people that live here in the summer and go to Florida for the entire winter, and you know, it's more important to them to know the security thing. And if they travel for work, or they are alone, or whatever. But for me, you know, if I was living in a regular house I wouldn't have security, so.

I ask her if it is important being on Long Island.

Yes, I mean, it's huge . . . you know, I can go back to my family in a half hour, but it's still breaking away a little bit [laughs]. And he doesn't have anyone left in Levittown anyway. I guess it's more like Dix Hills. . . . I'm comfortable here because of that. I would not have liked living on the south shore. My husband came from Levittown, which is very different. . . . We like it very much, and like I said, in order for me to leave this place, it would be a big step that we really couldn't do. We just like to stay here.

Buffy and her husband's return to Long Island illustrates how important place identity and place attachment can be when making decisions about where to live. Questions of "who we are" often relate to "where we live" because place is such an important component of how people define themselves. Place identity figures prominently in determining where a person lives, and contributes to feelings of satisfaction and a sense of security.

A component of place identity is "place attachment"—the social, psychological, and cultural bond that forms between individuals or groups and their environment. [Place attachment develops over time through personal involvement: living in a location, buying or decorating a home, telling stories about a particular landscape, and learning about the religious or cultural importance of a site all contribute to a sense of place attachment.[4]]

Moving to a new home in a gated community is a complex event both socially and psychologically. It necessitates taking on a new place identity, disrupting an established sense of place attachment, and reestablishing a sense of self and place in a new environment. This transition is easier when the area is familiar and offers a place identity formed in childhood. Buffy's story reiterates the intimate connection between place and identity, as well as landscape and self, and how place identity and place attachment play a role in residential decision making.

VANESSA—GROWING UP IN A GATED COMMUNITY

Vanessa greets me at the door of her Manor House home and invites me into her sitting room, just off a large entry hall. The house is a two-story colonial with five bedrooms, spacious and simply decorated in pale earth tones. A coffee tray sits on a low table next to the sofa with a plate of sugar cookies. As soon as I sit down, Maria, a domestic worker who Vanessa brought with her from South America, comes to serve the coffee.

Vanessa lives with her husband and two children. Her husband is an accountant who works in the city, while she stays home, prepares the meals, and takes care of running the house. They previously spent four years in Latin America and then lived at her mother's house on Long Island during construction.

When I ask how the children like living in Manor House, Vanessa says that they enjoy it, but wish there were more children. The son has a friend his age in the community, but her daughter has not met anyone her age yet. Vanessa lets them play outside without supervision, knowing they will be safe. But one of the things she likes about gated communities is that there are always people around. 7

Just before moving here, we spent fourteen months, the period of construction, at my mother's house. And she lives not far from here, in a typical urban suburb, and my older son loved that very much. He loved the fact that there were lots of children in the neighborhood and that he could go out and fall on the street, and there was always someone around and he could play in the front yard. They could have Rollerblades and—what do they call that?—street hockey. He was actually sad to leave my mother's house because he thought, "Well, now I'm not going to have that anymore." And there won't be any people in Manor House yet, 'cause we were among the first to move.

We previously had spent four years in Brazil just before coming to the States, and there we lived in an apartment and it had a common area, which had a pool, tennis court, and garden, and lots of security because that's very important. São Paulo is a big city, and we lived in the [center] city. It was an apartment building that had private grounds and was a private community.

We liked that because there were other children in the building and liked the fact that they would meet downstairs, or they would run into each other downstairs. So on the one hand you'd think kids are not going to like living in an apartment, but the fact that there were children close by where they could take the elevator and go down to their house and drop in [made a difference]. I didn't need to bring them somewhere to play.

. . . that's the kind of community we were living in in Brazil, and then before that it was also the same situation in Argentina, very similar, one apartment building with a common area and again they had made friends.

I ask Vanessa to compare where they lived before and where they are living now. She answers:

There are always advantages and disadvantages to everything, but I think, in terms of comparing them. . . . this is nice because they now just take their bikes, go out, and play around here, and I don't worry about them. That was the thing in São Paulo and Buenos Aires, I couldn't let them go beyond the gate, and they were really, confined, and that was a restriction for them.

[And then] Westbury, that's where my mother lives. Comparing it? The houses are very close together there, and there's a lot of woods. I personally like that. [But] I don't want to live on two acres and not see my neighbor. I considered that when we moved here because, when I started looking on Long Island, I looked from

Manhasset all the way to Cold Spring Harbor, when I was looking for a house and I saw that kind of living situation. More isolated with a house and two acres, which I guess a lot of people like, or used to like. Anyway, so we did consider that, and we saw houses that were in our price range, and they were nice houses, but I didn't like the idea of having lots of trees around but not seeing any neighbors—partly for security, and partly because I just like to see people. I don't want to be alone; it's not me. And I think that for the children, when we would look at these houses, on the one hand they had space and the trees around the house, and that was pretty to them. But I think that the fact that there would be no one around, I don't think that they would have enjoyed it as much.

Vanessa says that even though she looked at houses on larger pieces of land, she was really only interested in a gated community because of her previous experience.

As an expatriate you go to a city like São Paulo, or even Buenos Aires, Caracas, or Bogota, that has a certain amount of crime and a concern for security, you always look for that. So whether it is in an apartment or whether it's in a house, it's in a closed community; that's what you look for. When you go there and you haven't grown up there, you really don't know the city well. And it's like if you grow up in New York, you know where you go and you don't go, and you know how to handle the city. So for an expatriate, you just land in a complete jungle with a high crime rate—that becomes a main concern. There are options. You can have a house in a closed community like Manor House. In São Paulo you have those kinds of areas, gated communities in the suburban areas. They were all located a little bit far away from the part of the city where my husband needed to work. So we picked a place in an apartment complex, gated, closer to town.

I ask her if she would consider not living in a gated community. She replies that after so many years in Latin America—she practically grew up there—she only feels secure with gates:

No, I wouldn't have considered it. I mean, I felt a little more relaxed in the States than I would have, and maybe wouldn't have minded it, [but] yeah, I think having lived so long—fourteen years—in Latin America, and having that concern, the security concern, I came here predisposed to being concerned about security. I know [real estate] brokers would say to me, "Why are you looking for that [gates]? Why are you concerned about that? And "the less people you see, the better," and "this is so pretty." And "Do you want to see your neighbors, who wants to see their neighbor?" My eyes were totally different; it's obviously a different mindset.

She was born in Kuala Lumpur, in a very normal neighborhood, not in a closed community, but where one house was next to the other, and she could see her neighbors and all the children got together on the streets and in the front yard. And as her family moved to various places, they always lived in suburbs. Most of the time the communities were gated, but in Guatemala and Chile, where it wasn't a closed community, they had guards.

Her husband grew up in Latin America. Vanessa tells me about a telephone call she had with him when he was still in Brazil and she had moved to the United States to find a house.

He said, "If it were up to me you would find a house in a gated community where I don't have to worry about anything. Because I don't want to start with the garden and this and that. For me you can go get a townhouse 'cause I don't want to know. If you can find a gated community, a house in a gated community with a good commute for me, that for me is perfect. And that we can send the kids to public school, because I don't want to pay private school. If you can do that, it would be great."

And I said, "Yeah, but I don't know of any. The only gated community that I know in Nassau County has attached townhouses."

He said, "Well, if that's what it has to be, a townhouse is fine with me." And then, in reality, this was his dream come true. He goes for walks. Because he grew up in Latin America, and he grew up on a farm, and he often used to walk, had to walk on the farm and between his father and his uncle's. They lived in the city in a closed [gated] community, but every weekend was spent at the farm, so for him that's important, walking a lot; he'll go walking to all the areas that they haven't developed. He loves that.

In Latin America, there was socializing within the gated community. In Argentina they went to parties in the building, and in Brazil there were lots of activities for families and children. There's none of that where they live now, but Vanessa says she is not concerned about making friends in Manor House.

That's not important to me. I mean, quite honestly, I don't mind if it never happens, because I have my friends, and if it clicks, then that's great. But it doesn't matter to me. I like having them all around. If I see someone up the street and say hello, and how are you, and that's nice. If she's struck fire, that's great, but if we never become great friends, because we're all different, okay. And I like to live in a community where everyone is different. I don't think I'd want to be the greatest of friends, and we—we don't have to socialize. But it's nice when you walk out and say hello, and you might chat a little bit; that's nice, I like that.

Her mother, father, and sister live relatively nearby on the south shore of Long Island, but the rest of her family still lives in Latin America.

When they looked for a house in a gated community they visited many in the region, but chose Manor House.

What didn't I like about the others was the security. . . . The houses face each other. And here, as you can see, I have someone very close to me, and you can see I'm going to have someone very close to me on the side, but, back and front, I don't really see anyone. . . . So it's nice [that] I have a pretty view, whereas in the other houses you would look out and you had the other person's backyard directly touching your backyard behind you.

I wanted closeness, but still some privacy, like I had in Latin America. I like the way it's set up. Actually they designed this in quite a nice way because they provided for that [privacy], for the most part. They had the proximity on the sides, but [on] most of the lots they've been able to provide trees and a sense of privacy in back.

We [also] looked at various lots, but then we thought this is nice for the children. It's nice to be in a circle [cul de sac] where they have space to go and play, and there have been times when it's eleven o'clock at night and the kids are out playing on the sidewalk. I don't know what the neighbors think about that!

Vanessa laughs and adds, "We're all very happy with the lifestyle that we have here, and we like having security."

Vanessa uses the word *security* in many ways. In the first part of our conversation she means safety, in the second, privacy, and the third, an emotional sense of feeling protected. Her husband grew up living in a gated community in Latin America, and she has lived in one for at least half of her life. For this family, a gated community re-creates the past and reproduces an ideal environment because of the multiple kinds of "security" it provides.

The link between emotional security and the built environment is forged in a number of ways. Enlarging Marcus's idea that home is a symbol of self[5] to encompass the house and its physical surroundings, gated communities provide another layer of symbolic identification by adding a boundary created by gates, walls, and guards. This boundary acts as a psychological buffer experienced by residents as defended and secure.[6]

Another way to understand how emotional security connects to the environment is through the concept of relational trauma. Any trauma—from personal injury, loss of a loved one, or loss of a job or employment location—violates and ruptures relationships at multiple levels and brings into question basic assumptions about the world as a safe, predictable, and reasonable place. As individuals move through their lives experiencing everyday traumas that include neighborhood dislocation, change, and disruption, they can feel that their home, as well as their self, is threatened. In order to re-create a more secure base to counteract the impact of trauma, they choose homes within what they perceive as protective walls and gates.[7]

It is through the symbolism of gates and walls that the desire of gated community residents to re-create their childhood environments becomes intertwined with security. The gates and walls represent parents, protecting the individual from physical harm as well as providing the sense of psychological well-being originally experienced at home as a young child. The common desire of people to re-create the past, then, becomes integrated with residents' desire for emotional security—symbolized by the walls and gates—as well as elements of the landscape, architecture, and other features of their childhood homes.

Because the desire for security is psychological, even unconscious, it is difficult to appreciate its possible negative consequences.

Most people want security in their daily lives. Security, though, also implies regulating disorder to create a safe environment. And while many Americans want emotional security, most do not want to live in a police state.[8]

The social impact of gating provides the same paradox. The degree of control restricts participation and limits aspects of interaction and struggle important to furthering local democracy. How do we balance the psychological need for security with practices that maintain social and political freedom?

Gated residents perceive their pasts very differently, but the sense that someone is taking care of them is a constant. Many of the residents who mention security cannot explain what they mean, yet references to it permeate their conversations. In some cases, residents use *security* and *safety* interchangeably, but they are not the same. Security is emotional, an unconscious desire, difficult to articulate, and gating provides it. Gates and walls, for a variety of practical and psychological reasons, contribute to a sense of security similar to that experienced in childhood. Safety, on the other hand, is about protecting one's family and environment, and is the subject of the next chapter.

CHAPTER 5

Protecting the Children and Safety for All

"Interview me, interview me," clamors Alexandra as we walk toward her friend's house, "I want to be in the book."

"The book will be about you," I try to console her, "but I'm only interviewing parents, not children."

"Why aren't you asking me?" she counters. "I live in a gated community too."

I'm not sure how to answer. How do I explain that I must follow a research protocol approved by the university? Interviewing children requires written permission of their parents. But this is my nine-year-old niece; surely I can have a casual conversation with her.

"Tell you what." I stop and turn to face her. "I'll ask you one question, okay?"

"Great, and will you ask my friends, too?"

Uh-oh, I hear my internal voice cautioning me, what do I do now? I guess I can chat informally with her friends—no notes or tape-recording. But I need to ask something that interests nine- and ten-year-olds.

"If you could live anywhere, in any house, where would you live?" I ask.

"Do you mean here in San Antonio?" Alexandra looks at the curb.

"Yes, but in any neighborhood or kind of house you can think of."

"Okay . . ." she pauses. Her face wrinkles in concentration. She looks like a quiz-show contestant aware of the ticking clock.

"Take your time," I reassure her, "this is not a test."

Her face relaxes. "Well . . . " she drawls. "I want a two-story house on a hill with a stable nearby where I can keep my horse. It must be a safe neighborhood, new, with green all around and lots of flowers. The backyard has a swing set and a pool. Behind the house is water and a boat." She is combining the fantasies of her father, mother, and even her aunt.

"Would it be gated?"

She hesitates. "Only if needed."

"How would you know?"

"If there were robbers."

The street is quiet even on a Saturday morning. The sky is robin's egg blue, cloudless, but the ground is still cool and damp from the desert night. Soon the sun will be overhead scorching the grass and forcing me inside.

We stop in front of a two-story brick Tudor with stained-glass windows and ring the doorbell. Someone with a Spanish accent calls out, and running feet can be heard, first thumping down the stairs, and then shooting across the tiled entry hall. The door opens with a jerk as Alex's friend flies past, completing her skateboard slide.

"Hi," she giggles, holding on to Alex to steady herself. "You must be Alex's aunt. You look just like your sister."

She immediately grabs Alex's arm, pulling her out into the street. "Let's get our bikes," she suggests, "so we can get away from my brothers." Just then, two blond boys tumble out the door yelling something about lunch, time, and shopping—a cacophony of voices. I cover my ears as the four of them talk at the same time.

"Mother said you should wait for her here."

"We're having lunch soon, so you can't go."

"She said I could play with Alex."

"Leave her alone," Alexandra says, and turns to her friend. "Just ignore them; my aunt Setha wants to interview you."

The boys stare at me.

"Why would you want to ask her anything?" the bigger boy snorts. "She doesn't know anything."

Alexandra puts an arm around her friend. "She does too. My aunt's going to interview just us."

"If you'll stop shouting long enough, I'll ask you all the question." They are silent for a moment. This is my chance, I realize, and I dive in.

"If you could live anywhere in San Antonio, in any house or neighborhood, where would you live?"

"In a bigger house."

"In a nicer neighborhood."

"In a place with eight-foot walls and an armed guard where you'd be really safe."

"What?" I turn to the younger boy, surprised. "What did you say?"

"Well, anyone can climb over the walls here," he says pointing to the five-foot wall surrounding his backyard and swimming pool. "It's not safe here. I'd like a higher wall and more security."

I stare at him in disbelief. Is he really afraid or just infatuated with the idea of armed guards? Young boys are often captivated by guns, so maybe he is kidding or playing around to impress the others. I decide to talk to each child separately. I begin with Alexandra's nine-year-old girlfriend.

"Where would you live?" I ask her, gently pulling her aside.

"My favorite house is my aunt's in the Highlands. It's cream-colored with six bedrooms."

"Why would you want to live there?" I ask, startled by the coincidence. I had just visited this development with my sister because she was toying with the idea of moving there. The house was a bargain considering it was five thousand square feet and had luxuries such as a Jacuzzi in every bath and a fireplace in every bedroom.

"Because of how big it is. All of the rooms are a lot bigger, and it has glass stairs. That's why they have to move, my two-year-old cousin fell on the stairs."

Her older brother chimes in. "It's much safer, too. They have real guards at the gates, not a camera like we have."

"Do you really care?" I turn to the older brother.

"Yes, I'm afraid people can get in. A gate isn't enough to stop them. I'd rather live in Castle Hill where there are a lot of rich people. The houses are stone and bigger and better than ours. I like their high-security system because it's safer; Castle Hill has armed guards and a patrol car that drives around twice an hour."

Their mother, Susan, drives up in a black Suburban. She rolls down the tinted window and looks at the boys, Alexandra, and her daughter, and finally at me.

"Hello, you must be Alex's aunt." Then turning to her daughter, "Sorry to keep you waiting, honey, hop in and we'll go."

I smile gratefully. "We're finished here. Thanks for talking with me." Taking Alex by the hand, I drag her back down the street.

Walking slowly, Alex tagging behind, I think about what I have just learned. The children say they want more protection—higher walls and patrol cars. What are they afraid of? Robbers, Alex said. Why should she be so afraid of "robbers?" As far as I know her family has never been burglarized. Her friend's older brother is afraid that people can get into his house, while the younger one imagines someone climbing over the wall. Yet they live so far from other people, out on the suburban fringe. Are they repeating what they hear their parents say or is this some childhood fascination with guns and robbers?

Fear is a part of every child's life and varies over the course of a child's normal development and as a consequence of emotional vulnerability to perceived dangers. The content changes: a four-year-old may fear the dark, large animals, and imaginary creatures, while an eight-year-old's fears are a mix of ghosts and tigers and more realistic fears about bodily harm. Until recently it was thought that it was not until the teenage years that children begin to focus on societal violence and failure at school.[1]

A study of San Antonio, Texas, school-children between the ages of seven and nine, however, found that most of their fears were related to personal threats and injury, including societal danger such as street drugs, drive-by shootings, guns, gangs, and nuclear weapons.[2] Girls reported more fears than boys did, and poorer[3] children expressed more fears than middle-income children did. Clearly, the fears of children under ten in San Antonio resemble those of older children documented in earlier eras. In our increasingly violent society, young children may be prematurely encountering "an array of fears for which they may be neither cognitively nor emotionally prepared."[4]

Mothers in San Antonio have noticed this change. They are concerned about their children's fears of being hurt, kidnapped, or killed. Susan and her family moved to a gated community in part because the son was scared.

SUSAN—MOVING FOR A FEARFUL CHILD

Susan is too distracted by her children and the telephone at home, so we make a date to meet at the golf and tennis club during her children's swimming lesson the next afternoon.

The club is located inside a residential development with large, elaborate homes on quarter-acre lots. A uniformed guard checks the sticker on my windshield as I drive by the gatehouse. I park by the clubhouse and wander through its two restaurants, billiards room, golf shop, and party rooms decorated in red velvet with oak floors, stone fireplaces, and baronial details; it reminds me of a British men's club. Walking back outside, I hear shouts of children splashing on the other side of the densely planted parking lot. Tropical trees and short, frilly shrubs, elephant leaf ornamentals, and Christmas ferns crowd into planting beds, creating a verdant landscape.

Separating the pool and the tennis courts is a snack shop with a line of children waiting to order. The rest are in the pool slapping their arms against the water learning the Australian crawl. Deck chairs and Brown and Jordan tables with umbrellas encircle the large Olympic-sized swimming pool. Next to it, a toddler's pool is filled with parents sitting on the cement edge bouncing babies and young children in the shallow water.

I look around for a petite, blond woman in a blue Speedo bathing suit and find her sitting on a deck chair drinking iced tea. She is watching her two sons race, shouting encouragement to the younger one. She looks like a Miss Texas contender with her hair curled around her shoulders, perfect proportions, and large blue eyes. She waves me over, flashing a big smile, then concentrates on the end of the race. I hear the coach shouting, "Faster, stretch your arm out and grab the water." I sit on the deck chair next to Susan and join her in cheering on her sons.

Susan, her husband, Eddie, and their two young sons and daughter have been living in Sun Meadow for four years. They moved to Sun Meadow from Orchard Valley, just down the road. Orchard Valley was very popular in the 1970s, so when her husband got out of college, that is where he built his first home. It was a residential area with young singles and couples with children looking for a friendly neighborhood, and houses were modestly priced, between $100,000 and $150,000. Unfortunately, there was a murder-suicide on the next street that upset her son.

> You know, he's always so scared. He's had this fear that somebody was going to come in through his window. As a matter of fact, when we built our new house here, one wall was to have no windows, specifically because of his fear. It has made a world of difference in him since we've been out here. . . . It's that sense of security, that they don't think people are roaming the neighborhood and the streets that can hurt them. Whether it's a false sense of security, I don't know. That's what's been most important to my husband, to get the children out here where they can feel safe, and we can feel safe if they go out in the streets and not worry that someone is going to grab them. And we feel that way out here because of the gates.

Susan talks to other mothers, asking them whether they think that they are too lenient, and if they should be more vigilant regarding their children's safety. Would increased vigilance make her son feel even safer? Susan explains her concern:

> You know, we've got workers out here, and we still think "Oh, they're so safe out here," but you know, children get grabbed anywhere. Not only in nongated communities. We just get a little bit lax. In the other neighborhood where we lived, I never let them out of my sight for a minute. Of course they were a bit younger, too, but I just would never, you know, think of letting them go to the next street over. It would have scared me to death, because there was so much traffic coming in and out, you never knew who was cruising the street and how fast they can grab a child. And I don't feel that way in our area at all, ever.

Their son's fear has a lot to do with why they decided to move. To someone who lives in New York City, it seems unfounded to be so concerned about a child being "grabbed." It's not as if they are celebrities or have the kind of extreme wealth that would make them especially vulnerable to ransom-oriented kidnappings.

I ask Susan about her upbringing and background, hoping to learn more about her son's fear and their decision to move.

She grew up in a house in a small "cowboy" town, "way out in the country." When her dad retired they moved closer to San Antonio, but still lived outside of the city. She remembers only one hamburger joint where they could go on Saturday nights. They never went into the city. When she graduated from high school, she moved to an apartment in San Antonio, where she met her husband. Their first home was in Orchard Valley.

> What we liked most is that it [Orchard Valley] was a real neighborhood with lots of nice people with big families. On our street, I bet we had thirty kids just on our street. Everybody walked, everybody jogged. . . . You felt pretty safe there . . . until the last couple of years. Our next-door neighbor's girlfriend got mugged by two guys with ski masks with a gun. They stole her jewelry and her purse. Not only that, but the people on the next street over, their daughter got knocked down in her yard and almost raped. It just happened in the past couple of years.

She accounts for this change because the streets are dark and secluded. For a long time it was the only subdivision on a deserted road, and no one bothered them. They never had any concerns when it was just their subdivision, but when all the other subdivisions were being built around it, they started having problems.

I ask Susan how they chose their house and lot. The details of building the house reveal the same old story told by recent homebuilders: it took too long, it cost too much, and the builder never returned her calls. But like other homeowners who have built their own house, they love it now that it is complete. And they also like the community:

> We love all our neighbors. And we are the ones who are out there all the time and always say "we love this neighborhood" even when everybody is fighting and gossiping; I mean, it's a fun neighborhood. I think the neighbors have a lot to do with

it; a lot of us are in the same age group, we all have children, and a lot in common. We can all get together and have lunch, and hang out while the kids play in the pool.

I can picture mothers and children enjoying themselves on a day like this. A crystal-clear sky with a gentle breeze cooling the hot rays of sun beating down on us. The sounds of children shouting "Marco Polo," and the whack, whack of tennis balls being hit back and forth almost lulls me to sleep.

I ask what the most important reason was for their moving here. She replies,

> I think a better environment for the children. I've begun to feel safe, and be happy out here. [They will] grow up with all of the extras that they get from living out here, all the benefits. I mean, what a happy childhood to live out here, and to have these children grow up in this environment—what wonderful memories, what a great place to live! It has made a difference, and you can see it in the children. It's the community, the area, it's the people. I think now we're kind of taking this safety for granted. We hardly ever lock our doors. And we usually don't have our alarm on.

Eddie, Susan's husband, joins us, sunburnt and jovial from having just finished his thirty-sixth hole. I take this opportunity to ask him about his perceptions of why they moved. He agrees with what Susan has been telling me: they were concerned about their youngest son's fears, worried about neighborhood changes, and wanted the protection of gates and guards.

Many parents experience an extraordinary amount of fear about what could happen to their children. Barry Glassner, a sociologist who writes about the culture of fear in the United States, documents how parents are overwhelmed by the amount of attention given to child abduction and cyberporn. A *Time* article estimating that more than 800,000 children are reported missing every year created a national panic. Three out of four parents in a national survey say they fear that their child will be kidnapped by a stranger.[5] Criminal justice experts, however, estimate that only two hundred to three hundred children a year are abducted by non–family members and kept for long periods of time or murdered, while 4,600 (of 64 million children) are abducted and then returned.[6] But I am sure these statistics are of little comfort to worried parents.

Fear of crime has become a major social problem over the past twenty years. It has influenced school-aged children's behavior: school attendance is down, and more children are carrying weapons, ostensibly to protect themselves. Research in a southern Atlantic city found that 57 percent of middle- and high-school students used tactics of avoiding certain people and places, leaving the lights on, installing security locks, and requesting an escort when leaving home at night, because of their fear of victimization. A few learned a self-defense technique or carried mace or a whistle. The additional social and psychological problems that children must cope with because of concerns about crime add another burden to their lives.[7]

Heightened crime awareness among children can make them wonder about the need for better safety measures, such as the young boys in the opening vignette wanting higher walls and better guards in their ideal gated community. Another Sun Meadow resident, Karen, becomes concerned about her son's sense of safety when he begins to feel scared and wants a metal detector installed at his school.

KAREN—WORRYING ABOUT SURVEILLANCE AND SAFETY

Karen lives at the end of a cul-de-sac in a two-story baronial-style house with an ornamental slate roof. A brick walkway lined with red geraniums leads to the front door and a marble entrance hall and curved mahogany staircase. Karen, a young-looking woman in her mid-thirties, greets me at the door dressed in pink Bermuda shorts and matching silk golf shirt. I hear the beeping of what I assume is a security alarm being turned off as she invites me into her spacious library for the interview. Her youngest child is asleep, her nine-year-old is at day camp, and her husband is at work at a family consulting center. We only have an hour and a half until everyone returns, so I hurry to turn on the tape recorder as she begins the conversation. She starts by talking about problems with their security company, complaining that they do not do a very good job. I ask if there is a block watch or other surveillance organization. "Just the security that patrols the golf course. They're supposed to come down here once an hour. [They] drive through, and monitor the gates with security cameras. I mean, it's limited, but that's unfair to say: [at least] it's controlled-access entry." I ask her to be more specific about the kinds of dangers she imagines.

[The kids] getting hit by a car [while] playing in the road. That's one of my biggest fears, because they're not into watching and being cautious. Since we live on a cul-de-sac and in a gated community, you falsely have the security that no one is going to hit you. Probably my biggest fear is that there is all this construction going on because the construction workers draw a lot of illegal aliens working out here. I guess, not to stereotype it, but it's like that's the way typically you see lots of burglaries going on. The house next to you is being built, and then you have a burglary at your house. And they can take something and watch when you come and go. During construction I would be very, very cautious.

She emphasizes how the gates restrict traffic and make it possible for children to ride their bicycles around the neighborhood at an early age. She lets her older child ride anywhere inside the community:

But he always tells me, "I'm going to ride my bike." So that I know he's out there, and I can look for him. He really rarely goes off, and he won't go too far. Or he'll come and tell me, or he'll be with a group of kids doing it. I assume that my kid must have a real fear of a lot of things. One day, he says, "You know, Mom, I wish our school made us go through one of those things like they have . . . "

"What are you talking about?" I ask him.

And he says, "You know, he has to walk through and if he had a gun, then. . . ."

I just says, "Metal detector?"

He says, "Yeah."

I told him that [if the school needed one] we would not make him go there. We would go to another school.

Where is that [fear] coming from?

The thing that I see about the gates [is that] you're going to see very different kinds of gated communities. You're going to see this kind of gate, where it's controlled but it's very limited. If you want to come in here, you just sit there, and you wait, and when the gate opens you tailgate somebody. You know, we're told if somebody does that, get on the phone and call security, say somebody followed me in. But, you know, I don't think everybody does, all the time. I know it's happened to me, and I have not done it, even when I didn't know the person. Because there are so many workers, you've got people coming and going. And I guess the way I look at the security issue out here is those gates are not going to stop a burglar if he really wants to come in here. They're going to deter him, though. He's going to drive up and he's going to say, "You know, I'm going to go across the street here because the houses are just as nice, you know, they all look just as nice. But it's not gated, and there are other ways to get out."

Statistics show a burglar does not come down a dead-end road. They want two exits. Now, we've had a handful of burglaries out here . . . in two of the houses, but they were probably inside jobs. The kid had a party, the parents were gone, the party got totally out of control, [and] it turns out there was $2,000 in cash missing. Another house, the same sort of situation, where she's got teenage girls and a teenage son. They've got all kinds of people coming and going from their house with those kids . . . on End Street. [They] had some jewelry stolen. Not that you shouldn't take it seriously, but those kinds of things don't matter to me or if you get in the police blotter. You look to see your zip code in the police blotter, and it says where. It will tell you the street, and you'll call security and say, "What happened?" They'll just tone it down and just say, "Well, you know, I don't think it's anything to worry about."

I find it interesting that Karen draws a distinction between burglaries within the community and her general concern about protecting her family from crime. It's as if a burglary by someone from within the neighborhood is not as dangerous or threatening as crime committed by outsiders. Sally Merry, an anthropologist who studies perceptions of danger, found that familiarity—familiarity with other residents and with the locations where crime usually occurred—reduced residents' sense of fear.[8] In Karen's case, familiarity seems a reasonable explanation.

I ask her how she would characterize this community in comparison with other neighborhoods in San Antonio.

It's not the real world out here, although that may not be true, because if you look around in all the new developments, 90 percent of them have gates. I guess if you look at the mean price of homes being $90,000, the communities that are coming up with $120,000 to $750,000 houses are now gated. More and more, all the new communities that are built are all pretty much gated. And it's almost as a form of competition.

I think it's [gating] one of those nice things. I don't think people are so afraid. I think they have that same attitude that I originally had that crime doesn't really affect me. I think people have that sense of security, although it's probably false if you look at personal-property crimes like we have here . . . [but] if you asked me tomorrow if I was going to move, it would be only to a gated community. I think that the safety is most important; I really like knowing who's coming and going . . . I love knowing my kids can get on their bicycles and ride around the block, and I don't have to wonder are they gonna come back home.

I ask her if she thinks the environment of San Antonio has changed. She replies that she thinks that she is just more comfortable with the gates and guards than without them. "I don't think the environment has changed. Maybe it has, but in my mind it hasn't. Because I'm so insulated from it. I mean, if you look at the drive-by shootings, we have [one of] the highest records in all of the country. I mean, it's unbelievable, but again, that's only in certain areas."

Karen doesn't seem to understand her son's fear or draw the connection between his increased fear and her concern that the gates and guards provide a false sense of security. Further, news reporting can have an impact on children's fears. There was a famous kidnapping case in San Antonio a number of years before. Eleven-year-old Heidi Seeman disappeared on August 4, 1990, walking home after having spent the night with a young friend a mile from her house in the far northeast side of San Antonio. She was believed kidnapped and her decomposing body was discovered three weeks later in an isolated area.[9] The event so traumatized the city that even five years later a news article reported:

For many San Antonians, that fateful August, with its abduction-death of not only Heidi but another child, Erica Maria Botello, 7, remains a troubling memory. For Heidi's parents, Theresa and Curtis Seeman, the month of August exposes "an open sore" that cannot heal, a pain that has no closure. For Theresa Seeman, the anniversary—August 4—is a sharp reminder of what she says she learned that violent summer: "That evil exists in this world. And it is powerful," she said.[10]

In a computer search of the *San Antonio Express-News* from 1990 through 1996, I found over thirty-three references to Heidi's kidnapping and seventy-three references to kidnapping of children in general.

Karen's son's reference to metal detectors, though, suggests an additional explanation. Metal detectors are used in troubled urban high schools with high rates of street crime when other solutions for creating a safe environment have been exhausted.[11] They are an extreme deterrent for controlling violence and not necessarily appropriate for her son's elementary school.

A study by the National Center for Health Statistics found that whites and students who attend suburban and rural schools are less likely than blacks and Latinos and urban students to fear violence at school. Based on these findings, urban high schools began to utilize security measures and procedures. The recommended safety procedures, though, were not seen as necessary in the suburban and rural settings.

Adoption of safety measures, including metal detectors and security guards, resulted in reducing violence at urban schools during the 1990s. Yet during the same period, a spate of shootings, drug-related deaths, and suicides occurred in suburban schools located in affluent and often gated suburban communities across the United States. Massacres at Columbine High outside of Littleton, Colorado, Thurston High School in Springfield, Oregon, and Heritage High School in the Atlanta suburb of Conyers, Georgia, have even triggered copycat shootings such as the recent incident at Santana High School, in a southern California suburb surrounded by stucco-walled gated communities, in which a freshman killed two classmates and wounded thirteen others. Even with this comparative evidence, researchers cite competition for grades and jobs, the impact of a public slight, or exclusion by the dominant social group for the increase of violence in suburban schools, rather than criticizing the apparent lack of security precautions.[12]

Recent incidents in Plano, Texas, a white, affluent north Texas gated suburb, illuminates another aspect of Karen's son's anxiety. In the early 1980s, Plano made national news for teenage suicides; then, from 1997, a string of eighteen deaths from heroin occurred.[13] Officials and local media attributed this tragedy to black drug dealers from the inner city and predatory Mexican nationals who "infiltrated the suburban environment magically creating a demand that supposedly never existed before."[14] Matthew Durington, instead, argues that the racial dichotomy between youths who take drugs in the suburbs and the evil outside forces that supply drugs is a displacement of blame away from the suburb, where certain social problems are not supposed to occur.

Contemporary suburban adolescents—especially white males—actively borrow stereotyped elements of urban black popular culture (such as hip-hop) through dress, language, and behavior to transcend their identities and expand their cultural horizons.[15] This cultural borrowing occurs at the same time that these youths are resisting their parents' control and creating their own identities. Adults respond to this incorporation of black culture with a kind of "moral panic," not understanding why their children would want to take on these symbols of the inner city. White parents worry that their children will not be able to obtain middle-class jobs or get into college if they dress and act like their black teenage counterparts.

Some Plano teenagers using heroin can be identified by their black hip-hop dress, which the media has labeled "wigger," white kids acting like "niggers."[16] Middle-class parents and local officials are horrified when kids emulate the dress and culture of black inner-city youths, and fail to see the seductive tension that has developed between black and white teenage culture. Yet this tension was first created when "white flight" to the suburbs meant leaving the inner city and blackness behind. The racial history of the suburb influences the identity formation of adolescents who live there. It draws upon their ambivalence about race and class, and restructures their symbolic world in complicated and not always healthy ways.

In general, though, gated communities are seen as safe havens for children, especially in Queens, New York.

GLORIA—GATING IS GREAT FOR CHILDREN

Gloria just retired after working in the health care industry for most of her life. She is an active sixty-six-year-old who raised her children on her own. She lives in a sunny second-floor apartment in the gated condominium part of Waterview. Initially, she rented a condo as an experiment, and then bought her own place within six months:

> I was in Chicago, and my daughter lived in a high-rise that had a dry cleaner's, a video store, and a grocery store in the basement, and I thought they should have something like this in New York. And here all my children were grown, so I wanted to move into, you know, a smaller type place. My house had four bedrooms. So I found these condos over here that were high-rise. And, I looked at three different ones, according to the activities they had in the condos themselves. And I was on my way to sign the lease when I saw this little gated community [she laughs, remembering the occasion]. And I went to the gatehouse and asked do they rent these, and he said yes, and I looked at two and rented it. It was just so nice. The clubhouse was so nice, the pool, the tennis courts. It had everything I wanted, but yet it was secured. It was the first time I had moved into Queens. Previous to that I had lived on Long Island. And it was more like a house, in an area with houses rather than a big high-rise apartment. So, since it was my first move from a house, I thought this would be better, and I thought I would try it. I loved it.

Part of the reason she loves it is that as a working mother she was just too busy to have friends. But when she moved in she made friends instantly through her building and the clubhouse. There are three families in a building and a lot of single women and men, families with children, and retirees:

> We have people with children, older people, younger people. . . . It's not one age more than the other. And also since I moved here—and I have been here four years—and I have been on the board of directors for two years of the four years that I am here. And this year, I think that the amount of people with children has

tripled, because the kids are running up and down the streets. . . . But they don't have to worry about their kids playing in the road, or running across the street, or, you know, it's not like another community. And then they have the security guards patrolling all the time, so they keep the kids out of trouble. We also don't allow them to use the facility (the clubhouse and the pool) if they get into trouble. They are banned from the facility for a month. So they have to respect the security guards. And the same with the teenagers. I mean, the teenagers hang out on the steps by the clubhouse and stuff. But if there is any kind of problems the security guards just, you know, write them up. And if they get two or three write-ups they are out of the clubhouse, they are not allowed in for a month. So that's a big thing. So it's a form of control of the kids behavior. . . . It works very well.

It's the same with the parking. In here we have tons of tickets, by our security guards. . . . You park outside the lines you get a ticket, if you are too far forward of the line, if you park in illegal spaces, they charge $25 a ticket. If you don't pay it in thirty days it's $50. And if you don't pay your tickets they come off your [house price], when you sell. You never get away with your tickets, you always have them, and people know they are going to abide by the rules of the community. So it's a very respectable community.

When I ask her if she minds the rules, she replies, "Absolutely not. I have no objection to them. I mean, if you parked in my driveway without a visitor's pass, I would get a ticket . . . because you're not registered. You know, that really is security. We have no burglaries. I mean, we haven't had one in seven or eight years."

I ask if she is aware of any controversies or friction between retirees and families with children. She is not aware of any problems even though the community is quite diverse, and she estimates that it is about 40 percent Asian, 5 percent black, 1 percent Indian or Pakistani, 25 percent Jewish, and 20 percent Christian—typical of Queens.

Gloria goes on to explain that the reason so many families with children are moving to secured communities is that they don't have babysitters. The kids come home from school and can play safely because the security guards are watching them. The school bus picks them up in the morning just outside the complex. They also provide free babysitting for two hours at the clubhouse on Saturdays.

Residents believe that a gated condominium complex or housing development with a pool, play areas, and supervising guards creates a safe play environment for children. Some residents are not as pleased as Gloria is with herds of children "running wildly" through the neighborhood, but all agree that it allows greater freedom because of traffic curtailment and the guards' supervision. One could argue that the $400-per-month maintenance fee and the $100-per-month club fees at Waterview are a bargain if they include an after-school supervised play program and Saturday babysitting.

But this internal freedom comes at a high social and psychological cost. Are the children growing up in gated communities actually more afraid of people who live outside the gates and of being hurt by a random act of violence than other kids are? Are they more vulnerable to drug problems, suicide, or violence partly because of their racial and social separation from other children, especially blacks and Latinos, who become exoticized and whose imagined lifestyles are mimicked in a stereotypical and potentially dangerous way?[17] Evidence from recent years points to the possibility that both of these queries will be answered affirmatively. Certainly the interviews with Susan, Karen, and Felicia (reported in the first chapter) suggest that gating is one way to deal with children's fears, but at the same time, children might experience increased concerns about "workers" and "someone getting at them" living within these protected environments.

The feminist geographer Cindi Katz writes eloquently about how the state manipulates parental concern for their children's safety, inciting "moral panics" about specific incidences of child abuse, kidnapping or rape to gain control over neighborhood public spaces and other places where families live and children grow-up, (ie., the sites of social reproduction). She cites the growing child-protection industry as a way to remake the home as citadel and to sell private protective technologies. "Nanny cams" are installed to watch the child's caretaker and transistorized monitors record the child's location and heartbeat. This "hypervigilence," Katz argues, allows neoliberal politics to shift the responsibility for social reproduction from the public to the private sector, further shrinking the power of the state and relinquishing responsibility for providing a safe environment for bringing up children. These "moral panics" provide the rationale for privatizing child care and intrusive surveillance in the face of the government's inability to solve the problem of increasing child vulnerability.[18]

Is this also the case with gating, but in these circumstances reinforced by the economics of the private sector, the developer, and the construction industry? Thinking about gating from the point of view of child protection forces us to reconsider why urban and suburban neighborhoods are no longer seen as safe enough for children to play in freely. The freedom to play should be a right regardless of whether your family can afford to live behind gates and walls.[19]

CHAPTER 6

Fear of Crime

The first time I consciously noticed the psychological impact of guarded gates and surrounding walls was during college while living with six other students on a small *finca*, a coffee plantation, just outside of Santa Ana in El Salvador. We were working on an archaeological dig to determine whether the nearby pre-Classic ceremonial center was influenced by a Mayan trade route. The perimeter of the compound was encircled by a concrete block wall topped with broken bottles stuck at various angles in a cement cap. A corral gate with barbed wire and a guard with a machete were located at the entrance. Every day, the armed guard opened the gate and closed it quickly behind us as we drove to the excavation site. The gates evoked unknown danger lurking outside.

As an anthropology graduate student specializing in Central America and the Caribbean, I soon learned that walls and gates are ubiquitous throughout Latin America. They separate the domestic domain of women from the public domain of men, providing both a physical and symbolic defense against unwanted intruders. Early North American towns and forts, such as Roanoke, Virginia, also were initially surrounded by walls and barricades for protection. But walls and gates never became an established part of North American town planning. Instead, the wide open spaces of the western frontier, the democratic New England village green, and the fenceless landscapes of suburbia were adopted as spatial models. Cities in North America are not defined by walls and barbed wire, but by public streets and sidewalks lined with apartment buildings, townhouses, or detached bungalows and houses, while suburbs display grass lawns stretching like large welcome mats in front of one- and two-story single-family houses.

The gates and walls of Latin America that define public and private spaces now protect residents from urban crime and class-based violence. Latin American cities have experienced explosive population growth, social and political deterioration, and recurring economic crises. Middle-class residents are moving to the edges of the city or into gated neighborhoods where they protect themselves by living within a carefully circumscribed world. A New Year's visit to Caracas, Venezuela, in 1993 provides an apt example.

My host lives in a walled and gated compound, Bella Vista, on a south-facing hillside overlooking the city. I insist on visiting some poorer neighborhoods or at least taking a walk downtown.

"But that is impossible," my host says. "You'll be killed."

"How can that be," I counter, "don't you go out for dinner or to the movies?"

"No, not now," he answers, and goes on to explain: "You can visit the shopping mall; there's an armed guard, and you'll be safe. There are movie theaters and restaurants in the mall. But you can't walk on the streets and be safe anymore. You can walk in my neighborhood, or on patrolled streets, but basically you must go from one secured location to another, and not stray into other parts of the city."

I found it hard to believe him at the time, but he doesn't let me out of his sight, and I'm unable to find out firsthand if his perceptions are accurate.

In 1999 the homicide rate in Venezuela was 20 percent higher than the previous year, and in Caracas the number of homicides reached the hundred mark on some weekends. Twenty years ago, there were only a hundred homicides a year in the capital. In the past ten years, the homicide rate has grown 506 percent, and half of all property crimes are now accompanied by violence.[1]

In Caracas, as well as in Rio de Janeiro, São Paulo, and Mexico City,[2] walls, gates, and guards defend the built environment of the middle and upper classes, creating safe havens for living, shopping, and entertainment. In Latin America this design feature grew out of Spanish colonial architecture adapted for contemporary use, but during visits to Africa and Asia I discover that gates, walls, and guards exist in numerous third world cities.

During a field visit to Nairobi, Kenya, our friend insists we not go out at night, and none of the other guests leaves the hotel. Even taxi drivers are hesitant to take us to a restaurant. They worry about being car-jacked. We persist, leave the hotel grounds, and hail a cab in the street.

After dinner, a cab driver in a faded blue Ford Escort with torn plastic seats picks us up, then pulls into a service station just across the street. I assume that he does not have the cash to pay for the gasoline until he has a fare. When I offer him money, though, he explains that he has enough, but keeps the minimum amount of petrol in his tank.

"This way if car is 'jacked, they can't get very far." The driver laughs at our surprise. "Many taken every day. Good thing my car's so beat-up," he tells us in Kenyan-accented English as we return to the hotel.

The fear in Nairobi is palpable. Visiting an old friend from graduate school, I am dismayed to see a rape gate[3] and padlock in front of her bedroom door, as well as gates at the entrance to her house, and a guarded entrance to her land. She lives on the edge of Nairobi, locked and barricaded inside.

FEAR OF CRIME AND GATING IN THE UNITED STATES

Urban fear in the United States has not escalated to these proportions, but North Americans have begun to worry about car-jacking in suburban malls and being mugged on city streets. Recent statistics, however, suggest that incidents of urban crime have been dropping since the mid-1980s in cities throughout the United States. In New York

City, for instance, crime rates have fallen much faster than in the rest of the nation. From 1990 to 1995, violent crime dropped 44.4 percent compared to 6.5 percent in the nation as a whole, and in 2001, while numbers of homicides increased in many large cities, New York City's rate continued to decline another 5.2 percent.[4] Property crime has experienced a similar drop, with a decline of 47 percent in New York City compared to 9.7 percent in the nation as a whole from 1990 to 1995.[5] Urban crime rates, though, are still higher than those in the suburbs. For example, in 1997 the total number of crimes of all types was 95,751 for Queens, with a population of 1,966,685, compared to 29,770 for Nassau County, with a population of 1,298,842—about double in the city compared to the suburb. For violent crimes, such as murder, the difference is even greater, with 207 murders in Queens and 26 murders in Nassau County reported in 1997.[6] Yet fear of crime remains high, even in the suburbs.[7]

Barry Glassner points out that we are inundated with media reports that have created a culture of fear.[8] Violence is a staple in newspapers, with the "amount of crime reported being unrelated to the actual crime rate in the locale. Violent crimes are much more likely to be reported than less violent ones, often with important details, such as motive, omitted from the news report."[9] Reporters often need to overstate the actual threat of an incident just to get coverage in the news.

But urban fear in the United States is not based just on media sensationalism. There has always been an uneasy relationship between the suburb and the city. People began moving to the suburbs to escape the dirt, disease, and immigrant populations of the inner city as soon as trolleys and trains made it feasible.[10] For a majority of Americans, the distance from suburb to city, and from home to work, was maintained through a complex social discourse.

Lynn Lofland believes that fear of crime and violence is based on the possibility that strangers could invade one's private space in the city. The wealthy have dealt with this fear by living in separate zones and by instituting restrictive land covenants. Gated communities possessing restrictive land covenants and defended boundaries are merely an expansion of this residential pattern. Certainly, urban fear reflects media manipulation of the public, but it also has historical roots in American anti-urbanism, and in legal and design strategies for the development of exclusive suburban communities.[11]

The majority of my New York interviewees mention crime as one of the main reasons that they moved to a gated community. Many worry about being robbed or have had an experience that triggered these fears.

CYNTHIA—FEAR OF BEING ROBBED AND VICTIMIZED

Cynthia, an attractive blonde in her late twenties, greets me at the door wearing a white T-shirt and a short jeans skirt. I notice the beautiful landscaping, a rock garden and English perennial cutting garden, as I enter her Newport-model house and I am surprised by the ultramodern interior. Cynthia makes coffee while answering the telephone and telling workmen where to put the furniture arriving outside. I sit in the family room, next to the kitchen, wondering when we will start. She explains that she is always running around, doing a million things, so it would be hard to catch her at home when she is not doing anything. The house has been a lot of work, and her husband is not around much, so it is up to her to see that everything gets done. I admire her unusual sense of style—a mix of French café posters, a large dark green couch, and green and gold drapes with fringe and tassels.

She has lived at Manor House for over a year and considers herself a pioneer for having bought the house based only on some drawings. Safety is particularly important to her because as a little girl her house was robbed: "I was about ten and remember coming home in the car with my mother and my little brother, who was a year old. The door to the house was open. My mother went in and saw a man jumping out the back window."

She lived in Bayside, Queens, in a gated condominium development before she was married. Bayside is a nice neighborhood, she says, but thieves go there because they can find valuables to steal. "I lived in an apartment. I couldn't live in a house in Bayside, because I'd be afraid of being robbed. My car used to be stolen, because it's the highest crime rate in New York [in 1996]."

She has friends in other neighborhoods in Queens who have burglar alarms and dogs, but the burglars cut the wires or drug the dogs. So she decided she needed something more secure. She knows the police department is good in this area—they get paid well and do their job—but she seems unsure of the Manor House guards: "during the day it's great with James [the guard], who you've met. But at night, it's like anything else [she worries]. I feel okay because if I had a problem I could call the guardhouse. I remember the first night I stayed here by myself. I said if something goes wrong, who am I going to call? I don't know what to do."

Her husband would only consider a gated community anyway, she adds. He had lived in a private gated community with his first wife and loved it. He was looking for something similar when they found Manor House.

The telephone rings several times during the interview, and each time I stop the tape recorder. What I overhear of the conversations confirms that she is a very busy woman, outspoken with her friends, and gets to the point quickly. After she finishes her last telephone conversation, she adds that her brother also lives in a gated community, and that her friend's best man is going to live at Manor House. According to Cynthia, a gated community is the only sensible way to live, especially given the increasing number of burglaries in Queens and in the surrounding suburbs.

Not everyone moves when they are robbed or vandalized. Joel and I had our cars broken into at least three times, and endured one attempted car theft and one successful one during our twelve years in Brooklyn. Yet we are not considering leaving Park Slope and instead use other ways of coping, such as parking in a garage.

The overall fear of crime, however, is increasing, particularly in the suburbs. It has created a boom in the security equipment industry.[12] Between 1965 and 1992, the percentage of Americans expressing fear of crime increased the most in the early 1970s and then remained constant. And even with a 27 percent decline in violent crime rates between 1993 and 1998, there was only a modest reduction in fear and worry.[13]

The research linking fear of crime to the physical environment suggests that familiarity, avoidance, and surveillance play important roles in allaying that fear. Sally Merry studies the interactions and perceptions of black, white, and Chinese residents in a high-rise project in a large East Coast city and concludes that lack of familiarity plays an important role in the perception of danger. Eli Anderson illustrates avoidance as a coping strategy in his study of "streetwise" behavior of Philadelphians living in a neighborhood undergoing gentrification. Philippe Bourgois depicts the fear and sense of vulnerability experienced by residents of El Barrio in New York and identifies their strategies of avoidance and surveillance used to deal with street crime.[14]

Joel and I deal with our fear of crime with similar tactics: by avoidance—we park in a garage; by surveillance—we check what is happening on the street before we enter our house; and by familiarity—we know our neighbors and the area intimately. Cynthia, it seems, decided that living in a gated community was the best way to cope.

Previous victimization also plays a role in a person's fear of crime, and some studies even suggest that fear increases among residents in relation to potential victimization, such as when rates of crime go up in the surrounding area. Fears associated with specific offenses, however, may be quite distinct. Violent victimization is more traumatic than property victimization, and greater trauma creates more "spillover effect," such that victims begin to fear many types of criminal victimization. Burglary victims are better able to compartmentalize the event, and experience an increase only in their fear of burglary. This may be because in many cases people perceive burglary as an "outside" threat. But when the victim perceives the threat to be within the community, as in Cynthia's case, the fear of crime may be greater and more persistent.[15]

Another New York household moved to Manor House because of increasing crime in their Manhattan neighborhood. Even though the husband was able to protect them because of his "streetwise" knowledge, he decided he preferred to live in a relatively crime-free environment.

BARBARA AND ALVIN—STREETWISE AVOIDANCE AND VULNERABILITY

Alvin Belen shows me to his study, where his twelve-year-old son is reading. The boy greets me with a handshake, says "good morning," and leaves immediately.

I am struck by his respectful manner. I know from my initial telephone call that Alvin, who is in his seventies, also has an older daughter, and currently lives with his second wife and young son.

The house is in disarray with workmen everywhere. The study, however, is comfortable, with a brown leather couch, walls lined with bookcases, and an executive-sized desk. A miniature poodle sniffs my legs, wags her tail, and is about to jump in my lap when Alvin reappears with his wife, Barbara. Barbara is a youthful forty-five, small-boned and athletic, wearing a jogging suit and tennis shoes. Alvin is dressed in gray slacks and a white shirt, as if he were getting ready for work. He is retired and stays at home, while she runs her own business.

Alvin starts by telling his life story. He was born in the Bronx, moved to Greenwich Village, and then rented an apartment with Barbara on Fifth Avenue in Manhattan. They moved to Manor House because they needed more security and wanted space, comfort, and convenience. Alvin points out that his wife forgets that there was a doorman at their previous residence, just like a guard in a gated community, so they were just trading one kind of protection for another. He wanted a private community so he would not have to mow the grass and take care of things in the house. He also wanted to be able to go away and not worry. The people at Manor House check the house for you when you are not home.

> We never had any incidents, but we knew that it was not a safe area. Fifth Avenue is very dark at night once the stores close up, especially on weekends. You had to be very careful because you had banks, and you had people ripped off right on the street, cars broken into continuously, and windows broken. They came in from Central Park. [One day] I saw them breaking windows and robbing a car. They caught the perpetrators—I saw the cops take away the stuff and I know they kept it. They wanted me to testify in court, and I refused. Why? Because they paraded him in front of my window, and he knew I was on the second floor. Contrary to what they say about the city, don't believe it, it's not safe. Giuliani [the previous mayor of New York] does not publish what's happening in the real world.
>
> I'm a born New Yorker, from the Bronx, and I speak Spanish. I know what's happening all over. I'm one of the real people, up from the street. I speak to the cops, the Latino cops; they tell me what's going on. . . . I feel safe even in the city, because I know where to walk, how to walk. I'm streetwise. You have to be streetwise. You have to know where to walk and how to walk and what to wear.

He is sarcastic when I ask his wife if she is afraid in the city. She says yes, then he adds that she loves the smell of garbage and soot.

I ask him how he feels at Manor House. He loves it there, loves to cook, and thinks his neighbors are wonderful. He adds that he stays on the guards' case to announce visitors and to be "on the ball." His wife, on the other hand, is a city person. She likes the vibrancy of the city. Alvin cuts in to explain that he is the realist. She likes the city, he says, because in the city he did all the driving. She didn't really know what living in the city meant because she never took the subway.

This couple does not agree on why they moved. They were concerned about crime, but Alvin was the one to deal with it, and Barbara was sheltered by his "streetwise" ways. His urban coping strategies worked in Manhattan, and still work for her. He, however, is much happier living where he does not have to use his street smarts and can relax, not worrying about the safety of his house and car.

Another dimension of fear of crime is the sense of vulnerability, in which social or physical characteristics lead one to feel more or less afraid. For example, research demonstrates that the elderly are more fearful than the young, and women more fearful than men. But gender and age interact with other individual or contextual features that could make one feel more or less vulnerable. For example, one study found that while men are less likely to fear violent crime, there was no significant difference among men and women in their fear of burglary. Because there are two psychological components of fear of crime—cognitive (risk perception), and emotional (feeling afraid)—as well as various kinds of crime, researchers have had a difficult time clarifying the specifics of the crime-fear relationship, but generally agree there is a loose relationship that varies in response to the particular circumstances. In the Belen household the husband does not feel as vulnerable to crime as his wife does because of his previous life experiences, and yet he decides that he wants to move up socially and enjoy the safety and maintenance of a gated community.[16]

Unfortunately, moving up in class position may actually increase a person's sense of potential victimization. Those who occupy higher class positions participate in activities and lifestyles that place them at risk, thus increasing their sense of vulnerability. This, in turn, leads to household fortification.[17] Residents who are active and affluent agonize about protecting their property, and thus create homes that are "fortified havens against a threatening world."[18]

San Antonio residents also identify their fear of crime—or their spouse's fear—as a prime reason for moving to one of the many gated communities north of the city. Polly and her husband live in an upscale gated development with armed guards at each entrance, roaming crime-watch patrols, as well as the standard entry gates and surrounding walls.

POLLY—THE FEAR FACTOR AND SOCIAL ISOLATION

At first I cannot find the house, so I ask a group of children on bicycles if they know where Polly lives. The houses are uniformly large, two stories with ornate detailing. In the twilight it is hard to see the house numbers or any other distinguishing features. The children lead me to the house, shouting and laughing.

Polly is standing in the doorway looking for me, and waves at me to come in after thanking the children. She is a tall, heavyset young woman, about thirty, dressed in a white blouse, floral skirt, and sandals. She leads me into her husband's study with oak paneling and built-in bookshelves. We sit close together in leather chairs next to the one brass lamp. She apologizes, saying that none of the rooms is finished. They are trying to get every detail right, so it is taking a long time—three years so far—to decorate and furnish the four-bedroom, five-bathroom house. She is supervising painters putting the finishing touches on an original wall mural in the dining room. I ask if her husband will join us, and she replies that he should be home in about an hour and will join us then.

Her husband chose their gated residence: "I think it really mattered to my husband, just for the security. . . . I think he's a little overboard when it comes to the fear factor [he is afraid of] just crime in general." She thinks that she is not afraid because as a psychology major in college she learned that urban crimes actually occur on the south side[19] of San Antonio and not in the northern suburbs. Nonetheless, she feels safer and more comfortable living with guards and gates. "I certainly feel safe here because it's gated. It's not that I [don't] feel ambivalent, but I really like all this luxury. The one thing that's really striking is you don't get door-to-door solicitors."

She complains, however, about the inconvenience of having to call the guard to let her friends in the gate.

> Sometimes [the security guards are] stiff, sometimes they're totally lax. I notice with my friends that some of them can get through the gate, and I know I haven't called. And sometimes I've called, and they won't let them through. It's a hit-or-miss thing. Believe me, if you wanted to get into a gated community you could.
>
> Look at this community I live in. Do you think that I'm afraid that someone is going to come up to my door with a gun? No, I'm not. Is my husband sometimes? You never know [mimicking him]. . . . He has a big fear that the house is going to be robbed, and we always have to turn on the alarm system. When I don't, he gets angry.

She attributes her husband's fear of being robbed to growing up in an affluent urban neighborhood in San Antonio. His family did not live in a gated community, and even though they never had a burglary they were aware of their potential vulnerability. She, on the other hand, grew up in a small community where they left the front door unlocked more than half the time. There were no murders in the town's history that she can recall. There was only one publicized murder, but it happened in the city. Her husband's family had enough wealth to be concerned about burglaries, while she grew up far enough from the city that urban crime did not affect her life.

She thinks people live in gated communities because of fear. "Fear of crime, gangs, it's really out of proportion. . . . I just feel that the crimes that people are afraid of here—kidnapping and drive-by shootings—they don't happen here. Those are segregated in their own residential communities. It's happening over there. So I believe that fear is probably the biggest factor why people live in gated communities."

Polly offers an insightful analysis of the problem. She is aware that San Antonio's crime is concentrated in poorer, urban neighborhoods and not in the suburbs. Nevertheless, Polly and her husband feel afraid. Polly says that residents read about kidnapping and drive-by shootings or hear stories about burglaries in the suburbs, and it sets the "fear factor" in motion. Polly calls it a "crime movement" at one point in the interview—an interesting commentary that captures the "waves of crime" reported in San Antonio's only newspaper, the *San Antonio Express-News.*

For these residents, urban fear encompasses fear of being burglarized, robbed, or assaulted and fear of the people who are thought to commit these crimes. The gates, walls, and guards are thought to deter crime by keeping whose who are potential criminals out. It is of little comfort that the crime statistics suggest that they would be quite safe in traditional, ungated suburbs. Ultimately, urban fear, fear of actual crime, and fear of certain kinds of people all combine to form a worldview. Gated communities are a product of this mindset—they at once protect and segregate residents.

In the United States, though, gating does not necessarily reduce crime. Randy Atlas evaluated changing crime patterns in four gated communities located in Keystone Point, a middle- to upper-middle-class residential area comprised of six islands and three land entrances in North Miami. A guard gate was installed in 1991. Burglary and theft decreased from 1990 to 1997—there was a 14 percent decrease in theft and a 54 percent decrease in burglaries—but there were also spikes of increased crime. He concludes that gates do not make a significant difference in the crime rate or deter criminals, but they do make residents feel safer and increase the real estate value of the property and surrounding area.[20]

In another study using economic modeling to understand the impact of gating on crime, gates were found to divert most crime to other communities. But by diverting crime to other areas, it also had negative repercussions for residents who were not as well protected as those in gated communities. This crime diversion was ignored by the developers and not calculated in their costs, but led to excessive gating and increased expenditures in the surrounding areas. These unnecessary expenditures raise the question of whether private gating is an economically efficient means of crime control.[21] Further, where gating reduced employment opportunities, it significantly increased the overall crime rate in the region.

Social integration reduces fear of crime and increases resident's sense of well-being. Although it seems counterintuitive, taking precautions against crime actually may increase rather than reduce a person's fear of crime: those precautions lead to greater social isolation, which in turn produces greater perceived vulnerability and more fear—which residents deal with by taking even greater precautions—and thus becoming even more isolated socially.[22] Social integration reduces fear of crime and increases residents' sense of well-being. Thus, gating may create more fear of crime than it alleviates.

CRIME AND GATING IN MEXICO CITY: A LATIN AMERICAN COMPARISON

To place fear of crime in perspective, I decided it would be valuable to talk to gated community residents in Latin America, where the rates of crime are very high. Fortunately, Mariana Diaz-Wionczek, then a graduate student in environment psychology, had entrée into a gated community on the southern edge of Mexico City, and we were able to speak to a number of its residents. Their stories offer a counterpoint to the New York and Texas experiences, and bolster the argument that fear of crime in the United States is not necessarily about crime *per se* while in many places, like Mexico, the fear might indeed be directly related to crime itself.

Violence and fear of crime in Latin America are ubiquitous. Citizens of Latin American capitals live in constant fear—15 of every 100,000 people die as a result of violence—and this is a conservative number, since in Colombia the violent-death toll rises to 100 per 100,000 population. Much of this crime goes unpunished, further frustrating and terrorizing residents.[23] In this cultural context, gated enclaves have a long history as a crime deterrent.

Teresa Caldeira traces the history of urban spatial changes and economic crises in São Paulo, Brazil, from the 1940s to the 1990s and identifies the breakdown in government integrity and policing, and the subsequent rise in state corruption and fear of crime that produced fortified enclaves. In Brazil the closed condominium is the most desirable type of housing for the middle and upper classes. An "aesthetic of security" has evolved based on walls, fences, and guards creating a city in which the quality of public space and the possibility of social encounters has been drastically reduced.[24] And in San Juan, Puerto Rico, Law 21 permits residents in existing neighborhoods to seal off their streets and living areas.[25] Ivelisse Rivera-Bonilla reports that residents decide to close off their streets because of the rising crime rate as well as their desire to improve their quality of life and strengthen community solidarity.

Not so long ago, Mexico City was seen as a relatively safe place in comparison to the rest of Latin American capitals.[26] But from 1990 to 1995, reported murders rose 50 percent and robbery incidents increased sixfold. Kidnapping, once rare, rose to fifteen hundred per year. Some experts blame it on the increasing gulf between the rich and poor, while others fault the discredited justice system and inefficiency of crime-fighting institutions. Crime has become a career not just for criminals, but for police officers who are now the main organizers of drug dealing, car theft, kidnapping, piracy, and truck hijacking. Murder is rampant in Mexico City's suburbs, where the new rich are building elaborate homes next to established slums.[27]

Throughout the city, there are a variety of types of defended spaces, including individual houses with gates, walls, and a nighttime guard, or groups of three or four houses cordoned off by a perimeter fence patrolled by an armed guard. Gating is not a new tradition in Mexico, but has its roots in walled colonial architecture. *Urbanizaciones privadas* (private planned communities) existed as early as the beginning of the last century. In Mexico City the first wave of new construction of such communities started at the end of the 1960s, about the same time that Leisure World was established in California.[28]

Gated communities are not formed as common interest developments in Mexico, but as private subdivisions or condominiums; lots are purchased individually without maintenance guarantees or a required fee structure. Even though it is illegal to gate public streets, the number of gated communities is escalating both in the northern and southern sectors of Mexico City. Vista Mar is a recent example.

Vista Mar is located on the southern edge of Mexico City at the base of Ajusco Mountain, off the major urban highway, the Periférico, and was planned to be a part of the Tlalpan Forest, one of the most important ecological reserves in the city. This upper-middle-income community has four access gates controlled by armed guards and is surrounded by forest and a stone wall. No two roads cross, to prevent accidents, and all streets end in a "T" to discourage automobiles from driving by. Roads meander through the hilly terrain dotted with parks and gardens landscaped with semiarid plants and the local volcanic rocks.

House size and styles vary considerably: there is the classic modern with straight lines and volcanic rock details, the Mexican colonial, and the modern and postmodern designs that use contrasting shapes in the facade. A typical house has two stories: three bedrooms on the second floor, each with a separate bathroom; and, on the first floor, a studio or library, television room, a living room, dining room, kitchen, breakfast area, and living spaces for domestic employees.

The community is divided into nine hundred lots, four hundred square meters each, and families purchase up to three lots for an individual house. A four-hundred-square-meter lot costs 2,000,000 pesos ($120,000), and houses on single lots have been sold for between 3,500,000 and 4,000,000 pesos ($420,000 to $500,000). The lots are still being purchased, and more houses are currently being built. This gated community does include a few businesses—about 5 percent of the community—including a bank and hotel, and a few apartments owned by the tenants.

Two vignettes from Vista Mar illustrate residents' reactions to the rising crime in Mexico City. Sisters Maria Eugenia and Marta, want to feel safer, and like the Texas and New York residents, they think the gates will keep criminals from entering the community.

MARIA EUGENIA AND MARTA—WHEN YOU PASS THE GATE, YOU FEEL SAFER

Maria Eugenia and Marta are twenty and twenty-six, respectively, and live with their father and mother in a large, two-story modern house. They are both attractive, tall with long black hair, dressed in blue jeans and colorful T-shirts. Marta works in an accounting firm, while her sister, Maria Eugenia, is still finishing university. Both of their parents work—their father is a doctor and their mother a financial analyst—and their two brothers are away at boarding school. They moved to Vista Mar over six years ago from another neighborhood also located in the southern section of Mexico City. As Marta explains,

> We lived in a house near the UNAM [the largest public university in the city]. My father built that house. Living there we had the opportunity of playing in the garden and inside the house, but not outside the house because it wasn't safe. It was not a place to go outside and play with the neighbors. The house was a little isolated. I remember it with affection.
>
> We moved because of the traffic—the subway train was constructed nearby—and my father did not like all the people and congestion just in front of our house. Also, the houses were too close to each other without a garden or something to separate them.

They miss their neighbors. In Vista Mar they are more isolated from others, because there is so much space and the houses are bigger. But their new neighborhood is safer, and the green areas and the type of people who live there promote "coexistence." Marta continues:

> At the beginning, I felt far away from everything because the other house had a better location: two blocks from the university and three blocks to where my school and my friends were. . . . On the other hand, safety is getting worse . . . and now, living here, I feel different in terms of safety. The moment you pass a gate you begin to feel safe, while in the other house a lot of people and cars were there, and you never knew [what would happen]. I didn't feel this way before, but now that I think about it, this neighborhood is safer, quieter, and there are not a lot of people and cars on the street—only the people that live here.

Maria Eugenia adds, "I didn't feel isolated. Maybe because I knew a lot of people, and I was near my work. Things are near, bars and everything. You don't have to go out of the neighborhood, and also there is the additional security. I go out with the dog at nine P.M. and nothing happens."

Both sisters agree that they do not know or visit their neighbors. Marta says that she does not get along with them very well, while Maria Eugenia says that she waves hello and lends neighbors an onion when they need it, but otherwise has little contact.

Their father chose the neighborhood during one of their Sunday excursions to look at land and houses after the family had decided they had to move. They bought in Vista Mar because it was very private, secure, and quiet. Also, their father liked it because it was near a forest, and their parents now have a view of the forest from their room.

We ask them about the kind of people who live in the community, and Maria Eugenia answers:

> You can find all kinds of people. Recently, at the corner we had two cars filled with bodyguards taking care of their boss, and that bothered us. It looked as if he had a debt and needed security. But things like that you can see everywhere. People also say drug dealers live here, even that a very well known dealer has a house here, but who knows? On the other hand, businessmen and housewives that have their children in private schools also live here.
>
> Some people feel that they own the street, and they think that they can walk anywhere and do whatever they want. Then you see their behavior with the people who work at the gates, and you just know that they just like to feel powerful. The security guards are trying to do their work to benefit us; they are trying to create a safe environment, order, and these people bother them with anything that interferes with their feeling of comfort. They don't pay the maintenance fee, which is absurd because if they have the money to be here, they must be able to pay the fee, which isn't much. These are the type of people who live here.

Marta adds that in the time that they have lived in Vista Mar, they have gone to the tenants association to ask about some robberies that had occurred. They wanted to know about why they had happened. That is when they learned that less than half of the residents pay the maintenance fee. "[Only] 45 percent pay. I know a lot of people from the block, and a lot of them are in the group of people that don't pay. . . . I never imagined until then that there were so many people who don't pay. It's embarrassing, because I do not know what to say to them."

According to the sisters, the community was started by a developer who owned all the land, and each buyer who bought land also deposited money into a fund used for maintenance and security. But that initial money is gone, and instead a voluntary residents association runs everything, asking residents to pay fees to support them. Maria Eugenia has become involved in this group because of her concern over a series of robberies by people who worked in some of the houses and who provide security. People would go to church, for instance, and when they came back they would find their house empty.

As we end the conversation, Marta says that safety and tranquillity were definitely the reasons they moved. In fact, one time their father asked her if she felt all right about living in a gated community, and she told him that "after the gate I feel safe." And she appreciates it more each year: "Because safety issues in the city are getting worse every day. I am becoming very paranoid when I see a car behind me and [I wonder] how much time it has been there, following me. You are always at risk, and it's good to know that after you go through the gate the person behind you can't follow."

According to Marta and Maria Eugenia, crime is a compelling reason to move to a gated community. Unlike in New York City or San Antonio, kidnapping and murder as well as armed robbery are on the rise, and there is little to no police protection. Janina and her husband also moved for safety reasons, but understand that gates and guards do not always work.

JANINA AND HECTOR—AFRAID TO GO OUTSIDE

Janina and Hector are a middle-aged couple with three children ages eight through fourteen. Hector is a businessman, and Janina, like the majority of women interviewed in Vista Mar, stays home to take care of the children. They live in a rambling one-story modern house with large patios between the bedrooms and a perfectly kept lawn decorated with clumps of bird of paradise. When you drive up, you cannot see in the windows, since they are hidden by a stucco wall that faces the lawn and road. Upon entering, however, you realize that the wall creates an interior corridor garden filled with potted plants and flowers that the windows of the house look out on.

They have lived in Vista Mar for five years, and before that lived in a quiet and beautiful neighborhood near the airport. We ask Janina how she compares Vista Mar with their previous home:

I think that this is one of the few neighborhoods where you can feel safe . . . We started to feel unsafe when we heard about robberies and assaults [in Mexico City]. My father-in-law moved [here] first, and then we followed. . . . We made our decision thinking about our daughters. We wanted to have a garden without strangers from another neighborhood.

[We like] the little bit of security and the privacy. Not everybody can get in. It is very quiet, and they ask for your ID. . . . Sometimes we go out for a walk, but with everything that is happening now, we don't want to go out of the door. We knew about some house robberies eight to nine months ago [in the community].

We like the gates. We would like them to close some entrances and restrict the access even more, but the community is very big, close to a thousand families, and for that reason is difficult to do. We are happy—at least they ask for an ID at the gate. If you see someone or something suspicious you just call the association, and they immediately send a patrol or a person because they use radios. We like this kind of security.

The community is closed, and you have a gate at the entrance. You don't have this kind of arrangement in other neighborhoods. What you have [there] is some blockades and a gate. I think this is one of the few communities to have the privilege of being completely closed.

I know people in other gated communities. There is one that has only one entrance and one exit, but it has fewer families, only about two hundred. In the other gated community, they have also one entrance and one exit, and it is very restricted. They ask you for an ID number and talk to you by intercom. Here you can't do that because we have too many families. In some communities you can't get in until they call your house. I would like to have an intercom to know when people are coming, but still people get in by giving a fake name.

Janina and Hector discuss the different types of secured entrances that exist in Mexico City and conclude that they are doing as well as can be expected. They are not surprised that there have been robberies inside the community, because of its size and social diversity, but would prefer better screening of visitors. Still, they feel that Vista Mar is marginally safer than where they lived before.

In 2000, a year and a half after we spoke with these residents of Vista Mar, a new president, Vicente Fox, was elected, bringing down the authoritarian government that had controlled Mexico for most of the last century. President Fox opened the archives of secret government security documents and appointed a special prosecutor to investigate major cases of past government abuses of human rights. Residents feel that his openness to reform and commitment to taking responsibility for governmental corruption may arrest the tide of rising crime and violence.[29]

COMPARING FEAR OF CRIME

The comparison of gated community residents' fear of crime and violence in Mexico and the United States raises interesting questions. Residents in both countries are concerned about crime, and the majority say they moved behind gates to ameliorate the impact of crime and violence on their daily lives. Yet in the United States the crime rate is decreasing—and has been decreasing—rapidly, and in the suburbs where these communities are located it was quite low to begin with. In Mexico City, however, violent crime in the suburbs of Mexico City is escalating, and police protection has been almost nonexistent. Regardless of whether crime has been increasing or decreasing, the same discourse of fear is evident everywhere from Long Island and Texas to Mexico City, São Paulo, and San Juan.

Further, there is not a great deal of evidence that gates in fact deter criminal activity. Both the San Antonio and Mexico City communities report robberies by insiders, and the fear of crime has not declined. Residents say they feel safer, but then go on to talk about their worries concerning burglaries, kidnapping, assault, and whether the gates provide anything more than a false sense of security. Since the crime rate is the same outside and inside these communities, the reason that there is so little crime in the U.S. examples is that they are located in areas where the crime rate is already very low. In the northern county of San Antonio within the zip code area of the gated communities studied, you can look up reported crimes by the month on a San Antonio crime web page. There are almost no reported crimes in the entire area. It is not the gates that lower the crime rate, but the physical and social context and other demographic characteristics of the region. In Mexico City, residents have a sense that gating reduces car hijacking and drive-by shootings, but there are no statistics available as to whether this is actually the case.

Gates, in fact, may contribute to placing residents at increased risk by marking the community as a wealthy enclave where burglary is lucrative and by creating a social environment characterized by lack of social integration. The majority of residents say that they do not know or are not particularly friendly with their neighbors, which adds to their sense of social isolation and contributes to their feeling vulnerable and scared.

In Mexico City, where the actual crime rate is high and kidnapping is on the rise, it makes some intuitive sense that families who could afford it would choose to live in gated and guarded areas in an attempt to deter criminals who are not from within the community from entering. But in the United States, where most of the gated communities are in suburban areas, this rationale does not hold up. Fear of crime and violence may be about other fears that are not as easily expressed.

CHAPTER 7

Fear of Others

Against whom was the Great Wall to serve as a protection? Against the people from the north. Now, I come from the southeast of China. No northern people can menace us there. We read of them in the books of the ancients; the cruelties they commit in accordance with their nature make us sigh in our peaceful arbors. The faithful representations of the artist show us the faces of the damned, their gaping mouths, their jaws furnished with great pointed teeth, their half-shut eyes that already seem to be seeking out the victim which their jaws will rend and devour. When our children are unruly, we show them these pictures, and at once they fly weeping into our arms. But nothing more than that do we know about these northerners. We have not seen them, and if we remain in our villages we shall never see them, even if on their wild horses they should ride as hard as they can straight towards us—the land is too vast and would not let them reach us; they would end their course in the empty air.

—Franz Kafka, "The Great Wall of China"[1]

My husband and I have reservations about going to a Fourth of July party, but my sister coaxes us with the promise of margaritas and sinful desserts, finally winning us over. Dressed in New York chic, we cross the street to enter an imposing Santa Fe–style house decorated with Mexican furniture and colorful textiles, full of people talking, children racing about, and our hosts serving drinks and dishing out enormous quantities of food. My husband wanders out to the pool, while I stay inside where it is air-conditioned. My choices are watching television with the older men or sitting with our hosts' teenage son and his friends. I sit down with the teenagers, and I am soon involved in a spirited discussion.

"Should we go downtown after dinner to see the fireworks along Riverwalk?" the host's son asks. Riverwalk is the commercially successful development that revitalized the center of San Antonio.

"Will there be many Mexicans there?" a tall, gangly boy in a Nike T-shirt and nylon running shorts asks.

"It'll be mobbed with Mexicans; I'm not sure I want to go," a girl with heavy blond bangs responds.

I am struck by how they used the word *Mexican*. Yesterday I toured the local missions where the complex history of Spanish conquest and resettlement of indigenous peoples is inscribed in the protective walls of the church compounds. Surely, these young people learn about Texas history in school.

I interrupt the flow of conversation and ask them what they mean by "Mexican." A young man in baggy khakis and a baseball hat worn backwards looks at me curiously. "Why, the Mexicans who live downtown, on the south side of the city."

"What makes you think they are Mexican?" I ask, frowning a bit. "Because they speak Spanish?"

"They are dangerous," a young woman in a tennis skirt asserts, "packing knives and guns. Our parents don't allow us to go downtown at night."

They decide to stay and watch the fireworks from the golf course—at least they would not be with their parents—and wander off to find their other friends.

I remain at the table, my mind racing to bring together scattered bits of the history and culture of the region. Texas was originally part of Mexico, colonized by the Spanish. The majority of people who live in Texas identify themselves as descendants of the Spanish and/or Mexicans who settled the area. "Mexicans" can refer to the founding families of San Antonio, hacienda owners and other landholders, who make up a significant part of the political elite and upper class. "Mexicans" also can mean visiting Mexican nationals who maintain summer houses in the region and this neighborhood. There are people who legally immigrated to Texas but retain strong ties to their birthplace and call themselves "Mexicans." Finally, there are the "Mexicans" that the teenagers mentioned, a stereotyped group of what some locals think of as poor, undocumented workers who speak Spanish but who in fact come from all over Latin America.

The teenagers' discussion of "Mexicans" reminds me of T. C. Boyle's novel about a gated community in southern California. In one passage the protagonist is arguing with the president of the homeowners association about a decision to add gates to their walled suburban housing development.

> ". . . the gate thing is important, probably the single most important agendum we've taken up in my two years as president."
>
> "You really think so? To me, I say it's unnecessary—and, I don't know, irresponsible somehow. . . . I lean more to the position that we live in a democracy. . . . I mean, we all have a stake in things, and locking yourself away from the rest of society, how can you justify that?"
>
> "Safety. Self-protection. Prudence. You lock your car, don't you? Your front door? . . . I know how you feel . . . but this society isn't what it was—and it won't be until we get control of the borders."
>
> "That's racist, Jack, and you know it."
>
> . . . "Not in the least—it's a question of national sovereignty. Did you know that the U.S. accepted more immigrants last year than all the other countries of the world *combined*—and that half of them settled in California? And that's *legal* immigrants, people with skills, money, education.[2]

Does Boyle capture what these teenagers are feeling? Are they reflecting local attitudes about immigration and the permeable boundary between Mexico and Texas that lies just a two-and-a-half-hour car ride away?

But it is not just in Texas and California that residents of gated communities stigmatize immigrants as a source of fear. In New York as well residents identify "ethnic changes" and a changing socioeconomic environment as potentially threatening.

CAROL AND TED—IT'S ETHNIC CHANGES

Elena, one of my graduate students, and I arrive at Manor House earlier than expected, so we stop and talk with the guard at the gate. He is a young African American man with short hair, wearing a conservative uniform—blue shirt and navy slacks. He is quite cordial, and invites us into his small room. This is his second job in a gated community. He likes working here, but feels that the residents sometimes expect too much: "after all, we are not police." He had worked at the Homestead where the residents complained that the guards were not doing their jobs. At Manor Place it's better, but residents still do not want their rights infringed on. Elena asks him if he feels that living in a secure environment affects the residents in any way. He responds that it makes them more demanding and not very responsible. They expect the guards to relieve them of all obligations and problems, and to "jump to the rescue" even though the guards have no real power.

As Elena continues to converse with him, I reflect on how nice it is to have her with me on this interview. Elena was born in Romania, and has never been inside an American suburban home. In contrast to my experience, she is amazed that a couple with only one child would choose to live in such a large house. She provides her own cultural perspective and compares everything she sees to her life to Eastern Europe.

"Did you ask everything you wanted to?"

"It's great," she replies enthusiastically. "He feels that residents are too dependent on him, which will ultimately lead to problems. I'm not sure what kind of problems, but I can talk to him again later."

He waves us on, and we pass through the visitors' gate. It is a beautiful day, sunny and breezy. We drive along the winding road, passing a number of just-completed houses, all painted in pale colors, with shutters, porches, and landscape planting. There is subtle variation in style and design, but nonetheless the houses look remarkably similar to one another. Each is placed back from the curb with shrubs, grass, and flowers arranged in neat beds between the house and the street. The interviewee's Vineyard model has a garage and driveway tucked away on the side of the house, allowing ample room for a wraparound porch in front. We arrive on time, park the car, and walk up the driveway.

Carol and Ted Corral are waiting for us at the door. They are both in their early fifties, casually dressed in tan slacks and matching polo shirts. Ted is a large, red-faced man with a loud voice, while Carol is pale with blond-gray hair, more soft-spoken and gentle. When they learn that we drove out from the city, they invite us to sit outside to enjoy the sunshine on the patio. We decline because the noise from airplanes overhead and the ongoing construction would interfere with tape-recording.

They have been living at Manor House for eight months, and had previously lived in Great Neck for the past twenty-eight years. Ted admits that it was "traumatic" to move, but they "made it," and he is now trying to minimize the impact of the move on their lives.

Carol tells me that they were attached to their previous home because they brought up their children there and because it had been built for them. Prior to Great Neck, they had lived in Brooklyn. "A long time ago," Ted adds, implying that he couldn't really remember.

Elena asks about their life in Great Neck. Ted replies that it's a great community socially, and that the children had a good school. It's an affluent community and offers lots of benefits. Carol adds that most of her friends were made there when her children were small. Great Neck had everything, so they did not have to leave for entertainment, restaurants, or even adult education courses. "It's almost like living in the city," Carol says, "but better."

Ted describes the community as "very, very educated. . . . You know, so everyone goes on to college, and it stressed the role of family, and you know, it's just a wonderful community. But it's changing, it's undergoing internal transformations."

Carol says, "It's ethnic changes."

And Ted repeats: "It's ethnic changes; that's a very good way of putting it."

Carol agrees and adds that it started to happen "in the last, probably, seven to eight years." The changing composition of the neighborhood made them so uncomfortable they decided to move.

I ask about their prior residence in Brooklyn. Ted shrugs his shoulders. I say that I would like to know about why they left for comparison purposes, and finally Carol answers. She tells me they had moved from Brooklyn to bring up their children in a better environment. The school system was changing, and they did not want their children to go to school with children from lower socioeconomic backgrounds who were being bused into their Brooklyn neighborhood.

"Those kids were wild," she says, "and had a different upbringing." She wanted to protect her children from exposure to the kinds of problems these kids might cause. The neighborhood was still comfortable, but the school system was not "desirable," as she tactfully put it. They had both grown up in Brooklyn, but the neighborhood changed, so they decided to build their own home in the suburbs.

Elena asks how they found Manor House. Ted answers, "driving by." Carol says there had been an announcement in the newspaper, and people were discussing that it had gone bankrupt and then had reopened under new ownership. I ask how they decided to move here, and Ted answers that they were looking for something that would suit their lifestyle better. He adds that they chose a gated community because they wanted a secure lifestyle with no hassles and no responsibilities.

I ask whether they would consider living in the city again, and they both agree that moving back to the city would be out of the question. They had lived there for twenty-five years, but when they moved to the suburbs they had done so for a reason. They would never go back. Carol says the city was so different now compared to when she was growing up. "You're always on guard when you're walking."

She still loves the city, but does not want to live there. She wants to come home to tranquillity.

Dualistic thinking is a form of social splitting used to cope with anxiety and fear. It oversimplifies and dichotomizes cultural definitions and social expectations to differentiate the self from the other: Anglos from "Mexicans," whites from illegal immigrants, or whites from "ethnic others." The concept of splitting draws upon psychoanalytic relational theory, particularly Melanie Klein's work on the development of object relations. According to Klein, psychological splitting is the process of disassociation between "good" and "bad" representations beginning when the infant differentiates external and internal relationships by splitting the mother into good and bad, incorporating the good mother who can be identified with, and rejecting the bad. It is a psychological means of dealing with contradictory and often conflicting feelings.[3]

Psychological splitting can be used as a form of denial and resistance, providing a means of distancing oneself from an undesirable self-image and projecting it onto another. Social splitting is often used to project social fears onto a more vulnerable group, such as the Jews during World War II, or the homeless on the streets of present-day New York City. It also helps to explain the kind of us-versus-them thinking employed by the gated community residents to rationalize their fears of those outside the gates.

During periods of economic decline and social stress, middle-class people become anxious about maintaining their social status—what is referred to in these interviews as "the good life"—and seek to identify the reasons that their environment and social world is deteriorating. Social splitting offers a strategy that is reinforced by cultural stereotypes and media distortions, allowing people to psychologically separate themselves from people who they perceive as threatening their tranquillity and neighborhood stability. The walls and gates of the community reflect this splitting physically as well as metaphorically, with "good" people (the good part of us) inside, and the "bad" remaining outside.

Advertisements for gated communities evoke this social splitting and even go a step further in envisaging what is being defended against. For example, the developer of Sanctuary Cove, Australia's first gated community, told reporters, "The streets these days are full of cockroaches and most of them are human. Every man has a right to protect his family, himself and his possessions, to live in peace and safety." Based on his study of gated communities in Australia, Matthew Burke found that the solidifying of perimeter barriers led to a greater sense of residents being "insiders," and reinforced the reverse process that "designates those beyond the walls as 'outsiders' [as] inevitable."[4]

Some gated communities, however, are ethnically diverse to begin with. Waterview in Queens is made up of many ethnic and cultural groups reflecting the surrounding neighborhood. At Waterview, there are residents who move out when certain ethnic groups move in, while others develop relationships that defy simplistic dualities and begin to create a community with social and cultural diversity.

CONNIE—DEALING WITH ETHNIC GROUPS INSIDE THE COMMUNITY

Connie was one of the original residents of Waterview and moved in over sixteen years ago. At the time, she wanted a safe environment:

> And I guess I must have known it was some kind of gate or some kind of enclosing. I did want some security provided. I'm single and I wanted to know that I would be safe. I was very nervous; I never bought anything and was all by myself. I mean, I did not know anything about closing or anything or how to inspect an apartment. And I learned a lot, after the fact. And I got very involved right away in the board.
>
> [At first there were] three different developments. Condo one was built first, and then condo two, which I am part of, then condo three. I didn't know that there were going to be three separate condos. I was really very concerned about it because I felt there were going to be problems with everybody fighting as opposed to coming together. Which every once in a while there is; there is fighting.

At first, she says, people didn't know how to build themselves into a community. People were being ticketed for "stupid reasons," and board members were not being ticketed. Because there was a real shortage of parking space, people were parking wherever they could. She thought that the management should become more community-minded and on Saturdays or Sundays let people park wherever they wanted, as long as it wasn't a fire hazard.

"But nobody wanted that. People wanted rules, rules, rules," she says.

Connie tries to get along with her neighbors. She understands that there are cultural differences, but she wants to have a good relationship with them, since it is her home.

> I try to embrace my neighbors—like my upstairs neighbor, who moved in about two years ago. They are not supposed to have tiles on the floors; you are supposed to have carpet. Before they moved in I noticed they were putting in tiles. I had man-

agement send them a letter saying. . . . They acted like they did not know what I was talking about. They were Oriental or whatever but they kept saying, their culture was [to say] yes, yes, yes. And they never changed anything. So I sent a couple of letters and then I just decided, I have to live with these people. I do not want to have any bad feelings in my house karma, my house energy. So I decided to embrace them. I made a conscious effort. I went up to them, and I said look, we have to work this out. And they were really nice. They told me they would do everything they can to keep the kids not in the living room area where my ceiling is their floor. And I said fine, and I was not going to be demanding anything else. I think it proved okay. Every once in a while it is bad, and in the past once I went up to them [to complain]. What I really keep saying like a mantra is: These are your neighbors, and you have to learn to love them, with their kids and their noise level. And it's almost like, you don't really mind the child's crying because it's just a child. So that has helped me a lot, and they really are nice people.

But it is very interesting with all the different cultures that move in, and you know, the cooking, and the ways of being. The Koreans cook with a lot of fish. That's a bad problem here. . . . I'm down on the first floor [so] I don't smell the food. Food permeates through to the other floors. And it's a horrible smell if you are not used to it.

Connie is a clinical psychologist, and based on her professional experience she has a theory of how the community has developed.

People did not even say hello in the beginning, [when] you would walk down the street. I would walk down the street; they would act like you are not there. It was very upsetting. I used to say hello, and they would still act like they had never seen me. So then I finally figured, you know, people really aren't "not nice." What is it? And I think that (a) they are not used to saying hello, and that (b) they did not feel themselves as a community. And also most of them came from houses where they were not used to living right on top of people. So they are not [like] New York and Manhattan people, who are used to saying hello. In the last two years I think this development has really finally solidified. People are more friendly, people say hello more. It is just a different attitude here; it feels more like one.

She thinks that it has to do with the turnover in people. For a long time her upstairs neighbors were saying that "they had had it":

A couple of years ago a lot of people were saying, I don't like this place, I want to move. They were like complaining about different ethnic groups moving in, which I did not care about. But now most people . . . stay here, and [if they want a change or have a conflict with a neighbor] they move to a different apartment. It finally has its own identity.

Also, a couple of years ago there were a lot of different ethnic groups, we had the Sikhs here, we had, we don't have that many blacks here, unfortunately. I think there were many different [groups], but now it is mainly Korean. So it also could have been those changes have stopped.

Sometimes I also think people matured, so like the people who moved in fifteen years ago were all young and did not have children. There were a couple of older people who retired, or worked part time. I think that everybody was able to form their own group here, and meet the people who they want to meet, or not meet. So it's finally a community, and there are all different age groups.

I ask what has happened to the many conflicts over the rules and regulations that she had mentioned. Connie answers, "And that may have stopped too. Maybe that has also made it more of a community. Because I have not heard that many complaints . . . I think people have blended and learned to live with the rules."

Connie's experience demonstrates that when people of diverse ethnic and cultural groups live together, conflicts and differences are worked out and ultimately a more diverse kind of community is formed. It is not that residents do not notice the differences. Connie points out that Korean food has a smell that she finds distasteful, and comments on her neighbors' cultural style in dealing with conflict. But in her case, living in constant contact, having conversations, and working out disagreements evidently solidifies the sense of neighborhood. Yusef, an African American resident of Waterview discussed in Chapter 10, has a similar relationship with his Korean neighbors.

Compared to most large cities, the suburbs do not have many public places where strangers intermingle, and the relative isolation and homogeneity of the suburbs discourages interaction with people who are identified as the "other." M. P. Baumgartner's study of an upper-middle-class suburban town outside of New York City illustrates how this social isolation is transformed into moral expectation, and becomes a yardstick by which residents measure the social order and safety of their neighborhood. Those who disturb the town's "protected world offend its inhabitants by doing so."[5]

Baumgartner documents how local residents in this town are upset by outsiders appearing on residential streets. Strangers by virtue of their race or unconventionality are singled out as "suspicious" even if they are merely walking down the street. The physical organization of the street pattern—cul-de-sacs and dead-end streets—enables residents to monitor their neighborhoods and to spot outsiders who linger. Residents explain their behavior by citing their "fear of crime," by which they mean "predatory behavior by strangers." They voice concerns about poor blacks and Hispanics from New York City entering their town and preying upon residents. Despite the low rate of crime in the area, residents are overly concerned about people who seem out of place.[6]

Gating exacerbates this tendency to monitor and be concerned about "marked" intruders by creating a kind of "pure space" for residents. The more "purified" the environment—the more homogeneous and controlled—the greater residents' ability to identify any deviant individuals who should not be there.[7] A key question about whether something is a "pure space" is whether a person can walk there. Examples of such pure spaces include whites-only country clubs, exclusive shopping malls and affluent Bunker Hill in downtown Los Angeles, as well as a gated community like Manor House. Pure spaces expose differences and have clear boundaries that facilitate policing. They are characteristic of the North American suburb, where boundary consciousness is part of mainstream society. Gating only makes the boundaries more visible and psychologically salient.[8]

Gating also involves the "racialization" of space, in which the representation and definition of "other" is based on human biological characteristics, particularly racial categories. In the past, overt racial categorization provided the ideological context for restrictive immigration laws and discriminatory deed restrictions and mortgage programs. More recently, phenotypical characteristics are used to justify social prejudice and unfounded fears.[9] The thinking of one gated community resident in Sun Meadow, Texas, highlights how race still plays a dominant role in eliciting fear of the other in contemporary society.

HELEN—SEEKING PRIVACY FROM SOMEONE AT THE DOOR

Helen answers the doorbell after two rings, as I wait outside admiring her elaborately carved door with cut-glass panels. Through the glass I can see an atrium, two stories high, and an adjoining living room. It is a tan Scottsdale house with a red tile roof, similar in style to others on the street, but set at an angle on a corner lot to give it a distinctive flair. As Helen opens the door her fox terrier jumps out and runs down the driveway, barking at the children Rollerblading by. She waves to her son as he catches the dog by the collar, and then invites me inside.

Helen is in her mid-forties, plump with brown hair and hazel eyes. She is dressed for golf in yellow shorts and matching shirt. Helen and her husband, Ralph, are avid golfers and active members of the Sun Meadow Club. They purchased their home from the original developer before he went bankrupt, and have lived here for over ten years. They were one of the first families to move in. Helen, her husband, and son lived in a number of different cities before moving here, because of her husband's varied businesses. She is a stay-at-home mother considering starting a business when her son finishes high school.

They originally moved to Sun Meadow for the golf course, but now would only consider living in a gated community. When I ask her why, she replies, "Because after seeing that there are so may beautiful neighborhoods that are not [in] a secure area, [and] that's where burglaries and murders take place. It's an open door [saying] to people, come on in. Why should they try anything here when they can go somewhere else first? It's a strong deterrent, needless to say."

She feels that there is less crime in gated developments than in San Antonio in general. She knows people living in equally nice nongated neighborhoods who have had their homes broken into and who have been assaulted with weapons. The worst that has happened in Sun Meadow is that a few cars have come through and "messed things up." She thinks that it was probably kids. Only a few families have been robbed or burglarized.

Helen feels that her community is different because it is secured. Without the gates, she thinks, anybody could come knocking on your door and put you in a compromising situation. She illustrates her point by telling me what happened to a friend who lives "in a lovely community" outside of Washington, D.C.: "She said this fellow came to the door, and she was very intimidated because she was white, and he was black, and you didn't get many blacks in her neighborhood. She only bought it [what he was selling] just to hurry and quick get him away from the door, because she was scared as hell. That's terrible to be put in that situation. I like the idea of having security."

Helen and Ralph put on their burglar alarm every time they leave, although she thinks they may be overly cautious. She also keeps her doors locked, because she has had people walk in her front door thinking her house was for sale.

I ask her if she is concerned about crime in Sun Meadow. She answers, "No, not here, but in San Antonio." She goes on to explain that San Antonio, like any major city, has problems:

> There are gangs. People are overworked, they have families, they are underpaid, the stress is out of control, and they abuse their children. The children go out because they don't like their home life. There's too much violence everywhere. It starts in the city, but then the kids get smart enough and say, "Oh, gee, I need money for x, y, or z, but it's really hot in the city, let's go out and get it someplace else." We're the natural target for it. So being in a secure area, I don't have to worry as much as another neighborhood that doesn't have security.

She cannot imagine any city in the United States that does not have to worry, because so many people in the city live in poverty. She tells me about her friends living in a wealthy suburb who had their car stolen at gunpoint. They were going to move out of the neighborhood, which did not have gates or security, to a small town outside of San Antonio. When they investigated further, however, they learned that the small town had just as much crime as San Antonio. Helen concludes that it does not matter whether it is the city or the suburbs, you have to live in a gated community, or at least have enough property to have a dog, a security system on your house, and warning signs on your door.

Ironically, Helen's concern with crime developed after she moved into Sun Meadow, but living there reinforces the importance of having gates and guards for personal security. She is more concerned about someone walking into her house than with crime in general. Yet she is one of the few residents who specifically cites an example in which racial difference triggered a sense of fear. Like Ted and Carol Corral, who moved because of "ethnic changes," Helen alludes to her friend's experience as the kind of thing that she is frightened of. "She was scared as hell," Helen comments. Her story—although displaced on her friend—suggests how Helen would feel if a black person came to her door. It is also unclear in the first vignette whether the Corrals are referring to racial or cultural differences in Great Neck. They could be referring to the large influx of Iranian Jews into their suburban neighborhood or the increasing number of Latino immigrants on Long Island. In both cases, however, these interviews conflate racial and ethnic differences with an increased potential for crime.

Racist fears about the "threat" of a visible minority, whether it is blacks, Latinos, "Orientals," or Koreans, are remarkably similar. This is because many neighborhoods in the United States are racially homogeneous. Thus, the physical space of the neighborhood and its racial composition become synonymous. This "racialized" spatial ordering and the identification of a space with a group of people is a fundamental aspect of how suburban landscapes reinforce racial prejudice and discrimination.[10]

Why should Helen's friend feel fearful just because a stranger comes to her door selling things? In Brooklyn and any urban neighborhood or integrated suburb, this would happen all the time. Think of how many times religious groups distributing pamphlets and recruiting converts knock on doors in all but the most isolated settings. Except for gated communities and other kinds of communities with secured, restricted entrances, such as military bases, prisons, boarding schools, doorman apartment buildings or special hospitals, contact with people soliciting, selling, proselytizing, and campaigning is commonplace. In most neighborhoods the streets and the sidewalks are still public, and cross-cultural and cross-racial contact is still possible and even encouraged.

Another aspect of "fear of other" to consider is how the talk about the "other," the "discourse of fear," is used by residents to explain why gates are important. Two examples, one from San Antonio and the other from Long Island (post-9/11) illustrate this point.

KAREN—THEY CAN SLIP IN AND OUT

Karen was introduced in chapter 5 as the young mother with a fearful son living in Sun Meadow. She is worried about the porous boundaries of her gated community, and we talk about her concern with the workers in her neighborhood in the following exchange:

"One thing you did say is that the undocumented workers concern you. Or is it that they are construction workers, or undocumented workers in general?" I ask her.

Karen responds, "It's like they can slip in and slip out. Where there's no record of these guys at all. They're here today and gone tomorrow."

"I was trying to get a sense about who the people are."

Karen looks puzzled. "Mean like now? If you asked me tomorrow if I was going to move, it would be only to a gated community."

When I probe about who the workers are, she switches the conversation to her reasons for moving to the gated community. Such a digression indicates an intentional shift away from a sensitive or socially inappropriate topic. Following her lead, I ask her for clarification.

"To a gated community? Why?"

Karen says, "I think that the security is most important; I really like knowing who's coming and going. I like knowing I'm not going to come home and find my house burglarized. Once you've been violated like that, it's really hard, I think, to continue living without one [a gate]."

Karen's words keep ringing in my ears: "It's like they can slip in and slip out. There's no record of these guys at all," just like in Boyle's story.

A careful examination of the words Karen chooses and the pattern of her speech can be used to get at what Michael Billig calls "the dialogic unconscious." Billig argues that the psychological processes of repression can be studied through what is said and what is not said.[11] For example, the evidence of racism is often "repressed"; that is, hidden not only from the interviewer, because it is socially unacceptable to talk about class and race, but from the interviewee as well because these feelings are psychologically unacceptable. Conversational interaction thus can have repressive functions as well as expressive ones, so what is said can be used to get at what is not said.[12]

For instance, Felicia in chapter 1 tells a story about her daughter feeling threatened by day laborers. She ends the story by explaining to her daughter in the story (and indirectly to me) that they are "workmen," the "backbone of our country." In this conversation she uses what is called a "disclaiming statement," a statement that displaces the feelings or attitudes expressed and turns what was said into something thought to be more socially acceptable. Conversation is often used for these kinds of social maneuvers and reflects the social sensitivity of the topic. In this example, Felicia highlights her acute understanding of social categories and then uses those categories to legitimate her discursive goals.

Another example of disclaiming occurs when Carol and Ted in New York begin talking about the deterioration of their urban neighborhood. Carol offers that "it's ethnic changes" to Ted, who is trying to articulate what happened that made them leave. He then repeats her phrase, "ethnic changes," to characterize the more elusive transformations that he was trying to get at.

All of the speakers use very vague signifiers for people outside the community, particularly "they" (without an antecedent), "anyone," and "everyone." For example, Karen's contention that "they can slip in and slip out." This linguistic strategy serves to create an anonymous and unknown dangerous other.[13]

Barry Glassner, who argues that news reporting capitalizes on our greatest fears, proposes that it is easier to worry about "Mexicans" or "workers"—focusing on symbolic substitutes—rather than face our moral insecurities and more systematic social problems. The attack on the World Trade Center on September 11, 2001, certainly adds to New York residents' concerns. Linda, a single mother living in Pine Hills, Long Island, expresses them well.

LINDA — SEPARATING OURSELVES FROM THE GREAT UNWASHED

Linda is a young mother of two boys, ten and twelve years old, in her early thirties. She is trim and keeps fit by running daily. She is a little nervous at being interviewed, but she is able to think about her surroundings and reflect on what her experiences have been there. Divorced, she lives in her recently deceased mother's house. It is a three-bedroom house, well furnished, although it is showing some signs of age. The entrance to the house is up a winding path, and the entry porch is set parallel to the road, making it feel very private even though it is an attached townhouse. Linda moved to Pine Hills two years ago, but her mother bought the house over fifteen years ago, when it was first built.

Her mother had moved to Pine Hills because she wanted to be in a setting where there would be neighbors close by, and to have the safety of the gate. Linda laughs and says:

> The security of the gate. Five dollars an hour, when they're asleep. I don't know how much security the gate is worth. Some of the guards just let you fly right in. The others have to strip-search you. It really depends. I guess that has been my experience with coming in. Some of them are okay, others want your fingerprints.
>
> [For her mother] it was just basically being less isolated on a big piece of property, and a couple of years before that we had something [happen]. There were helicopters flying over this area. I mean, this may be going back ten years, I don't remember specifically when, but some inmate, they were looking for someone who had escaped who had a murder record. That was quite freaky. You would look out in the backyard and there'd be woods out there, and you'd wonder who is out there.

Linda goes on to say that she tries not to get a false sense of security.

> Because, you know . . . people can come in here on foot. There's a golf course right behind us, and anyone could be wandering around on there, and decide to traipse through here.
>
> Honestly I don't know how useful the gate is. The gate is useful in preventing vehicles from getting in; that is, if the person at the gate is alert and competent. . . .

Most of the time I do get a call if somebody's coming. What can I say about the gate? We did have some robberies here some years ago. . . . I'll try to summarize this: [it's] good in preventing robberies whereby, you know, somebody would need a vehicle to load a whole lot of loot into a car or a van or whatever. But as far as preventing people on foot, it's ridiculous. You know, if anyone would have an interest in coming into this community and causing some kind of havoc or whatever, I think there are many ways they could get in.

Linda tells the following story to illustrate her point:

One time, one of my neighbor's boys, the little one, was missing. And this woman, I mean, she was white as a sheet, and she was really going to have a nervous breakdown. And we couldn't find him. He was actually in another neighbor's house with his friend, playing. I had called that house to find out, not realizing they were away, and there was a workman in the house. And these boys didn't know the workman. The workman just walked in there, went into the kid's room, and started working. So she wasn't at ease [because it was so easy for the workman to walk in without any adults being home, and that her boy was there with a strange workman].

You know, we are not living in very secure times now. . . . I can tell you that after a couple of robberies some of the older residents here felt comfortable with hiring a security car for patrolling the grounds. So they did try to do that.

To get in there is a password. I generally don't give mine out, unless it's a close friend or somebody that I know, or somebody who has my key and needs to get in. Usually, the people at the gate, they know you and they just let you in. A lot of people have automatic openers for the gate. Actually, I don't have one of those, I have a card that I can just slip in, and get in.

But Linda thinks that it is more than just security:

This is my theory: Long Island is very prestige-minded. And I think the very fact of having a guard at the gate is akin to living in Manhattan in a doorman building versus a three-flight walk-up type of thing. There's a certain "pass through the gate" type of thing; this is a private community. That actually, sadly enough, may be part of it. You know, other than the safety issue, just a kind of separating ourselves from the great unwashed, shall we say.

And I think with the gate thing, there is an increasing sense of insecurity all over the place. I think people are beginning to realize they are not really safe anywhere in middle America. We have had so much violence occurring, the school shootings, you know. That could be part of it.

In this interview Linda tells a story about a workman who walks into a house, without anyone even noticing. This occurs in conjunction with a mother's fear that her youngest child is missing. Again an outsider is feared, even when he had nothing to do with the incident. Just his presence evokes comment.

Whether it is Mexicans, black salesmen, workers, or "ethnic changes," the message is the same: residents are using the walls, entry gates, and guards in an effort to keep perceived dangers outside of their homes, neighborhoods, and social world. Contact incites fear and concern, and in response they are moving to exclusive, private, residential developments where they can keep other people out with guards and gates. The walls are making visible the systems of exclusion that are already there; now the walls are constructed in concrete.

Social splitting, purified spaces, and racialization help to explain how this kind of dualistic thinking develops and becomes embedded in local culture. Residents talk about their fear of the poor, the workers, the "Mexicans," and the "newcomers," as well as their retreat behind walls, where they think they will be safe. But there is fear even behind the walls. There are workers who enter the community every day, and residents must go out in order to buy groceries, shop, or see a movie. The gates provide some protection, but residents would like more. Even though the gates and guards exclude the feared "others" from living with them, "they" can slip by the gate, follow your car in, crawl over the wall, or, worse, the guard can fall asleep. Informal conversations about the screening of guards and how they are hired, as well as discussions about increasing the height and length of the protective walls as new threats appear, are frequent in the locker room of the health club, on the tennis court, and during strolls in the community in the evening.

The discourse of fear encompasses many social concerns, about class, race, and ethnic exclusivity and gender.[14] It provides a verbal component that complements—and even reinforces—the visual landscape of fear created by the walls, gates, and guards. By matching the discourse of the inhabitants with the ideological thrust of the material setting, we enrich our understanding of the social construction and social production of places where the well-to-do live. But what is being defended? In the next chapter I argue that "niceness" and being willing to pay the price of perfection has to do with the defense and maintenance of cultural "whiteness."

CHAPTER 8

Niceness and Property Values

It was just so nice. The clubhouse was so nice, the pool, the tennis courts. It had everything I wanted, but yet it was nice and secured.

—Manor House resident

While we all want to live in a perfect community, our ideas about what is perfect vary. Park Slope, Brooklyn, with its mix of town-houses, apartment buildings, and condominiums from various historical periods, accommodates a wide range of family types—singles, couples, and families of all ages, nationalities, and cultures. It is politically active with hippie remnants and countercultural lifestyles that remind me of graduate school in Berkeley, California. On the other hand, there are graffiti on buildings, trash on the street, and a high incidence of car theft compared to other parts of the city. I handle these daily nuisances by painting out graffiti, picking up trash, and parking in a secured garage.

"It's a trade-off," I say to my suburban friends, "living in the city with the diversity and street life I enjoy, balanced by cleaning my sidewalk and paying to park my car."

In many suburban places, "offenders" or "outsiders" are said to violate the public order by ignoring or challenging local standards of cleanliness and aesthetics. Residents may become annoyed, for example, by poorly kept buildings, run-down yards and gardens, and rusting automobiles parked outside. In one New York City suburb, citizens consider a school bus parked in a lot across from the town hall a visual blight that hurts the appearance of their neighborhood. Signs, shop décor, and street furniture in suburban towns are subject to local scrutiny to prevent the area from becoming disorganized and "filthy" like nearby cities.[1] Cleanliness and orderliness indicate the "type of people" who live in a place, and establish a norm of middle-class civility.

The less attractive physical and social conditions in a locale—for example, unregulated public behavior, diminishing quality or maintenance of property, and lack of capital investment—may, in fact, contribute to an increased sense of community disorder and fear of crime. Rapid neighborhood changes and signs of decay also result in a heightened concern for safety.[2] Residents perceive and read ecological changes in their local environment as part of an ongoing assessment of their social worth as well as the stability of their housing market. It is therefore not surprising that subtle visual cues are closely attended to. Indeed, in some cases, shifts in such cues can generate crises.

One strategy for minimizing neighborhood deterioration is to live in a residential development with strict rules and regulations. Many gated community residents say they have found the perfect place to live, and include the CC&Rs, as well as the gates, walls, and guards, as part of this vision. They make trade-offs to live in these restricted environments and adjust their personal, social, and economic values to fit their new home environment.

LAUREL—TRADE-OFFS IN TRADING UP

It's a cool spring morning. I feel exhilarated by the sunshine and blossoming trees. Humming a few bars of "My Favorite Things," I park in front of a beige Hampton-model house. Azaleas with pale pink flowers line the walkway, and I notice a Jewish menorah in the window. Mrs. Laurel Morton greets me at the door and invites me inside to sit in the living room. The house is conservatively decorated with dark red velvet sofas, crystal lamps on marble end tables, and cherry wood chairs. Laurel is a wispy blonde, thin and blue-eyed, in her early fifties. She has had health problems, and I am grateful that she is able to see me. I like her immediately—something about her straightforward demeanor—and I feel comfortable in her home. Her small black dog, a toy poodle, jumps up and settles on my lap. I laugh, saying I don't mind, and play with the dog.

Laurel has been at Manor House for eight months. She lives with her husband and her daughter, who is in high school. She also two grown sons, who visit on the weekends. Their previous residence was a large four-bedroom house in suburban Long Island. By 1986 they wanted more property, but the market was too high to purchase anything at a reasonable price. Instead they renovated the kitchen, bathroom, and master bedroom and added a swimming pool. But Laurel's husband still wasn't happy, and she did not feel safe in her previous Long Island neighborhood; her husband travels and keeps late hours. After a neighbor was robbed, an alarm system was installed.

She had known about Manor House, but thought it was going to be attached homes like other gated communities in the area. The work on it had stopped for a number of years, and they thought they should see what the new developer had to offer. She did not really want to move and wanted to stay in the house where she raised her children, but she was the only one in the family who felt that way. They have a second home, also in a gated community, that they use for vacations and skiing.

When I ask about community life, she says she is not able to make a judgment yet, as things are too new. She thinks the social life will pick up once the clubhouse opens. She is surprised that there are so many young people, given the cost of the development, but most residents are in her age group and income bracket. She does not think Manor House will become too neighborly, considering her brother-in-law's experience living in in a gated community. Homes are expensive, and people are in a later stage of life: children are grown, friends are established, and they do not need to be neighborly. She thinks the people at Manor House come from different worlds and are too wrapped up in them to be looking for community. There is not enough to unite them, no common experience to form bonds, and too much keeping them apart, in spite of similarities in income and status. Laurel says that if she were raising a child she would not live here, because she would want her children to have a choice of friends from their religious background. But now she wants a nice place to live. And Manor House is perfect in that way.

Her husband knew the builder of Manor House, and knew of his good reputation as a developer. The homes are well built, and they're safe investments. Her husband also thinks about appreciation more. He feels that the detached houses, in a good location, are bound to increase in value.

When I ask whether there is anything the family misses about their previous home, the conversation takes a sudden turn.

> The one thing I don't like about condominium living is that everything has to be cleared [by the homeowners association board]. One of the first things we realized is that we didn't have a storm door on the front door.
>
> I said, "That's crazy," especially when we let our dog out; she jumps on the door and you can hear her when she's ready to come in. "We've got to get a storm door. Henry, go out and buy a storm door."
>
> And he said, "I can't go out and buy a storm door." We just had the storm door put in this week, and that was eight months ago. It had to pass the committee.
>
> I said, "Henry, get on the committee."
>
> You can't buy the strong wood one either. They choose the storm door, and you pay for what they choose. And if you don't like it, tough.

Laurel continues talking about the restrictions imposed by what she calls "the committee." I am surprised, because many of the other residents do not seem to mind the restrictions; in fact they tend to like them because they limit what people can do. But Laurel finds these limitations problematic, and considers them a negative aspect of living in Manor House, one of the trade-offs she has to make to have the orderly environment she wants. Laurel continues, "If I want to put in planting, especially in front, it has to meet community standards. I mean, logically I can understand they don't want somebody putting in sunflowers all over the place, but if I want to plant my tulips, I have to get it approved first by the committee. That's the part I don't like. But I've decided to accept it."

I ask her if she thinks other residents feel the same way. Laurel replies:

> I know my neighbor does. I was surprised when she moved in. [Where she lived before], she had a magnificent garden she put in herself. I'd ask her [talking in a whisper behind her hand], "What are you going to do about your garden?"

She said, "I'll plant here."

"But don't you realize you've got to pass, you know . . . " I said.

"I'll do it in the back, they won't notice," she confided.

"You've taking a chance," I warned her.

Laughing, I ask: "So what do they do, come and look at your backyard, at your tulips?" Laurel looks at me.

I don't know. I was speaking to the man who is the landscaper and told him about our concerns on our property, on making changes.

I asked, "Why can't I just plant? I have to plant my bulbs now, or I won't have anything in the spring." This was last fall.

He said, "Well, you know, we have a committee, and you have to tell them what you want to do, and I'm sure they'll let you do it, but. . . ."

According to Laurel, the committee is made up of tenants. Her husband has been to a number of meetings, but they do not have enough people to really have a sense of the consensus of the community.

It's totally ridiculous, especially if you want to make a rule. The committee that's going to run the development, who decides things like whose house gets painted, or what color, you know [does not represent the community]. Once the developer is out of the community, they'll make some logical rulings, like if you want to do planting it has to be in the backyard, unless you do something very limited, because they don't want anything outrageous, which I can understand. I think it should be whatever you do in your own backyard, it's your business, but in front it has to meet certain requirements.

I ask if they allow pets. Laurel replies that they would not have moved in if they did not allow pets. But they have put in some rules about it since some people let their animals run everywhere and do not pick up after them. Some gated developments are even more restrictive and do not allow pets even to visit. The committee even gave them trouble about putting up a television satellite dish when they moved in.

She does feel safer than she would in a nongated community. The guards call when people who are not on the list arrive (the list is submitted by residents on behalf of frequent visitors), and no solicitors are allowed. Her sister moved to a gated community in Florida and loves it, but it is not the same as Manor House. The area outside her sister's gated community is not a "good area" to be living in, she says. It's run down and doesn't have the same quality of housing.

"It seems like people in Florida are walling themselves off," Laurel says, "but at Manor House it's a 'good area' to begin with."

"What do you mean?" I ask.

"That my sister's situation is different—she has to have gates." Laurel stops and gestures with her hands, warding off imagined outsiders.

"I really have to go now," she says, ending the interview.

Getting into my car, I think about how glad I am to learn about the pitfalls and trade-offs of homeowners associations. I am not sure, however, that Laurel and Henry's dislike of the rules has much to do with the fact that Manor House is gated. Any community interest development has covenants, rules, and regulations.

What makes a perfect community? The people who live there, the beauty of the surroundings, the sense of belonging that evolves over time? Everyone has their own notion of what it would be. "Niceness" is an important aspect of the ideal for gated community residents. Gating, in fact, has been called "government by the nice," referring to the CC&Rs written into deeds dictating even the colors a house can be painted, the weight of family dogs, the type of furniture or curtains that can be seen through one's picture window, and the color (white), number, and type of Christmas tree lights.[3] Some homeowners associations even regulate behavior; a woman caught kissing her boyfriend in her driveway in the evening was fined and threatened with expulsion.[4] Residents in Pine Hills and Waterview in New York talk about board members who survey the community daily looking for infractions.[5]

What exactly are gated community residents saying when they talk about wanting a "nice" environment? One component is cleanliness and orderliness. Another is an underlying concern with maintaining one's home as a financial investment.

retail value

Constance Perin points out that Americans are both "neighbors" and "traders" when it comes to real estate. In homeowners' calculus, the physical appearance of the development—and particularly their street or block—matters the most, and residents endeavor to keep their neighbors "up to snuff." And it is important for neighbors to maintain a firm line between the value of money (and resale value of their home) and neighborly love. The reason for such concern is that about 64 percent of American households put "just about everything they have into buying a house," and the maintenance and appreciation of house value is dependent on how well everyone else keeps up their house and grounds.[6]

Based on this reality, it is not difficult to understand why most gated community residents accept the extensive set of covenants and restrictions that indirectly bolster the value of their house and property. Residents cannot change the exterior of their house or the landscape, thus ensuring a certain level of quality and consistency. Even though residents complain about the restrictions and inconvenience, the CC&Rs provide an extra measure of safety and security—financial—in addition to the walls, gates and guards.

REBECCA—MAINTAINING THE VALUE OF YOUR HOME

I arrived at Rebecca's late in the afternoon on a cold, misty December day. Her house is located across from the mansion, with a beautiful view of its grounds and its Victorian splendor. She greets me, laughing about the gloomy weather and early winter darkness. The gas fireplace casts a warm, though somewhat unreal, glow on the modestly decorated family room: two leather armchairs across from a brown-and-beige tweed couch with a rustic wooden coffee table between them. On the table there is a bowl of dried fruit that she invites me to try. The sweet, moist apricots are fragrant, reminding me of summer. Rebecca smiles at my enjoyment, transforming her tired, lined face into that of a younger woman. Her stocky figure is accentuated by her rumpled blue jeans and oversized black T-shirt, with thick-soled loafers and striped socks.

Rebecca's reasons for moving to a gated community were simple: she wanted safety and no hassles. Property value and choosing a good location were her other major concerns. She and her husband moved in only four months ago and are still getting settled.

Before moving to Manor House they had lived in nearby suburban areas:

We stayed in a suburb north of the city for fourteen years, because there's a wonderful thing, the community. The children were very small, there were sidewalks on the street, there were other young children on the block and young parents on the block. It was friendly and warm, and hard to move, but I wanted a larger, nicer house, and better school. And that's how I moved to Long Island. I loved it there; that's why I was there nineteen years. I had a pretty house, the schools were good, and it was very pretty, you know, lots of trees, and it was hilly. But I started to work, and got tired of the house. I knew of this piece of property, and wanted to live here. I wanted a gated community. I wanted the services of going away and having the lawn taken care of, the snow removed, and not having to fetch somebody myself. I wanted a new kitchen, a new bathroom, all the new pretty things and I did not want to renovate my house. I thought that this would be a very good financial investment, because there are very few—no, let me take it back there—there are no communities like this on Long Island.

She had her heart set on Manor House because of the convenient location, and because it was "nice, nicer than any other community." She wanted to be the first one in, to get a prime piece of land, and picked the best lot, right across from the clubhouse. She now has everything: newness, luxury, safety, scenery, and value.

"What about community life?" I ask.

There is no contact at this point with other people except we're all going through the same experience, we all come and watch our houses being built, and when I drive by and see someone, we talk. I ask them when they are going to move in, and everybody seems anxious and is very friendly. So it's a very nice feeling. We're all going in at the same time, having the same experience, which is nicer than moving into an established neighborhood where people have their own friends.

Rebecca and her husband are relieved that they know what the other houses will look like beforehand, and that the architect uses only traditional styles. There are no modern houses—just the three models that were available when they moved in, and now three more. They are all the "New England line," using only four colors: soft beige, yellow, gray, and white.

She is pleased with her new home. Her friends love it, and so do her grown children. Her children also live in a gated community, but it is an older one with clustered houses. She thought that Manor House was a better investment. "New sells well," she adds. The clubhouse, exercise room, and mansion all add to making it perfect.

Rebecca shows me her favorite spot, where the family room abuts the kitchen with a view of the mansion. She invites me to look out the window, where glass sliding doors lead out to the deck. As she opens the doors, I put one foot out.

"Don't go out," she says. I look back.

"This is a big deck! I can see the mansion," I say as I venture farther.

"The floor is going to get wet," she exclaims, grabbing my arm. "Don't step on it." She looks at her waxed parquet floor, then at me.

"I'm sorry, I didn't realize it was raining." I try to step directly onto the mat by the door, but miss, slipping sideways, leaving a puddle where my boot touches the wood floor. Rebecca runs to the kitchen, gets a towel and wipes up the water.

We continue our conversation after I dry off. Rebecca talks about how Manor House is perfect for people at her stage in life. She is in her late fifties, and her husband is sixty-three. He is still working, but once he retires they might need a one-story home. One great thing about Manor House is that she will be able to sell her two-story colonial-style home easily and move into another model.

> I feel I have my hands on the pulse of things, and especially in my age group, the empty-nesters. We're the prime people for this because we don't want to take care of land anymore and don't want to do all the chores. I think there has to be more adult type houses, meaning, you don't need all the bedrooms, you don't need a maid's room, and ranches [one-story houses] would be attractive. This development sold very few ranches, because they were not attractive architecturally. Yet we're in an age group where people prefer the ranch. We don't want steps because as we get older, we want it to be easier. There are no beautiful ranches here, and I keep telling them that if they really made ranches—I mean made some nice ones—people would come.

Rebecca's husband telephones for the second time during the interview, and I overhear her say she will have dinner ready when he arrives.

"I guess we'll have to stop," she says.

"I'm so sorry," I respond.

"Well, I don't think this will be our final home," she adds. "Maybe we can talk again."

"I thought you said it was perfect?"

"It's nice in many ways, but it won't be my permanent home." What is nice is her selection of a good piece of property and a limited number of house styles and paint colors so her house retains its market value.

As I leave, I think about Rebecca and her ideal home. Image and investment, along with safety and hassle-free living, are what many gated community residents look for. I know it is not true for everyone, including my sister and her family. They are interested in making friends in their neighborhood, and although they want their house to maintain its value, it does not dominate their concerns. Still, gates, rules and regulations, and governance by a strict homeowners association may help to maintain housing values.[7]

Evan McKenzie in *Privatopia* writes about the problems and disputes that emerge from rigid enforcement of strict rules and regulations. He is worried about the loss of first amendment rights and the residents' inability to challenge board rulings because they have signed contracts. Unfortunately, new owners often are not aware of the extent of CC&R restrictions at the time of purchase. Nor are they cognizant that they have agreed to abide by an arbitration panel, appointed by the community association industry, rather than having legal recourse for litigation of disputes in the public court system. New residents do not understand that, because they are living in a private space controlled by a corporation, much like a mall or office complex, they have waived many of their free speech rights.[8]

The case of Bear Creek, Washington, a five-hundred-resident walled community with private streets, sewers, gun control, and design control regulations, illustrates the difference. Bear Creek prohibits flagpoles, firearms, visible clotheslines, satellite dishes, street parking, and unkempt landscaping. The president of the homeowners association boasts that they have moved ahead of government by being able to enforce these restrictions through covenants that in the public sector might run afoul of constitutional restrictions and statutory limitations.[9]

Local government can use zoning ordinances and enact design review standards to regulate the landscape, but to be enforceable the standards must be objective, allow for due process, and serve the public's health, safety, and welfare needs. Property owners are entitled to a hearing on any government decision to restrict the use of private property, and if the restriction creates a hardship, property owners can apply for a variance. Further, if the zoning ordinance or design standards are deemed excessive, they can be considered a "taking," and the property owner must be compensated for any financial loss. These same protections are not available to a property owner living in a private, gated community because "these constitutional and statutory limitations do not apply to private agreements."[10]

Yet, even residents such as Laurel, and Iris, below, who are surprised and dismayed by the board's strict enforcement of the CC&Rs, still feel it's worth it.

IRIS—WORTH THE AGGRAVATION

I arrive at the Manor House home of Mrs. Iris Gerald at eleven in the morning. She has to take her son to school in two hours, giving us just enough time to complete the interview. The sales manager recommended her as a woman who was in touch with the other mothers at Manor House and thought she could provide a young family's perspective.

Iris is a slim woman of medium height in her early thirties with long, straight brown hair pulled back in a velvet headband. She is wearing a pair of faded jeans and a white T-shirt, without makeup or jewelry. Her four-year-old son is running around the entry hall waving a plastic machine gun. She mentions that her eight-year-old daughter is at school as she guides me around the rambunctious boy. She ushers me into a sunny day room off the kitchen. I choose the chair closest to the window at the kitchen table, trying to get as far away from the blaring television in the next room as possible. She seems friendly and relaxed, and watches as I set up two tape recorders.

"I lost my last interview because the tape recorder broke," I explain. She smiles sympathetically, tapping her manicured fingernails on the tiled table.

What I can see of the house is cozy, comfortably furnished with a modern black leather sofa and armchair set, a television mounted on the wall, and a white kitchen table with black-and-white chairs. Iris lives in the Hampton model with a small balcony overlooking the day room from upstairs. I imagine her four-year-old falling off the balcony as he runs by, gun in hand, but she says she has not had any problems.

She loves the location and her custom-built house; the community pool and tennis courts are also a big plus. She does not want her own pool, but a community one is perfect for the children. Her son darts out the front door to sit on some rocks. I ask if she is concerned about him playing outside alone. She answers that it is a little dangerous because of the construction. Even though the workers know him, they don't always see the little kids, so she has to watch. The other mothers do the same. They congregate for playtime at three each afternoon in front of her centrally located house.

Iris and her family have been living at Manor House for ten months. Their first home was an apartment in Bayside, Queens, a duplex with a converted basement. It was a neighborhood where people stayed for only a short time and then moved on, and she found it difficult to find parking on the busy streets. They bought their first home in New Hyde Park, a "family-style" neighborhood built in the 1950s, with a diverse mix of people, churches, shopping, and good schools.

"Why did you move?" I ask as her son interrupts, brushing up against her like a kitten, asking to have his hair blown dry. Iris runs her fingers through his hair, humoring him as he rubs his back on her bent leg.

"It was a nice size, a three-bedroom ranch, but we needed more bathrooms, and it had no family room or library. We just outgrew it."

When I ask her to compare the two homes, the first thing she mentions is cost.

"That was a home in the $300,000 range. You can't really get this house for less than a million." She goes on to explain that they have made a lot of friends in Manor House, and have developed very close relationships.

And that happened in the beginning because you come and check the progress of your home, and everyone is in the same boat. You're having problems, and everyone commiserates. You see something positive, and everyone is happy for the same reason. We all complain about the builder and how they maintain things. They never have anything ready on time. They're not as forthcoming as they should be. And I don't think anyone will tell you differently.

Iris explains how people bonded by going through the building process together: "Struggling through the same struggles draws you together." She knows about twenty families in the community: four of them are close friends who vacation with them, share birthdays, and spend time at one another's homes.

Another reason for moving is that their financial situation improved, so they were able to upgrade their home. She feels that it was a good move, and that the neighborhood will retain its value. She likes the space and the comfort of the house, but feels that investment and safety are more important considerations.

They do not have friends who live in gated communities; the people in their old neighborhood are not moving. They decided to make this change on their own. I ask what the major difference in the two neighborhoods is, and she responds that she feels more secure here. Even with the construction going on and numerous workers moving about, she feels safe. She also feels better about her car and parking space. In the old neighborhood her car had been stolen from outside her door, even though it was a safe neighborhood.

They were attracted to Manor House because they could have their own home built and customized according to their needs. It is not more of a community than their previous residence—if anything, it is less so—because many people have other residences, and they are not there all of the time.

I ask if she has any concerns about living in a gated community.

Well, it's not about the gated community, but the homeowners association. And yeah, a homeowners association is a pain in the neck, because if I want to change my front door, I can't. If I want it brown tomorrow, I can't do that, or if I want to put a statue on my front lawn—not that I would want to do any of these things—but it does protect you from the crazy neighbor who wants to paint the house red. It definitely has some negatives and some positives, but for my personality and way of life, I don't mind it. I chose the neighborhood because I like the style of the homes, and there would be nothing that I would really do, because I like what I have, and I'm not looking for anything that would be against the homeowners' association. Everything is included for me.

Iris remarks that she had had problems in her old neighborhood, where all the neighbors had to approve if you wanted to build an extension on your house. At Manor House no external changes are allowed. We talk more about the amenities she now has compared to her old home. She thinks it is unique because of the view and all the trees and grass. She is happy with everything—the built-in stereo, the heating and air filtration system. She and her husband take walks in the evening while their children bicycle on safe roads.

I ask whether they are active in the homeowners association. Iris answers:

> No. And my husband is not interested either. The problems that exist here are minor, really. I guess if you chose to do something that the homeowners association doesn't approve, I guess that's a negative. The maintenance fees are pretty steep, and if you don't use the facilities you still have to pay. Also, fees will go up as everything is finished. I don't know that I'll use the indoor pool—probably not.

But she says she knew this beforehand and chose to move because of the overwhelming advantages.

Her son comes up and takes her hand.

"When is she going to leave?" he asks.

"Soon. Don't be rude," she smiles at him; then, turning to me: "I guess we'd better stop."

"That's fine," I reply, happy to end the tug-of-war for her attention. "I have learned a lot, especially about the homeowners association. I think it's fascinating how it makes it the kind of community you want."

"Yes, yes it does," she says, watching her son run up the stairs to the balcony. He waves. We wave back. "I love the neighborhood and how it looks. The homeowners association protects it for me."

On the way out I notice the detailing in the entryway and living room. A landscape painting hangs over an antique sofa; there are two tufted chairs placed at either end of the sofa. I ask if her son is allowed in the room. She shakes her head, throwing her long brown hair back, and laughs. She says good-bye.

Iris chose this community because she likes the style of the houses and the maintenance of the landscape. Therefore, the restrictions are acceptable to her. She feels safe because it's more protected. She does not want more property and likes being close to her neighbors. Her time revolves around the children, taking them to school and playing with them when they return—a family-centered lifestyle. Manor House seems perfect for the family, and they have even created a small social world made up of other families.

The aesthetic control of the landscape is one strategy by which "niceness" is expressed and used to mark a residential development—and the people within it—as middle class or upper middle class. Aesthetic management has long been used by elite families to demarcate their estates and buffer their property boundaries. Through their power and influence in the local context—bolstered by historic preservation and conservation easements—elites have successfully protected their geographical settings throughout the United States. In a similar vein, middle-class families imprint their residential landscapes with "niceness," reflecting their own landscape aesthetic of orderliness, consistency, and control.[11]

Even within the middle or upper middle class, people with varying amounts of wealth or disposable income may have different ideas about what the landscape should look like and the amount of aesthetic control that should be exerted to keep it that way. Eddie (Susan's husband, mentioned in chapter 5), for instance, expresses his annoyance at the degree of landscape control when I ask him what the difference was between their old neighborhood and Sun Meadow, the gated development where they currently live. He distinguishes the different socioeconomic groups living in those two neighborhoods, and how much landscape control they require.

> The difference is that in the old neighborhood, they were a bunch of people who had no preconception of what their life—or what everybody else's life—was supposed to be like. Out here, everybody not only has a conception of what their life is, but they dictate what your life and house are supposed to be. They think because they've made it, [you] should be influenced by how they made it; and so you have a conflict, a clash of ideas, because everybody has made it in a different way. Or they think that they are so smart, that you should do it their

way. And that's not necessarily right. In our previous neighborhood, everyone pretty much minded their own business.

Eddie reiterated the story of the original developer's bankruptcy, and how the residents who purchased their homes and lots from the first developer assumed that Sun Meadow would remain expensive and exclusive. After the bankruptcy, however, the land went into bank receivership, and many lots and completed houses were sold at a discount. I have been told that the initial houses sold for over $500,000 (in 1993), while in 1995 houses could be bought for as little as $275,000 to $300,000. By 1999, the real estate market had recovered, and houses currently sell for close to $450,000 to $650,000, depending on size. This fluctuation in price often happens with large-scale residential developments, and occurred in New York as well as in San Antonio. The social consequences, however, vary in each situation. As Eddie describes it:

> Here you have a group of people who were thinking that a certain type of person was going to move in, and then [instead] you have another type move in. You have some people that probably really don't belong, from a financial [point of view], but because of the economy, well, now they're allowed to come in. So you have a really diverse group of people in a very small area. And they all don't necessarily think the same way or want the place to look the same way.

Socioeconomic and cultural differences make creating "niceness," much less "the perfect community," harder. Thus, the greater the social and cultural diversity of the gated community, the more extensive the rules and regulations. Yusef, who lives in Waterview, Queens, is frustrated living in a socially and ethnically diverse gated community, where there is tremendous pressure to conform to an ever increasing number of rules. Board members survey the streets and houses constantly and work hard to maintain "niceness" and orderliness in this densely populated gated community in Queens. Because of the diversity and density, there are frequent disagreements over noise, parking, cultural style, children, and cleanliness. He chafes under the pressure of the CC&Rs, but accepts them in order to live in a middle-class environment.

YUSEF—THE WRONG KIND OF RULES

When I arrive at the Waterview gate, Yusef isn't answering the telephone so the guards won't let me in. On the third try, he picks up. The gate actually prints out a visitor's pass with your name, license plate number, and the address you're visiting. The pass has to be displayed on your dashboard, and handed back when you leave. There are cars everywhere, and every available parking space is numbered and reserved. It takes me quite a while to find a spot. I finally ask a security van driver where I might find a spot, and he directs me to a parking space about three hundred yards away.

When I get to the apartment Juliette, Yusef's wife, shows me to the sitting room, where I can look out the window. There is a party going on on the ground floor outside the building. A dozen people are sitting outside, barbecuing, drinking wine and beer, and having a good time. Juliette comments that sometimes it does get a bit noisy, and that people can be inconsiderate. The apartments are close together; noise is something that living in a gated community doesn't protect you from.

Yusef and Juliette are a young African American couple who have been living at Waterview for four years. They moved from a nongated community in "a beautiful neighborhood" in Brooklyn. They wanted to buy a place instead of paying rent. Yusef explains:

> We went to look for a house, and we couldn't find a house that was the type that we wanted. And I came down to thinking that a condo was going to be less in price, and so it was, okay, if we can't get a house for this amount, maybe that amount would get a condo that was nice. They took us to a lot of places. They showed us co-ops. We were not interested in co-ops. And we finally came to this place, and saw it, and I fell for it, and here we are. I think the selling point was the fact that the place was spotlessly clean and it was near the water, and we have a cool breeze coming in. I thought I would like to live near the sea or a river. And the gate and other things came after.

When we were looking, the broker showed us condos not in an area that we wanted to live. And there was nothing particular, nothing attractive about them. They were quite plain and ordinary. So we said, "We're not interested in these." He says, "Oh, the price is lower," and we said, "You have to listen to what we say. We don't want you to give us something that is very, very expensive. We told you about how much we were willing to pay. But we don't want to see something lower [in price]. Give us something that matches [what we can afford]."

Yusef talks about the kind of neighborhood he was looking for. Cleanliness was very important, as was an orderly environment. He also wanted a place that was nice, and—ideally—friendly. I ask him to compare their new home to their previous neighborhood, and he says,

> I think to compare this place is not fair because they are two different things. This is a gated community, the other is not. There is a gate here that stops everyone who has no right to be here from entering. That in itself is a big plus. So you have the kind of security that the other place did not have. . . . It doesn't mean that someone who really, really wants to come in here cannot manage to come in. But it is very rare for someone to be that desperate to come into a place where they have no big interest. People who have no reason rarely come in. I think it makes you feel secure. We have been here for about four years, and I have not heard of any case of robbery.

Yusef and Juliette have not met many of their neighbors and do not find it easy to meet people unless they go to the gym. There are some things that they dislike about the community.

> Things are a little regimental, because there are rules and regulations here. I mean, if you don't like rules and regulations, and most adults don't. I got fined because my car leaked oil. There was a tiny spot. And that oil thing, we were looking for it. We went outside, "Where is the oil?" I asked, and he [the board member] wasn't quite sure where he saw it, and finally they withdrew the $25 [fine]. They advised me to go to do it [fix the car]. I paid $700 to have it done.

They also have problems with their neighbor upstairs because the floors are not very solid.

The daughter, who is now four years old, jumps about the whole place. It wouldn't have been so bad if it was just the daughter's jumping disturbing us. If the parents, especially the father, recognizes that they are disturbing us. The father's attitude is, I live in my own apartment, I can do what I like, I bought my apartment, I can do what I like in my apartment. I say yes, you can do what you like, I'm sure we have the right to do what we like, to enjoy our apartment, without someone really knocking at our head when we want to sleep, or want to study. And he had the impudence to say, "Why do you study in the house, what is the library for?" He said, "You are so full of yourself, why are you studying in the house? People don't study in the house"—that's what he tells me.

The wife is a very nice lady, and the two little girls are so nice that you just forgive the old fool, because the family really works, and I told him, if you didn't have the family you have, you're a goner, because I [can] make sure that you are out. Because he went to have his place carpeted, a plush carpet, and the legal position really is that if the place carpeted that way for up to 70 percent of the floor then it's okay. But that's for normal usage, not for a child who is overactive and jumping and thumping. So we just ignore it. I said to the mother, "If I hear the jumping over and over and over a long time then you are really overdoing it. But if she jumps and the jumping stops after a little while, then fine. It can start again." So we have been managing, but the man is really so ignorant. We are not on speaking terms with the man. I say hello to the daughters, I say hello to the wife, but not to the man. That's the position.

I ask if this conflict could be solved through the governing board here, but Juliette said that the governing board was not interested, and gave them an address of the local mediation center. They went to the mediation center, and their neighbors lost their case. "We decided to take them there after it had been proven that they didn't comply. They knew that they didn't have to go. It's not obligatory for you to go to mediation; you can refuse to go. But if they took you to court it would count against you. It seems that you are the aggressor really because you didn't want to make peace when it was offered."

I ask Yusef if he would recommend this community to others.

I would recommend [it to] those that I know very well. Those that I think are not going to find the rules and regulations very unacceptable. Those people who want a quiet life, who understand that they have to pay a price somehow, to live a quiet life, will enjoy being in a gated community. If you are going to have a place that is secure, then you have to have people who are controlling entry. But some people may not like that they are controlled, and [yet] the same people are asking for security.

I think that the members of the housing association have quite a lot of power. They will say, for instance, you cannot have a fire grill on the second floor, on the balconies. So you can imagine someone who lives on the second floor who bought a fire grill before they knew that they can't use it. And they have power to fine you an amount that is quite heavy, and if you refuse to pay it they have power to put a lien on your property. I find those things are the price you have to pay.

One explanation for why some residents—especially those living in Waterview, Pine Hills, and Sun Meadow—are willing to accept these apparently excessive restrictions can be attributed to their anxiety about maintaining their middle-class lifestyle and socioeconomic position. Yusef was annoyed with his real estate broker when he showed him houses in price ranges that were lower than his ability to pay. He wanted a condo that matched his class status, not a lesser place to save money.

Niceness—keeping things clean, orderly, homogeneous and controlled so that housing values remain stable—is also a way of maintaining "whiteness." Whiteness is not only about race, but is an historical and cultural construct. Karen Brodkin writes that many groups now considered white were not originally. In *How Jews Became White Folks* she illustrates how Italians, Irish, and Jewish immigrants became "white" only when they assimilated economically and culturally in the middles class.[12]

Whiteness also refers to the privileges of being a member of a socially unmarked class. Blacks and Hispanics, as well as other members of minority or immigrant populations within the United States, are racially and ethnically identified by socially contructed notions of phenotypic traits; these "traits" are used to mark groups as different from being "white." Whiteness, on the other hand, is the assumed norm—socially, physically, and even politically—and dominates national ideas of beauty, social class, and goodness. Whiteness provides access to education, elite taste cultures and behaviors, and allows a group to prosper within the dominant culture. In places like Long Island, New York, and San Antonio, Texas, being "middle-class" and being "white" overlap such that one social status can be taken for another.[13]

Baby boomers across the nation are worried that the critical advantages of whiteness and a middle-class life, the so-called cultural capital, that families pass on—knowledge, contacts, and inherent privileges—are being lost. For the middle class, and especially the lower middle class, downward mobility during the 1980s and 1990s due to economic restructuring and shrinking job opportunities meant that their children are facing diminished expectations, and are living in less affluent communities with fewer amenities. The deterioration of middle-class suburban neighborhoods, escalating housing prices, a flat job market, and limited job advancement all enhance the fear that the economic future is not as secure as it was for the previous generation, when there were expanding employment and housing opportunities.[14]

One of the ways that previous generations heralded their arrival in the middle class was to buy a home in the suburbs. Now this symbolic arrival is not enough, because many of the traditional middle-class suburbs are situated in areas with decaying physical environments, increasing heterogeneity, and, in some cases, rising crime. Gated communities, with their increased "security" and strict enforcement of rules and regulations, are an attempt to bolster residents' middle-class status. By regimenting the environment, keeping it "nice" and filled with "nice" people, maintaining the resale value of one's home, and putting up with increasing privatization and restrictions, residents hope to keep the threat of economic decline and loss of class position at bay. This underlying social and economic anxiety is a crucial factor in middle-class residents' search for security.

But even upper-middle-class residents, such as Laurel and Rebecca in Manor House, worry about the resale value of their homes, even though they did not necessarily experience the financial pressures of the past twenty years as acutely as the middle class did. For them, the CC&Rs simply provide additional reassurance that their investment is secure, well maintained, and protected.

CHAPTER 9

Private Governance, Taxes, and Moral Minimalism

When I enter the neighborhood where I stay in East Hampton, I drive by a gray wood sign that reads, "Oak Hollow, A Private Community." For a long time I could not make out what this meant. A private community without gates or guards—why advertise it? Is it to make it seem more prestigious or just to keep strangers out? One of the first things I did was to call the president of the property-owners association to ask if they could take the signs down. They seemed so unnecessary, way out in the woods. But I quickly learned that these signs are important for a sense of identity and security. The "privateness" refers to its development as a common interest development with rules, regulations, and fees for maintaining the collectively owned bay beach, hiking trail, and reserve areas.

I attended the property-owners meeting this year to learn more about the workings of this form of private governance. The latest problem is a genteel struggle over the mowing of the three-foot shoulder that runs along the road. The substance of the argument is whether to pay for additional mowing of the grassy edge that is currently cut twice a year by the town. But the essence of the conflict is housing values and implied norms about whether the community looks unkempt and disheveled or neat and trim, and implicitly whether the people who live there are unruly or refined. It's a discussion about how the mowing destroys the wildflowers many of us cherish and damages the undergrowth, or whether the neighborhood should protect housing values by presenting itself in a more fashionably elite style.

Oak Hollow is a rustic-looking subdivision with heavily wooded lots, too many deer, no curbs or lights, and wild grasses dotted with oak trees and pines along a ragged asphalt road. My husband and I chose the area, as did many of our neighbors, because of its laid-back character. It's "rural"—"rundown" the new neighbors say—aesthetics suggest a quiet and tranquil house in the mountains or countryside rather than the heart of East Hampton. But newcomers buying or renting in the area prefer another image, one with trimmed grass and open vistas, the "estate" front yard reminiscent of the large multimillion-dollar cottages along the ocean; not the modest country housing of the Northwest Woods. These aesthetic and implied moral arguments overlay economic considerations and are at the crux of the property-owners association debate. They characterize the deliberations of private governance organizations throughout the region.

Voluntary associations are part of American life and character. Alexis de Tocqueville commented in 1835 that "Americans of all ages, all conditions, and all dispositions, constantly form associations . . . religious, moral, serious, futile, general or restricted, enormous or diminutive."[1] Residential associations, however, are relatively recent and can be traced to Gramercy Park, which formed in 1831 in the center of New York City.[2] The concept of a private community was first proposed in 1898 by Ebenezer Howard, father of the British Garden City movement. He imagined a proprietary community funded by private investment capital and managed by a residential association. In *Garden Cities of Tomorrow,* Howard described a utopian community with planned streets, gardens, and housing governed by the residents. His ancillary goal was to convince potential investors to support his innovative plan.[3]

Homeowners associations (as well as property-owners associations or landowners associations) are a special kind of residential association created by the covenants, conditions, and restrictions of a common interest development. Elected boards oversee the common property, and each home is purchased with the CC&Rs as part of the deed. As discussed in the previous chapter, an extensive set of rules and regulations are mandated by the CC&Rs, and homeowners associations as private entities also can make their own rules.[4] In an overwhelming number of cases, particularly when racial discrimination is not an issue, covenants are treated as private agreements that need not comply with the constitutional standards that apply to the laws adopted by public local governments.[5]

In 1962 there were only 500 homeowners associations in the United States, but by 1970 there were 10,000; in 1980, 55,000; in 1990, 130,000; and by 1992, there were 150,000, with over 32 million people. While in 1970 only 1 percent of American housing units were in a homeowners association, condominium, or cooperative—the three main instruments of collective private ownership of housing—by 1998 this figure had risen to 15 percent. Today, in major metropolitan areas, 50 percent of all new housing units are being built and sold as part of a collective housing regime.[6] This increase is a social revolution in governance, with private organizations now responsible for collecting trash, providing security, and maintaining common property. Private enforcement of covenants has replaced municipal oversight in regulating the environment by zoning, and new ground rules—voting rights determined by property or home ownership and not citizenship—are being put into place. The greater flexibility of private governance arrangements, it has been argued, have many advantages, and there are land use planners, developers, and economists who feel they should be made available to existing neighborhoods in order to replace extant zoning controls.[7]

Today there are more than 230,000 homeowners associations, each serving an average of about two hundred residents.[8] The majority of associations have responsibility for the buildings—apartments, townhouses, and single-family houses—as well as for the surrounding developed areas and landscape. The typical operating budget is between $100,000 and $200,000 per year, but some operate with more than $1.5 million. Other small property-owners groups, like the one at Oak Hollow, run on as little as $10,000 per year.[9]

Homeowners association boards make decisions that affect every aspect of community life. These decisions and the functioning of the board are monitored constantly by residents and evaluated in terms of how decisions resonate with the values and preferences of individual households. George Moore, who has lived in Pine Hills since its inception, is aware of both the positive and negative aspects of private governance in practice.

GEORGE—APATHY AND PARTICIPATION IN GOVERNANCE

George Moore is straightforward and easy to talk to about living in Pine Hills, New York. He is in his early forties with graying hair, but looks fit and healthy. He has just put his two preteen children on the school bus when I arrive, his wife having already gone to work. The security guard had trouble getting through to him as he was standing outside waiting with his children—and did not hear the phone ring. It was only after I had pleaded with the guard that he tried again. I was on the verge of giving up and going home when the guard finally got George on the telephone and raised the gate to let me in.

His attached townhouse is spacious, with polished wood floors and windows that look onto the street in front and a large garden in back. It is sparsely furnished, with colonial-style wood furniture. The backyard rises to a crest, where there are trees and a fence that divides it from the adjoining golf course.

The houses at Pine Hills looks very much the same from the outside, but there is actually quite a mixture of types: rows of attached townhouses, some duplexes, and a few single-family houses. According to George, the townhouses sell for between $500,000 and $600,000, but the managing broker says that they start as low as $300,000.

George was one of the first three or four people to move to Pine Hills. He calls the period when it was just a building site the "Wild West." The developer had constructed four model houses, and there were just three other couples living there in 1987.

George and his wife saw the house as an investment opportunity and were there the first day lots went on sale. They put money down, and by the next day the prices had gone up $20,000. By the end of the week they had gone up $40,000. "We looked at each other and joked, 'Wow, we're going to make a lot of money. [Even] if the housing market falls, it's a nice house, we could have two kids and be very happy here. The market fell, we have two kids, and we have been very happy.' So, you know, it kind of worked into that. From that [perspective], it has been very good to us."

Their first residence was a cooperative in Suffolk County, Long Island, but that had only one bedroom. When they decided to have kids, they began to look for a place to move. They had seen a gated community before:

> My sister had a boyfriend in the early 1970s, and I remember visiting him in Staten Island. He lived in a townhouse condominium development. It was a gated community. I was very impressed, and I formed an opinion that, wow, this might be the future of living, never really knowing that years later I would be living in a gated community myself.
>
> What attracted me to this development was that I am not much of a handy person. Outdoor work does not thrill me. I would rather spend it outdoors doing leisure things. I like the idea of a no-hassle living environment where virtually the grounds are taken care of.
>
> We travel, we do a lot of entertaining, so I like to come and go without worrying about a house. It was more the freedom aspect, the lifestyle aspect, that the townhouse afforded us. Also, I grew up in Queens, the western part of New York City, but it's still Queens, and to have a backyard this big, to be able to watch a sunset without another house, the sun sets right back there . . . I never saw anything like this in Nassau County. So the spaciousness of this development was very appealing.

Also his kids love it. When they moved, there were other young families just starting out. "It's a mix here of families our age with one or two or three kids, and empty nesters who sold their big homes and moved here for more carefree living. As a matter of fact, my parents live four doors down. And my wife's sister lives across the street with her husband and two kids. So we have family right in this neighborhood."

I ask George if there a sense of community.

> Yes, [but] it is fractionalized based upon the age groups. Not everyone intermingles between the empty nesters and the young kids. As a matter of fact, there's some mini-wars going on with people who really don't like the kids playing in the street,

and they think they are causing too much noise. And young parents think it's very healthy for the kids to be out in a safe environment. There have been some conflicts. The community has recently put a "no hockey in the street" rule, where you cannot put your hockey nets down. They are very big on roller skating and hockey in this development. So there have been some, we'll call it restrictive tendencies towards children's activities. Although they are not anti-children here, they try to strike a balance for the homeowners in general.

I ask how conflicts are dealt with.

There's a board of directors. We run this as a corporation, and there are bylaws and meetings. Apathy runs rampant in a homeowners association like this. People just don't show up for meetings. So people who do [show up for meetings] become caretakers for the community. Because [it is a] volunteer board of directors, there are always questions like "Why are they doing that?" Well, why aren't you there to say anything? It's kind of like you snooze, you lose type of approach here. So . . . you have to go along with what the majority rules. And are we always happy with it? No. For instance, we have had broken window panes where there is a temperature seal that's been cracked. So one of our windows is badly discolored. We can't really replace it on our own, because it's technically part of the community. The community wants to get them all done at once, so we have been waiting two years for this one pane of glass to be fixed. Should I just break down and spend it on my own? Well, no, it comes out of our monthly maintenance. I want the community to deal with it, but we have to do it on their terms. When they can get enough of the community together. Those are the little things that could be tweaked. But you can't let those bother you. The benefits outweigh those little risks.

Actually we are considered a cooperative, not a condominium, because the town vetoed the petition to build these as a condominiums, but they had no jurisdiction over a cooperative. When we all signed on the dotted line we were buying a condominium, and that was preconstruction. And then, of course, the issue came up that the town was blocking building it, so we really had no choice but to become a cooperative or lose the opportunity. Seeing what happened, the board of directors adopted a "we'll run this like a condo versus a co-op," so we have more flexibility than a normal co-op would.

Early on, my wife did volunteer to be on the board, and we were just starting our family and our business. We run our own business, so we really put more time and effort into growing that. That's why, although we have opinions about things that aren't going the way we would like, we understand if you are not involved: lead, follow, or get out of the way.

But there are some things that they would like to change.

I'd probably get a pool put in, because I think that would add to a sense of community, having a rallying point. Although it could be a source of dissension because you have so many people populating an area. I guess sometimes good neighbors are the ones you don't see. Maybe we have kept such good acquaintances with everybody because they're not always around. From the limited skirmishes we have had with kids in the street I can imagine what a pool would be like if kids were in the pool with the other people who are not as friendly towards children. So maybe it's a good thing that we don't. But I like the fact that if we did have a pool it would be something centralized for the development.

Also, there's no meeting space. I mean, when we have meetings it's normally done at the community center in town. And I think that's part of the problem, part of the apathy. It's hard for people to get out. I mean if it was down somebody's block [it would be easier]. In the early days, when there were only five or six or ten families, we'd do it in somebody's house, because we could. So it was very community back then, because you did invite people in, because there were only fifteen or twenty people in the neighborhood. But as it grew and grew and grew, of course, we could not do that. So I think that detracts from the sense of running the community well, not having a centralized meeting place.

George makes a number of important points about how difficult it is to keep people actively engaged in community governance. Since he is too busy to participate, he accepts the board's decision based on the philosophy of "you snooze, you lose." He recognizes the apathy characteristic of residents who let the board make the majority of decisions. Yet at the same time, he wishes there was a common pool or a community center that would bring people together. George also points out that his gated community is actually a cooperative and not a condominium because of difficulties in getting condo approval from the local municipality. Although they are actually a co-op, they are run as a condo, implying that there are different rules of governance.

The difference between co-ops and condos lies not only in the structure of ownership, but also in the degree of control residents have in selecting prospective tenants. In cooperatives, residents become members of a corporation or limited partnership that collectively owns a building or group of houses. You become a shareholder and purchase shares that entitle you to a long-term "proprietary lease." Individual shareholders do not actually "own" their units, but own a percentage of shares within the cooperative. Condominiums, on the other hand, are real property, usually with individual ownership of the house or apartment, and common ownership of facilities, land, or buildings. Fees covering maintenance, taxes, and improvements are distributed to all residents in both organizations, but in a condo arrangement, an individual can often sell or rent his or her apartment without the approval of the other residents or the condo board.[10] In the cooperative, however, the co-op board must approve every buyer or renter and has broad powers to grant or withhold approval.[11]

George suggests that a busy lifestyle with multiple responsibilities is the reason gated community residents are frequently not involved in board politics and community conflicts. M. P. Baumgartner, however, offers a different explanation. She argues that upper-middle- and middle-class suburbs in the United States are moral systems, organized to promote what he calls "moral minimalism," a cultural system of controlling community conflict by external and structural means. Upper-middle-class suburbs are physically and socially structured to provide privacy and separation, and households maintain considerable social distance. Neighbors have "weak ties" to other people in the community, but although not strongly linked, they can recognize one another. Residents monitor their environments closely, "identifying those who do not belong," yet at the same time they are sheltered by the privacy made possible by these loosely held relationships.[12]

The upper-middle-class suburb, then, is a distinct kind of neighborhood that combines diffuse interpersonal associations, homogeneity, autonomy, and independence with an absence of strangers. While this pattern of social organization may not characterize all suburbs—there is quite a range of suburban types—when it does exist it allows suburbanites to keep conflict at a minimum, and to manage problems that do arise by avoidance rather than confrontation. In these circumstances, moral minimalism results in a distaste for the pursuit of grievances or censure of wrongdoing. Only when the resident can be assured that someone else will bear the burden of moral authority, enabling them to remain anonymous and uninvolved, do they approve of or practice any overt exercise of social control.[13] Gated communities share many of the characteristics identified by Baumgartner, and residents, in fact, search for intermediary institutions so they do not have to talk to their neighbors.[14]

Private governance enhances the ability of residents to keep interpersonal and neighborhood conflict at a minimum. The complex CC&Rs guarantee that most problems are resolved before they start. In the New York area, both the homeowners associations and the village and municipal organizations work together to reduce intracommunity conflict, and the covenants extend and elaborate land use zoning codes to incorporate an ever widening set of moral and social concerns.

Moral minimalism and the use of land use planning and zoning codes as moral codes are reflected both at the level of local governance and in the preferences and concerns of gated community residents. For example, in the village of North Hills, Long Island, disputes between residents are supposed to be resolved by the homeowners association, but actually end up in the village court. A mosquito problem occurred when one homeowner, whose garden is situated a few feet higher than the surrounding land, watered her plants too much. The water accumulated in puddles in her neighbors' lower lot, creating a breeding pond for mosquitos, for which the lower neighbor was blamed. The neighbors would not deal with the problem, nor would the board, so the managing agent called the North Hills village court to decide what to do.[15] Another example is Yusef's problems with his upstairs neighbor in Waterview, Queens, in the previous chapter. Moral minimalism within these communities necessitates that external—rather than internal—governance resolve these conflicts.[16]

Incentive zoning practices also reflect implicit moral codes that exist between the village and the developer. Developers approach the village board saying, "We need more flexibility in designing our subdivisions."[17] The village is willing to allow some relief, but wants to receive some benefit in exchange. Although the village is not supposed to negotiate fees, in practice, negotiations with the village mayor occur throughout the zoning review process. In the end, a compromise is reached that satisfies both parties. Thus, the fees paid to the village for zoning changes are completely negotiable, and there are no standards for the calculation of the fee. Every single item on the building application list, including the fencing, has to be approved or negotiated for a fee. This exchange is acceptable because the village has very low taxes compared to other municipalities and wants to keep the tax burden to a minimum. And low taxes are made possible by offering limited public services and using the fees paid by developers to provide public amenities.[18]

New York–area gated community residents also have moral concerns, but these are expressed in terms of an aesthetic code that conceals their social and economic objectives (as discussed in the previous chapter). For example, Kerry (introduced in chapter 4) is pleased with the controls exerted by private governance. She is a gardener and was delighted that there would be some areas for planting flowers in her Manor House home. When I notice all the flowers, she explains:

> They're [the homeowners association maintenance company] putting in a garden of shrubs and trees in the back, but we're going to do all the flowers, and they will do the twice-a-year maintenance. So there is a certain amount of leeway that they allow us on our property. I mean, there are certain things you cannot do: "Well, gee, can I put up a little gazebo in our backyard?" [Kerry mimics herself.] "No." [Kerry responds as if she is the homeowners association.] There are certain structures you cannot build. Which I understood going in. There are limitations. The fact that people can't do whatever they want makes me happy, because I don't want ugly structures. Someone might think it's beautiful, and I think it's atrocious. And I'll have to look at it.

"You don't mind, as long as you know that other people are not going to put up something as well," I say.

"Exactly," Kerry replies. "If it goes for them, it goes for me, too. So that's fine."

Laurel, Iris, and Rebecca (from chapter 8) also agree. Iris comments that a homeowners association "is a pain in the neck," but that it protects you from the neighbors who want to paint their house red. For most gated community residents in the New York area, the importance of private governance is as a means to control the environment—and the people living within it.

Another aspect of private governance is the complexity of setting up the board as well as staffing it to maintain the properties and enforce the rules and regulations. Gloria Taylor is on the board of the Waterview homeowners association in Queens, New York. She explains how complicated the system of governance is in her condominium complex.

GLORIA—FEES AND GOVERNANCE ORGANIZATION

There's four boards. . . . When the builder built this complex he started out with one series of homes, condo one. And then he built another series, and that's condo two. That's how they get their loans to build [by completing one part of a large complex and selling the homes and then building the next with the profits from the completed one]. And then he added condo three. And I am in the third condo. And then the recreation board, that is the homeowners association that I am on. Regulations are made for the whole complex through the recreation board. We do take the advice of the condos if they want something put into effect. But when they put out parking tickets, each condo gets their money from the person, because they are in charge of the selling of the unit, the closing, [and] when there's a sale they can collect the money if they [residents] don't pay [their fines]. So the condos receive the parking ticket money, not the recreation board.

The repairs to the outside are done by the condo, and inside is done by the owner. Except the hallways, [which] like any public area is done by the condo. Our condo estimates that this summer we will do seven driveways and we will paint two buildings.

I ask what happens if some emergency comes up.

We have four maintenance men in just condo three. And we have two in condo two, and two in condo one. And in the main homeowners association we have three maintenance workers, a receptionist, a manager, and an assistant manager. If the pool is open we have a lifeguard, and we have instructors for the different classes.

This is all paid for out of our fees: a maintenance fee and a recreation fee. Everybody pays both fees. They would get foreclosed if they didn't pay. We take them to court. But in the recreation association we have a very small percentage of people who don't pay; it isn't even twenty people or twenty units.

Gloria points out that in her gated community there are at least two levels of governance and separate fees. These fees are collected and allocated by the board to pay the staff that maintains and runs the development. In this sense, a gated community is similar to any private company or concern that bills its clients or "taxes" its members for the right to receive services. Because of the nature of these financial arrangements, a gated community is considered part of the private realm. Yet many of the rights of residents are "public," in the sense that they are shared collectively with others and therefore belong to the public realm.

Chris Webster argues that gated community debates frequently espouse overly simplistic notions of the private and public realms. Adding a third category—the "club" realm—modifies this dichotomy.[19] From the point of view of public goods theory, access to and consumption of a good or service is what makes it public or private. "Public goods" have the quality of nonexcludability, so that once they have been provided, everyone benefits regardless of whether they pay or not.[20] Cities or suburbs, in this scheme, are made up of small *publics*, each of which may be thought of as a collective consumption club.[21]

These consumption clubs assign legal property rights over neighborhood public goods by property market institutions (ownership, real estate assessments) and are not different from other governance institutions, in which included "members" (taxpayers) share goods and "nonmembers" (nontaxpayers) are excluded. A comparison can be made between municipal governments supplying collective services on the basis of taxes and gated communities with their own management companies, local service budgets, and contractual regulations providing goods and services based on fees. Rather than focusing on the distinction between public and private, it is more fruitful to ask whether gated communities deliver more equitable services to "club" residents.[22]

The current growth in private communities—gated and nongated—is one response to municipal governments' failure to provide adequate neighborhood services because of "free riding" (use of services by those who do not pay for them), and local governments' inability to supply services in rapidly growing areas. By "bundling up" a variety of public goods within a residential scheme and recovering costs through sale prices and fees, the house-building industry and market has become a "neighborhood"-building industry and market.[23] For the people living inside gated communities it is an efficient solution, because residents are legally required to pay fees, the community needs and desires are homogenous, and would-be residents can choose their package of communal goods according to their personal preferences.[24] Critics, on the other hand, are concerned that gated community residents will vote to reduce municipal expenditures they do not use, resulting in increased crime risk in the general vicinity and other forms of service inequity. But from an economic point of view, the gated community is an opportunity to experiment with new ways to provide goods and services that distribute them more efficiently to those who can afford to join the "consumption club" than current governmental strategies do.

The Mitchells, who retired to Sun Meadow, illustrate this point. They lived in an incorporated town within San Antonio, where they liked the schools, had their own police department, and purchased services from the city. But they found the services supplied by San Antonio expensive yet merely adequate, and therefore decided to move to Sun Meadow, where services were initially provided by the homeowners association.

Economic recession and the decline of real estate prices, however, also altered the level of services and tax structure, particularly in Texas, because Texas is extremely reliant on real estate taxes—rather than income taxes—like many other Sunbelt states. Because of this dependence on real estate taxes, Texas is representative of the trend toward privatization of municipal services. Pamela and Wayne, who live in the Links, offer their perspective on how taxation, private governance, and land planning influence the fees and services in their development and other gated communities.

PAMELA AND WAYNE—MUNICIPAL PLANNING AND GATED COMMUNITIES

Pamela and Wayne live in a Florentine mansion just inside the guardhouse at the Links. The entry hall is set with inlaid marble and stone pillars, furnished with French empire antiques. Pamela squeezes my hand as she greets me. She is tall and slim, with long blond hair, wearing white satin lounging pants and a silk cowboy shirt. Wayne towers above her, casually dressed for work on a construction site. We met at a dinner party; I asked if I could interview them to get the perspective of people who had been involved in the design and planning of gated communities. They agreed, and invited me to their home.

Their section of the development was planned with well-to-do retirees in mind—mainly doctors and lawyers—and other professional retired people do live in their immediate neighborhood. Most of their neighbors moved from even bigger homes—one because he plays golf, and another because she wants to be close to a hospital. The majority of their neighbors are white, but also include a black retired general, a black insurance agent, and Mexican nationals who "keep a shopping home here."

Wayne is familiar with the municipal consequences of developing large-scale gated communities outside the city, in terms of metropolitan planning and governance, and the ability to provide city services to communities.

A lot of what's happening in these gated communities is that local government continues to annex.[25] As they annex, the level of service goes down, not only for the annexed areas, but also for the inner parts of the city. [The idea is that] we'll get more money, and everybody will benefit. [But in fact] they get more taxes and dilute the level or quality of services.

So developers say, "Well, I have got to have my own amenity package, I have to have my own gated community." All that is, is a reflection of the inability of the government to deal properly with the problems at hand. They create another level of service: homeowners associations in these gated communities. So the type of development we get is because the city is ambitious in terms of annexation.

I see problems with gated communities in the future. . . . The reality is that when gated communities are annexed, the city does not take responsibility for repairs of streets [and infrastructure]. Homeowners associations have to provide that.

Wayne believes that the links will be annexed within two years. It means that residents will have to pay city and county taxes as well as their homeowners association maintenance fees. Tax assessments also will change with annexation, and resident taxes will increase. But the city will not take over responsibility for the private streets—or for anywhere that's not public, for that matter.

Residents will have to pay more taxes, but they won't necessarily receive more services. Wayne explains that the city does offer some services, such as police and fire protection, but because the community is gated, there are still problems of access. According to him, homeowners associations in gated communities are setting back San Antonio's ability to have proper levels of municipal services with appropriate taxation.

For Wayne, one of the biggest drawbacks to gated communities is what's going to happen with taxation, annexation, and the relationship to the city and municipal governments. The critical issue is the provision of city services and equity of taxation. He feels that there ought to be an equitable breakdown as to what you pay for and what you receive. "And when these private communities get annexed, they're going to be paying an exorbitant amount of tax for what benefit they get, and the inequity gets even further out of line."

Local governments promote economic growth through territorial annexation. As population and businesses expand, Sunbelt city governments try to capture the benefits of this urban growth through the annexation of adjacent unincorporated areas. San Antonio grew from 69 square miles in 1950 to 160.5 square miles in 1960, 184.1 square miles in 1970, and 253 square miles in 1973. Local government revenue per capita has increased from $262.64 in 1970 to $1,514 in 1990.[26] The city also controls subdivisions and land use planning for five miles beyond its legal boundaries.[27] Wayne verifies that this pattern of rampant annexation has not slowed.

Gated communities in many cases precede annexation as a result of extreme urban sprawl—that is, urban/suburban expansion without municipal infrastructure. The gated community serves as a government-like service provider. Eventually public government catches up, but it may be too overstretched and indebted to provide adequate services, except to impose a new level of taxes to support the older city. Gated community governance remains, with the public government on top of it. There may be some gated communities that form inside cities, in an attempt to provide their own services, but generally the gated community precedes annexation, which is when the problems for residents concerned about taxes start.[28]

While annexation bolsters municipal revenues and broadens the city's tax base, it has a downside for gated community residents in terms of double taxation—paying fees to the homeowners association and paying high real estate taxes. Gilbert and Marie moved to Sun Meadow in an attempt to escape some of these taxes, and to purchase private services at a reasonable cost.

GILBERT AND MARIE—TAXATION AND PROVISION OF SERVICES

Gilbert and Marie Walbaum live a split-level brick ranch with a three-car garage big enough for their golf carts. They retired in 1989, moving first to Florida and then to San Antonio. Their four children and six grandchildren visit on holidays and during the summer. They are both still active—Marie is sixty-nine and Gilbert is seventy-one—and involved in the homeowners association, a bridge club, and their church. The day of the interview, however, Marie had the flu, so I interviewed Gilbert alone.

They initially retired to a subdivision near a town of five thousand people in

Florida. He was active in the homeowners association, in which property owners already had control and decision making was easy. In Sun Meadow, the developers still own a majority of the lots, so working on the homeowners association is much more frustrating. They left their first retirement community because it was never completed and not gated.

I ask him about the decision to move to Sun Meadow. He answers:

> I wanted a clean, safe place to retire. The country has changed [for the worse]. It [crime, poverty] didn't affect me too much, but it affected some friends of mine. I felt bad [to have to move into a gated community], and I don't like some things about gated communities. Gated communities are not treated properly by the government [in terms of taxes and services]. You know streets are a large part of the city. If they [government] don't have to build them and maintain them, then that's big money [the government keeps]. . . . What I'm saying is [what] bothers me is the [political and social] makeup of the city, and how the city is governed, the reactions of the city directors. So if it [living in a gated community] keeps them out of my business a little bit, maybe it's worth it.

Gilbert thinks that gated communities are not treated well in terms of taxation. Part of his motivation for moving to a gated community is that there is a private government, a homeowners association, providing services within the development. As he put it, "Anytime I can keep the government out of my business, I do." His attitude jibes with the Sunbelt conservatism and right-wing politics espoused by a number of the San Antonio residents. He thought that being in a gated community would keep the government out, but now Sun Meadow is to be annexed by the city. When he purchased his home, they were two and half miles outside the city limit. But now "we're going to be a gated neighborhood in the city."

Gilbert is disappointed that the city is going to annex Sun Meadow. He agrees with Wayne's prediction that Sun Meadow residents will be taxed for services they will not use. For Gilbert and Wayne, triple taxation (city taxes, county taxes, and homeowners association fees) is inequitable, especially when street maintenance and water are not provided. They expect that what city services they do get will be mediocre.

Some gated communities have applied to receive a rebate on their property taxes for services they pay for privately. The executive director of Woodbridge Village in Irvine, California, went to the state assembly in 1990 to make a case for deducting homeowners association dues from federal and state income tax, but was not successful. The passage of California's Proposition 13 in 1978, however, placed severe limits on local governments' ability to increase taxes, making it difficult for government to provide adequate public services. Because of the resulting lack of services, private communities argue that they are forced to provide their own services and therefore deserve a tax credit or deduction for doing so.[29]

In New Jersey, a group of private homeowners associations succeeded in pushing a "Municipal Services Act" through the state legislature that provides rebates on property taxes residents pay for trash collection, snow removal, and street lighting. The New Jersey chapter of the Community Association Institute, the national association of homeowners associations, also continues to lobby for rebates on taxes paid to maintain public roads.[30]

In San Antonio, the northern suburban counties have organized a "homeowners taxpayers association" to combat higher taxes. Their web site encourages members to protest any kind of tax increase, including sales taxes. Arguing that the taxes in the northern counties are the highest in Texas, they want to roll back the San Antonio property tax and monitor any new proposed public construction or unnecessary public program.[31]

For Gilbert and Marie, private government represents local control of decision making and keeps "government out of our business." For Wayne and Pamela, it is San Antonio's lack of municipal planning, rampant annexation, and the resulting inequality in rates of taxation in relation to the provision of services. These issues are not mentioned by the New York and Long Island gated community residents because New York City is no longer expanding by annexation and hasn't since 1898. The level of taxation is relatively low, especially in New York City, but also in the parts of Nassau County where villages and townships charge developers fees that cover many public expenditures. Another reason that residents in the Northeast are more amenable to taxation than those in Texas is the difference in their political cultures. Many gated community residents in Texas mirror the conservatism and right-wing politics of the Sunbelt region, while the Northeast's liberal democrat tradition influences the politics of New York gated community residents.

One question the contrast between Texas and New York raises is whether homeowners associations actually provide an organizational structure to accomplish things that the government or municipality has chosen not to address. To examine this question, I briefly want to return to what we learned at Vista Mar, in Mexico City (discussed in chapter 6). Maria Regina, the president of the residents association of Vista Mar, explained how gated communities are organized and managed. According to her, providing adequate security and services became so important that the residents created their own form of private governance, without the legal underpinnings of a common interest development—much less the support of the municipality or state.

Maria Regina—Inadequate Security and Maintenance

Maria Regina is in her early thirties, dressed in a white silk blouse and skirt. She lives in a modern one-story stone-and-glass house with her husband, son, and a maid. During the interview, she receives various telephone calls from residents about operational issues, but even with the distractions she gives thoughtful answers to my questions. She mentions that there are subtle class differences in the community:

> Some are decent people with more or less economic power. We have a lot of new rich with inferior cultural background, and this may cause some problems . . . .They have jobs in the *central de abastos* [market and distribution center] or they are truckers. They have money but not education, and this can cause problems with those that may not have a lot of money but are educated.[32]

She later attributes these class and cultural differences to differences in participation in the community. But she gets along with everyone, and has a group of friends that she visits. It is a good relationship, because she is free to stop by for coffee or to borrow an egg, and you can ask a neighbor to watch your house while you are away.

Maria Regina explains that in Mexico City, gated communities are not formed as common interest developments but as private subdivisions, with lots purchased individually without any guarantees or a required fee structure. At Vista Mar, a team of seven women are in charge of the administration of the residents association and take care of maintenance as well as relations between the neighbors and the authorities.

Since the beginning, Vista Mar has been closed by four gates. The gates are illegal, as it is not constitutional to restrict access to public roads, but people are gating their communities throughout their area because the state cannot provide adequate security. Gating has a cost for the residents, since the state will not provide maintenance for the streets or police surveillance in a private area. For this reason, the residents association has imposed a maintenance fee even though they do not have the legal power to force residents to pay. Part of their work is to convince people that if they want to live in a gated community they have to pay a fee to have the necessary services. Only about 45 percent of the residents pay the fees—she attributes this to cultural differences—so of the four entrances, one is reserved only for the people who pay. The fees also cover the three parties a year that are attended by everyone.

Maria Regina's team oversees the maintenance of the 1 million square meters of the entire community and 120,000 square meters of garden areas. They also clean the two hundred vacant lots to reduce pests and limit security problems. They provide lighting and water service and charge to bring water to the houses, since the community is not yet connected to the city water network. They coordinate the gardeners, office workers, and policemen, and hire the security employees.

When I ask her why the team was made up of only women, she explains that a group of fifty neighbors—all women—had been meeting regularly. When they heard that the developer wanted to destroy one of the existing gardens to build more houses, they decided to take over the administration of the community. They already knew about many of the problems, such as irregularities in site development and construction, including a tower that is higher than the three stories allowed by local restrictions.

Residents have been ignoring the restrictions that were set up originally. Because Vista Mar was built in a semiecological zone, the developers were only allowed to construct houses with significant green areas, and houses could not exceed a certain size. Unfortunately, though, builders were violating these internal regulations, because they were not codified in state or municipal law. The women's group was concerned that if they didn't take over the administration and begin to enforce the regulations, they would lose the gardens that were so important to the children.

So even when there was no supporting legal structure, such as a common interest development or other form of governance other than state regulations for the subdivision development, residents created a quasi-governmental system to handle the administration of the community, to collect fees for services, and to make decisions that benefit everyone. Even if only half of the community pays the fee, it is adequate to maintain the grounds and hire security. No one even mentioned the existence of rules and regulations for house design—much less as an aesthetic or moral code—and house style and decoration varies considerably. Instead, class designations—for example, "new rich," "decent people"—pervade the Mexican gated community discourse, categories that are dependent on intrinsic characteristics of people's background that work to sort residents into their "proper" places.

When examined from the New York residents' point of view, private governance minimizes conflict by setting up an *a priori* set of rules and regulations that determine what residents can and cannot do with their property. It also provides a strict standard for the appearance of their homes and gardens, reducing the possibility of conflict when neighbors do not mow their grass often enough or if they put their garbage out too early in the day. It reinforces suburban moral minimalism by predetermining who is willing to live with the level of rules and regulations imposed by the homeowners association. That is not to say that some residents don't try to buck the system, fighting the design review board or homeowners association over the control of their home. My husband recently passed on to me a story from the *New York Times* that reports on a couple in Sacramento, California, who are fighting to have a yellow house where only earth-tone colors are allowed.[33] But as a general rule, CC&Rs and homeowners' associations work to minimize conflict in most upper-middle- and middle-class suburbs.

In San Antonio, on the other hand, private governance, from the residents' point of view, is less about moral minimalism and more about the efficient provision of services at a time in which the city is expanding too rapidly to keep up with taxpayer demands. Here the contrast is between newer Sunbelt cities that are growing rapidly and the Northeast, where the urban population peaked earlier in the twentieth century and then stabilized or even decreased with subsequent suburbanization. Further, the differences in political culture influence residents' concern with governance; Texans, even recent immigrants, are interested in lower taxes and less government interference, and New Yorkers are generally more liberal regarding taxation and the role of government.

Finally, the brief example of a gated community in Mexico City suggests that a residential association can become a vehicle for collecting fees used to provide security and services not provided by the state. In the absence of adequate state or local government, private governance forms voluntarily, to fill in the services and supply the needs of the community. These regional differences provide a more nuanced explanation of why people choose to live in private communities. Residents' needs and preferences respond to the local historical, political, and geographical context of the area as well as to the psychological and social concerns of the individual homeowner.

From the perspective of cities, the building of private communities has the advantage of providing the "front-load" infrastructure construction costs. Municipalities and towns that cannot fund new development but want to expand their tax base rely on real estate developers to produce new housing through incentive zoning mechanisms. The benefits of this strategy became even more apparent after the passage of laws like Proposition 13 in California that restrict the power of local government to finance activities through property taxes.[34] Common interest developments become more attractive and lead to privatization of government responsibilities in situations in which the local authority does not have the financial capability to build the infrastructure needed and when rapid population growth and annexation leads to an inability to provide basic urban services.

This is not to say that this expansion of private governance is a desirable or inevitable solution. Unfortunately, debates about public and private governance have not been as important in the United States as they are in most of Western Europe.[35] The European political climate of social democracy views private governance with suspicion, growing out of a World War II experience with closed and clandestine political groups and local social and political oppression. In the United States, private governance, in the form of business improvement districts in large cities and homeowners associations in the suburbs, has grown exponentially through the last two decades, eliciting relatively little comment.[36] Evan McKenzie thinks that private governance has become more common because the common interest development industry, housing developers, and local municipalities benefit from it and promote it because it's in their best financial interest.[37] The supply side of private governance (and gating) is driving the expansion of private communities, even though it is not necessarily the best (or most efficient) solution for residents or, much less, for society at large.

CHAPTER 10

Easing the Way to Retirement

When my adopted grandparents, Letha and Tommy, retired, they moved to a mobile home park in Orange County, California. Walled on all sides, with concrete lions marking the entrance, it was like a gated community but without the gate. Off the entrance was a locked clubhouse and swimming pool area enclosed by a cyclone fence. Each mobile home had a narrow garden of colored gravel, wood chips, or grass decorated with plastic deer, pagodas, or playing card designs of diamonds, clubs, hearts, and spades traced in stone (photograph 18).

Residents had to be over fifty-five, could not have dogs or children, and grandchildren visits were restricted to the weekends. Looking back, I find it hard to believe that such strict regulations existed, but I remember as a teenager trying to hide behind Letha's four-foot ten-inch, two-hundred-pound body when a man from the park office came to the door. Anna and I couldn't play outside or use the pool on weekdays since we weren't supposed to be there. One widower who married a younger woman—forty-eight years old—was asked to leave because his new wife did not meet the minimum age requirements of the community.[1]

As my grandparents aged, large numbers of Vietnamese families

Photograph 18. "Letha in her mobile home park in Westminster, California." Setha Low. Author's own.

moved into the surrounding neighborhoods, and Westminister became known as "Little Saigon." Malls marked by Chinese entrances and Mongolian dogs guarding red-and-gold pillars flourished along the Bolsa Avenue shopping strip. Each time I visited I found that Tommy was driving farther from home to find what he called a "regular" grocery, and after he died I found it difficult to find milk,[2] much less Letha's favorite hamburgers, in Vietnamese food stores (photograph 19).

As Letha approached her ninetieth birthday, she and many of her neighbors found themselves frightened by teenage Asian gangs and increased crime. They were shocked at the cultural strangeness of what they saw as their neighborhood and they were surprised at having lost control of their community. They added an electronically controlled gate and heightened the five-foot cement block wall to eight feet to protect themselves from the perceived threat.

In the end, Letha moved to San Antonio so she could be near my sister, and she died shortly thereafter. I am sad that the end of her life

Photograph 19. "Bolsa Avenue Mall in Little Saigon, Westminster, California." Setha Low. Author's own.

was marred by a growing sense of fear and cultural exclusion in Westminister and wish that local solutions to bring old-timers and new immigrants together had been tried. Reflecting on Letha's dilemma, I find it instructive that the mobile home park residents felt that it was necessary to add an electronic gate. Gating provided a sense of community for these elderly white, working-class retirees, created greater safety and psychological security, defined their community boundaries from those of immigrant "others," and made it "nicer" as the surrounding neighborhood was being transformed into another cultural world.

Many people decide that a gated community provides the safety and amenities they are looking for in retirement. Retirees, however, have other concerns as well, including the layout of the house and the social life of the community. Ruth Roth, for instance, chose Manor House on Long Island even before her husband's retirement in preparation for the kind of living they would want in ten years.

RUTH—SOCIAL AND RECREATIONAL NEEDS

Ruth Roth greets me at the door and invites me into the family room. She is in her early sixties, soft-spoken and relaxed, dressed in a long purple skirt and matching jacket. The family room is decorated in classic blue-and-white striped sofas and Windsor chairs. She serves coffee from a silver teapot and places it carefully on a teak coffee table. Ruth was a teacher before she retired, and begins by telling me about the compromises they had made in their residential choices before moving to Manor House.

I'm going to begin by telling you what led me to Manor House, because I think things evolved. I'm going to be married forty years in July, and we've lived in three homes. The first one was at the beginning of our marriage, when we had little children, and bought a home that was affordable, [but] needed a great deal of work. We chose it because we wanted our children to have a fine education, so we compromised in many ways. It certainly was not the home of our dreams, but it was a home that we could make into something. We worked for several years repairing, changing, ripping out, and doing most of it by ourselves. We lived there for twenty-three years.

When our children were adults, my husband suggested—he's always an innovator—that we sell the house and make a change. We sold the house in one day and that was very difficult, but it prompted us to hurry and find something very quickly. In three weeks we bought a house that was fifty-five years old in a neighborhood with lots of families. The house was a center-hall colonial, had a main level, upstairs bedrooms, an attic that was three flights up, and we finished the basement, so we're talking about four stories of living. It needed a great deal of work. This time it was more affordable for us to tear out the kitchen, change the bathrooms, finish the basement, and landscape. We did lots of things to the house and made it our own, because when you buy a resale, it really is somebody else's. We lived there for six years.

Then once again my husband—who I mentioned is an innovator—said, "Now in ten years I don't really want to be walking up four flights of steps. I don't want to be doing all the things that I have to do here." We also had a termite problem, which is something that comes [with] an older home.

"The house is beautiful," he said, "but I don't see myself living here in ten years. I really want to sell the house."

I wasn't too happy about it because I really loved the house. But I began to look. I saw other people's homes that needed repairs and might have had termites. I looked for two years and finally said, "If I don't find something that I like better, I'm not going to move."

So I put it on the back shelf for a while. One day we were driving home on Cove Hollow Road, and I saw the sign, Manor House. Now I had looked at townhouse condominiums and didn't like the sameness and being connected to another person's home. But I called from the car and asked to make an appointment. There were really no homes on the premises, only plans. My husband felt that he wanted a ranch, but when I looked at the floor plan of the ranch, I wasn't too happy because it didn't have a family room. Then I saw this model, which had all the living on the main level with the master bedroom, which we would be using, and the guest bedrooms upstairs. So it served his purposes: it had one-floor living except if we were to have company, and it had a family room. He still kept saying ranch, and I said ranch doesn't have a family room, so he compromised and we bought this model because it basically is one-floor living. I don't have to go upstairs unless I have guests. I also loved the fact that Manor House was accessible to the parkway, and my husband needs the railroad. The rail line is the best line to the city, [and] you can even get a parking spot.

So, one reason that this appealed to me was that it was brand new. I had always lived in other peoples' homes that I felt were not my own. It was a beautiful feeling after being married for thirty-nine years, like a fresh beginning. It's a very exciting thing to do.

Their first neighborhood was on the south shore of Long Island. Her children were able to walk to school, and since she worked in the community it was convenient for her family. "My children didn't feel that I was absent from their lives, because they were only minutes away from where I worked." But once the children were grown and had moved to their own homes, other concerns came into play.

Ruth worried what it might be like to live in a private community. Neither of her children live in one, and she values her privacy.

I didn't feel that I wanted to be in this kind of community, first because I am very independent and I value my privacy, and I didn't like buildings that were connected together or shared patios or facilities. I was afraid of giving up my individuality, but I didn't feel that about Manor House because the homes are separate. We have a lot of space, [and] we have our own property.

I looked through all of the documents to see what the community would be like, how many homes would be here. I knew that this particular lot could not have a house opposite it, and would offer us privacy. We call it a colonial, but it's the "Vineyard"; each model has a name. Next door is the smaller ranch. They're all different styles and different colors. You don't get the feeling of everything being exactly alike.

They were distressed, however, when not enough houses were selling to support the common facilities and maintain the guardhouse. As retirees living on a fixed, (though high) income, they worried that the fees would escalate. "We bought this at its conception and had the development not sold well we would have concerns, because our upkeep would become extremely costly if they didn't sell enough models. But we believed in the property, and we believed in the fact that [if] it had the convenient train station and was a premium property, it would do well."

Before moving to Manor House, they considered living in their Manhattan apartment. Now that they are retired and the children are grown, they want to spend more time in New York.

It was wonderful at the beginning. This was the empty-nest syndrome for us; we went to the theater, and we were enjoying all of the luxuries. But once we moved to Long Island we found we were very close to the city, and that we loved coming home to the country and a garden. I felt so sad seeing the homeless, and elements of the city are very unpleasant on a daily basis. I'm in my warm car in the winter, and in my cold car in the summer. I can drive to a shopping center and put my bundles in the trunk of my car. I'm very comfortable with living in the suburbs. In New York we were doing a tremendous amount of walking [which was harder] if it's hot and if it's raining and if it's cold. We realized that it's a much less friendly feeling, and we decided that we really didn't want to live in New York permanently, that we prefer just going in for a very short trip. And so we sold our apartment.

Manor House offers Ruth a new house and convenient access to New York without actually living in the city. She hopes that the amenities of the swimming pool and clubhouse will provide the social life and recreational center she wants in retirement. They feel that their home and the community fits this stage of their lives.

As I drive away, I reflect on gated communities as a retirement solution. Ross W. Cortese opened Leisure World "new towns" in Seal Beach, Laguna Hills, and Walnut Creek, California, in the early 1960s as a form of segregated housing for the aged. Retirees who moved to Leisure World were attracted "by the strict security measures in place"—the walls, guarded gates, police patrols, and even checks on the criminal records of new applicants. Leisure World was one of the first places where average Americans could wall themselves off, a prototype of exclusionary living for the middle class. The age restrictions, security patrols, gates, and walls created self-sufficient enclaves of senior housing.[3]

At Leisure World in Silver Spring, Maryland, Edward Blakely and Mary Gail Synder observed security guards boarding buses to see that no "undesirables" entered the development. There are walls, gates, fences, ditches, and barricades to protect the seniors, as well as organized activities and recreational facilities.[4] Even though Manor House was not designed specifically for retirees, it offers some of the same benefits, including the increased security and recreational center of the Leisure World model. What is different, however, is that the community is not segregated by age.

Sun Meadow, on the other hand, was originally designed for retirees. Located on a golf course, with tennis courts and swimming pools available in the nearby country club, it offers many of the amenities of Leisure World. Elizabeth and Mitchell Booth are a couple who moved to Sun Meadow because they wanted to live in an exclusive, golf-club retirement community.

ELIZABETH AND MITCHELL—GOLF CLUB RETIREMENT

The Booths' grandchildren are arriving tomorrow, so Elizabeth and Mitchell decide it is better to complete the interview late in the evening than to fit it in during the visit. It's dark as I drive around the development searching for their one-level, Southwestern-style house. The house is right out of a Mexican western, with a stucco facade that looks like adobe and wooden beams protruding from the roof. A lighted terra-cotta tile path leads to a heavily carved wood front door.

Elizabeth sits close to me in a leather chair, and Mitchell, who directs the conversation, sits next to her on a matching couch. The house is spacious and decorated with Mexican artifacts. Photographs of their daughter and her children are displayed everywhere.

They are retired, involved in the community, the church, and their grandchildren. Mitchell plays golf, and Elizabeth is what she calls a "golf widow." Mitchell is sixty-three, hardy and wind burned, and Elizabeth is fifty-nine, a small, plump woman with graying hair and a warm smile. Mitchell is a retired production manager; Elizabeth has always been a homemaker.

They moved into their house in 1986. As one of the first families to move in, they bought their lot and house from the first family that started the development. The original plan was for Sun Meadow to be a community for older people, empty nesters, and retirees, but it didn't turn out that way. It was seven years before any houses were built after they bought their land. Mitchell explains, "The original concept of the whole development was for older people, because younger people wouldn't be able to afford the houses. But the market went down, way down, so that's one of the reasons it's different."

When they first got married, they rented an apartment in Dallas. They moved to San Antonio in 1961 and bought a small, eighteen-hundred-square-foot house. In 1968 they moved again, this time to a larger house in Corral Run—an incorporated town within San Antonio—where they liked the schools; they lived there until they moved to Sun Meadow. They used services that their town purchased from the city. The elementary school was right across the street from their house, and the high school was just down the block. It was a nice, stable neighborhood and good for their daughter. They liked their neighbors, the schools, and the shopping. But they left because of the quality of the city services. Mitchell recalls, "We disliked the services supplied by San Antonio. Corral Run contracted out the electrical and the water and everything through the city. We had our own police department, but it [had] just opened."

Elizabeth adds, "And a mayor, but really it was just like living in the city."

Mitchell, however, had always wanted to live on a golf course. At first

Elizabeth was against the move, since she liked her neighbors and local church. She thought she might be lonely or that it would be too quiet. But Mitchell just "kept at her." Two houses on their street were broken into, and there were more people and more traffic, so there were also factors that pushed them out of the neighborhood.

They got the plans and walked onto what was to be a thirty-six-hole golf course. They wanted a piece of wooded land that would be big enough for a three-thousand-square-foot house.

They finally bought a lot when they were offered $25,000 off the initial price if they would start construction by June 1986. It was the start of the real estate decline in the region, and prices were dropping quickly. Originally, lots were $175,000 on the golf course and $100,000 across the street. House construction was calculated at $80 per square foot.[5] A few years later, lots listed for $170,000 to $190,000 were selling for $40,000. Mitchell concludes that "the reason we have a lot of young people is this was the same price as [a] nongated, nongolf community, and I think it did change the [original] idea." In December 1986, they moved into an unfinished house.

Elizabeth says that the gates are a bonus, offering increased safety and security. She feels better being in a gated community now than before. Mitchell adds that "once you get into a gated community you want one." They would not buy a house in a community that was not gated now.

I ask if they have any regrets, and Mitchell answers:

> If the concept had been correct, then our home would be worth more, and there would not be so many families. Even if we did move, the base value of the house and land has been eroded by the number of lower-cost houses in the area. For instance, I have a friend who paid $360,000 for his house. He now has it listed for $278,000. It does change the overall price base. It was to be the premier retirement development in San Antonio, but now it won't be.

I ask they if they would move again. Elizabeth replies, "We would love a gated community with a guard. The system at Sun Meadow allows another car to follow you in when you are buzzed. Cars do it all the time."

But even if Sun Meadow were not a gated community, there are some people who would come for the golf club. Originally, the owners of the development and of the club were the same. Then a Japanese corporation bought the club for $15 million, and Mitchell feels that this changed the management's attitude. Before, they needed to keep the club up to attract home buyers. When they were owned together, the idea was to keep the community and the club very exclusive. It costs $20,000 to join the club, and joining the club was a requirement for buying the land. With the separation, lots dropped from $190,000 to $45,000 on the golf course, and conflicts have arisen between the club and community members. If the community and club had stayed together, the profit made by the housing would have gone into the club and community. With the separation, one does not benefit the other. Further, there have been disagreements about the golf path: residents want to use it, but the club says it is too dangerous—residents can get hit by a golf ball or by a moving cart. Residents, however, do not understand why they cannot use this resource, which is on their land. It would have worked out better for the Booths if the golf course had remained exclusive and if Sun Meadow had remained more of a retirement community.

There are a number of concerns facing the community. A new shopping center is being built behind the development, and some residents are worried about increased traffic. Some residents want a higher wall around the development. Others are disturbed by school bus safety and traffic in the morning. Problems for families with school-age children are different from those without children, which is another reason Mitchell argues that Sun Meadow should have been only for retirees.

Interestingly, two of the gated communities—Sun Meadow and Manor House— have experienced a financial crisis and bankruptcy, which restructured the costs and concepts of the initial developments. The decline in real estate prices following the 1987 stock market crash and subsequent recession depressed prices in both developments in their early phases. In San Antonio, the country club was sold and the land and square-foot construction costs plummeted. Some lots went into bank receivership or were bought by other developers. The initial developer lost control of the overall design, and a variety of developers who built lower-quality houses took over.

In New York, the drop in real estate prices occurred just as Manor

House was first being marketed as an exclusive gated community. The owner/developer went into bankruptcy, and the land was purchased by the current builder. Again, the concept of the community changed, not as dramatically as in Sun Meadow, but the prices of homes did decline and many of the original amenities were eliminated. The resurgence of housing prices was faster in New York because of the growing strength of the Manhattan-centered financial markets in the 1990s in comparison to the sluggish recovery of the oil-based economy in Texas.

Socially, however, the results are quite similar. Both communities originally targeted wealthy retirees by publicizing enhanced security and luxury amenities. But the real estate decline and economic recession in both regions allowed another group of buyers to purchase homes, thus changing the community's socioeconomic and age composition.

Retirees also are drawn to gated communities because of the "easy-care" lifestyle provided by the CC&Rs and board structure that manages and maintains the landscape and buildings. Attached-townhouse gated communities are particularly attractive to retirees interested in scaling down their lifestyle and reducing the amount of work they put into maintaining their house and landscape. Pine Hills on Long Island offers retirees both, but also has few recreational amenities. Unlike the Booths, Bernie and Myrna Schnacter were looking to minimize the hassle of upkeep, and were not particularly interested in whether their community provided friends or recreational activities.

Bernie and Myrna—Maintenance and Minimalism

When I first arrive, Myrna asks me for some identification in a firm but pleasant way. She says that after 9/11 she is more anxious about trusting people and letting them into her house.

Bernie and Myrna are a retired couple who have lived in Pine Hills for thirteen years. Myrna is a plump, spry-looking lady who wears big glasses. She is enthusiastic about life and spends much of the interview buzzing around in the kitchen, commenting occasionally and adding to the conversation, while Bernie and I sit just outside the wide entry door to the kitchen. Bernie is intense, with a full head of gray hair and bushy eyebrows. He is very engaging, open, and communicative, and seems genuinely interested in the discussion. Dressed in a checked flannel shirt, khaki pants, and slippers, he seems very relaxed and at home. Their furniture is contemporary, giving the house a modern look. Bits of driftwood sculpture sit on a burr walnut coffee table that Bernie also uses as a foot rest.

Pine Hills was their first experience with a co-op or gated community. They had lived in private homes until their children became old enough to live on their own. When this happened, they found the house they owned to be too much of a burden.

> So we came here because a lot of the exterior work was to be done by other people. We did not have to worry about gardening and things like that. We could devote our time to more useful things for ourselves. The fun of mowing a lawn was gone.
>
> We came in here pretty much at the beginning. This section had not even been built yet. We chose this piece of land just on the basis of a trip up here and looking at the topography, and since we decided to buy here we decided to select our own [lot]. Since we were early in the development, we picked this particular site, which is overlooking a completely wooded region, on a cul-de-sac, very quiet, very private. And for thirteen years we have had absolutely no complaints. Well, maybe one or two.

I ask Bernie where they had lived before.

> We lived in an apartment for a while in Bayside and then, using the GI bill, we bought a home on the south shore of Long Island. We lived there for about five years, and then sold the house and moved to the north shore. We lived there for twenty-three years and it was from there that our children went out on their own, and we came here.
>
> I found an ad in the Sunday *Times* and it looked very attractive. It was a rather cheesy-looking drawing. But the text attracted me. So we just decided to take a ride out here one day. We had been to several other condos. That was the thing we liked—contemporary rather than colonial or traditional style. And so we took a ride out here. And it just caught us. So we went back, discussed it, figured out our finances, and came back a couple of times and talked to the builder, and finally one day we decided, "Let's move on this before someone else gets it."

We had never lived in a gated community. We knew a couple of friends who had purchased [homes] in gated communities in Florida, and in California. But this was our first time at it, and it was just something that was there. I mean, had it not been gated I still think we would have bought it here. Security was not a primary reason, [although] we had been burglarized before, and were completely wiped out. There have been a couple of burglaries here [in Pine Hills], but we have had alarm systems in our house ever since the burglary. We have one here now, even though there is a guard down there. We have an individual alarm system. We became very skittish after that incident. . . . They got out of there with a five-hundred-pound safe. They wheeled it out of the house and they stole my wheelbarrow from the garage and loaded the safe onto it.

Myrna comes into the room and changes the subject back to why they moved, gently reminding her husband what I had asked about. She likes to finish his sentences and move the conversation onward. Myrna explains:

Since you want to know about gated communities, we decided that maybe we would like to sell the house and get out of the responsibility of a house, as there was basically just the two of us. We took a look around, and even went to a realtor, and we decided that we would have to sacrifice our privacy to go to these gated communities, because of the sharing of the backyard and the attached units. We said this is not for us, we just can't give up the independence that we had. . . . so we dropped it.

"Remember," she turns to Bernie, "we looked for about a year or so, then we dropped it."

"It was not long after we found . . ." Bernie begins.

"The ad in the paper." Myrna says. "And Bernie said, 'Let's look at this.' You know, we liked the drawing, bad as it was. But you carried it around in your pocket for three months."

They are happy with their house; it serves their needs and accommodates visits from their grandchildren. Bernie describes the house.

We have three bedrooms, we have a large master bedroom, and two smaller ones, which up until about a year or so ago our grandchildren used very often. They lived only a mile from here. A boy and a girl, and they each had a room there, and even their toys and everything were here. We had the basement finished after we moved in . . . I had my desk, and a private business I ran for ten years, which I am now retired from. And so it provided a convenient three-story venue for recreation, entertainment, and sleeping.

They have not had any problems with the construction of the house, and are amazed when they go to meetings that other people are always complaining "about this or that or the other thing and I am saying to myself, I wonder what I have that I can complain about. I don't, so I won't."

Bernie attends homeowners association meetings but is not on the board.

The board has remained pretty well a fixed group of five people for several years now. We keep reelecting the same people, because they are very good, and the gal who heads it is a stickler for keeping the rules of the co-op going. She walks around this place maybe twice a day to check on broken things and on complaints of people and just to make sure that the roofs are not pulling apart. So she is on top of it [even] though she can be a little bit cantankerous. Nevertheless, she is a very efficient head of the board. So I am very pleased, we are both very pleased with it.

We think that we get a very good return for our monthly maintenance charge. The board itself maintains a surplus slush fund, and when it is necessary they will tack on a certain fee to our monthly charge to pay for an additional painting job or replacement-of-windows job or some other thing that suddenly came up, or whatever, and it is perfectly reasonable and makes sense.

Bernie and Myrna both reiterate that the maintenance of the house is the big plus for them, and really the reason that they left their south shore home for a gated townhouse community.

Maintenance, not having to worry about the exterior of the house, was a big plus because [in their previous home] we always had problems with something on the outside, I mean the shrubbery, or the lawn, or the . . . bugs or some draft or the roof blowing off, or the gutters not draining the water away. All of that exterior stuff, I mean the hours of work and the worry taken away from us. Naturally, the interior we concern ourselves with, paint jobs, carpeting, flooring, whatever is necessary inside, we take care of ourselves.

Socially, the community is not as friendly as where they lived before. People are cordial but not very involved in one anothers' lives. Except for the families who live on either side of them, they do not see their neighbors.

But most of the time, people are usually passing each other in the night like two trains, you know, cars coming in and out, waving. Or at the meeting maybe we will see each other. Our friends that we made years back are still our social friends. Nobody in this development right now interacts with us day to day on a social basis. We are just very friendly, and everybody has their own lives and goes their own way.

They are also not sanguine about how effective the gate is for keeping the community safe.

You wonder when you look at a gate like that; we are exposed all around, we don't have electrified fences or barbed wire. And if anyone was really interested in doing any harm they could easily circumvent the gate. I am sure they could come in through the golf course, they could come in through the woods. And so that is why we have individual alarm systems. For sure a lot of the other people in the development also have alarm systems. But maybe it is a deterrent, and I am willing to pay my share of that aspect of it. I mean, there is the main gate: a person looking to do something certainly would not be able to get in here with a vehicle. So that stops that. So anything they want to do they would have to do with a knapsack.

I ask them if there is anything that they would change. Bernie tells me about a swimming pool that the community was considering, but they thought it would only add to the community's problems and increase their financial liability. There was also talk about building a clubhouse, but they also felt that was unnecessary. Bernie concludes, "But minimalism is what I like about this place. . . . If they had a card room we would not go to play cards. Or social dances or tea or whatever—we would not do that very often I am sure. So it is just fine the way it is. The families here are, most of them are working families, some are retired. And it seems to be a lot of rentals, too. For us it was perfect."

Ira Davis is retired as well. He is also uninterested the social and recreational aspects of gated communities. In fact, he is <u>delighted that there is so little socializing.</u> What he was looking for was a controlled environment with strict CC&Rs to retain the value of his house, and the convenience of a condominium or cooperative that would take care of the maintenance and repairs. His needs are similar to those of nonretirees except for the emphasis on not having to take care of his home and garden.

IRA—QUIET AND TRANQUILLITY FOR RETIREMENT

Ira is a semiretired salesman in his mid-sixties who works out of his basement on a part-time basis. Balding, tall, and a few pounds overweight, he seems content with his life. As a retiree, he enjoys going to the city, to the theater, and he attends baseball games. He has the lifestyle he wants.

His Pine Hills townhouse is spacious and clean, decorated with reproduction antique furniture. The white carpet in the sitting room even shows the lines where the vacuum cleaner had recently gone over it. His wife remains upstairs doing some cleaning, and even though I ask her to join us, she declines, and Ira makes no effort to include her.

They are the original owners of this unit, which they purchased thirteen years ago. For the previous forty years they had lived in an expensive single-family house that they decided to cash in.

> We were looking around for co-ops and condos. . . . This was one of the largest places we saw, space-wise. And a terrific layout, and of course it was less expensive than what we were coming from. So I could put some money in the bank at the same time. That's why we bought it.
>
> It was a gated community, but there was no one at the gatehouse full time then. There was only someone there in the daytime, and restricted access at night. They can come right over the fence from the golf course. The security is that no one can come in with a car, because of having to go through the gatehouse. Anyone by foot could come over the fence from the golf course.

Ira and his wife like their house because it is very spacious for two people, and they know the local area. It also has limited amenities.

Yeah, we are happy, because . . . it doesn't have a pool, which we did not want. It does not have tennis courts, which we did not want. So it is strictly living. There are no recreational facilities.

We are pretty private people, and as I said, we don't socialize with anybody in the development at all. Even the next-door neighbors, because they are much younger, they are the age of my kids, so we can't socialize with them. Except once in a while [they] have a barbecue in the backyard. That's about it. So we get along with everybody.

There's a lot of people with children. It runs the gamut. There's a lot of rentals also. I would say about twenty units that get rented. And the renters don't stay that long, which is a problem because renters don't really keep up a neighborhood. But they are pretty strict, and the place is well run.

The head of the board of directors is very, very conscientious, and really watches the whole place as if it was her own house. So that's why everything is pretty neat and nice and so on. And there are rules, which people break. Stupid things like don't put the garbage out in a plastic bag, put it in a can. And there are no pets allowed, except for people who had pets before the rule was passed. The board of a co-op is unilateral. It can decide whatever it wants.

We moved from the house to a co-op/condo because I didn't want to pick up a piece of paper anymore, I didn't want to mow the lawn anymore, I didn't want to be responsible for anything anymore. And I'm not. That, plus the fact that the house price had risen so high. Of course, had I stayed there, in my house, it would have been worth a million dollars now [laughs]. But you never know.

I ask if their townhouse has gone up in value. Ira answers, "Not a great deal. What happened was, from the time we bought it dipped, and it came back about two years ago. So now if we sold we could make a profit. And we could sell; this particular unit is very desirable. We could sell this one, one-two-three. The layout, it's very popular. They sell one-two-three when someone puts one up for sale."

I ask if his wife feels the same about the place. He replies, "Yeah. We like it very much here. It's very private, very quiet, which is very nice, because I sleep with the window open. And we don't mind the kids. The grandchildren come and visit and play ball in the grass. We don't care. It's not my grass. It doesn't belong to me, it belongs to everybody, it's a co-op. And it's maintained."

But after telling me how great it is at Pine Hills, Ira says that they had been considering moving to the city.

> Well, there are no problems here, [but] we would like to move to the city. We looked at two-bedroom apartments in the city, to rent first, to spend a couple of years renting, to look to buy. And renting is $3,500 a month. Well, forget it. I pay $800 here, including taxes. So I'm not going to go to—I can't afford to go to the city.
>
> That's the whole thing. I mean, being retired I'm now basically on a fixed income. I'm not going to take most of my income to pay rent, when it would be the equivalent of one floor of this place. I got a two-car garage, I got a full basement, a total of four stories, two porches. Can't beat it.
>
> Instead, we drive to the city. Because you can park on the street on the weekend, below Twenty-third Street. We find a parking space, then we walk to the theater. We go to the city at least once a week. We take advantage of all of that. And some people out here don't go anywhere. They are so provincial it's ridiculous. And I am active in a folk music society in Huntington. I play the guitar, and I do my folk music and all that stuff. Life is nice, it's very good.

I ask Ira if they plan to stay there. He says,

> We are going to stay here, unless . . . my son just rented a house in lower Westchester County, about an hour from here by car. If we could find a place up near there, or inland from the coast in Connecticut a little bit, and we could come out with some money after we sold this place so that we could help him buy a house, then we might move. Otherwise . . . there's nothing, you know, you can't find any place around for under five or six hundred thousand. It's ridiculous, it really is. So we'll stay here, for the foreseeable future. Until we find we can't walk up and down the stairs anymore, but I think we have a ways to go.

Ira and his wife touch upon additional aspects of being retired, such as maintaining one's class identity in the later stages of life. After working for a lifetime, and having a particular income as status marker, some retirees like Ira find it difficult to scale down their living to accommodate their fixed income. Instead, Ira used his social affiliations, cultural activities, and friendships as strategies for identifying who he is.

For example, it was very important when they moved to Pine Hills that there was no socializing, and no pool, tennis club, or clubhouse. If they had had young children, Ira says, they would have considered moving to somewhere that had those amenities. Ira's explanation is that he and wife are educated, professional people, and at this stage of life they didn't want to end up living in a community where they would be drawn in to socializing with people they would not necessarily choose to mix with.

His concern about maintaining his social status is reinforced by his lengthy discussion of the value of his previous house, and his emphasis on the fact that they were trading down to Pine Hills in order to free up some cash. Perhaps, in this sense, he thinks of himself as socially "above" the other residents? Certainly, he was keen to avoid socializing with those who might be athletes or crane operators who also live there. It also casts his remark about the provinciality of some other residents in a different light. He stressed that he and his wife have no friends in this community. All their friends are outside, and he prefers it that way. Similarly, he has no desire to talk to somebody who, say, was a fantastic gardener and had made a lot of money and moved to Pine Hills. He doesn't want to end up being drawn in to socializing with people just because of propinquity. In this way, Ira and his wife distinguish themselves from the other residents and maintain their previous self-image and social standing.

Of course, for other residents at Pine Hills, the gates and guard indicate relatively high social standing to begin with. Attached townhouses that cost between $300,000 and $600,000 are expensive, even in the Nassau County housing market. The high prices are indicative of the affluence of the surrounding area, the golf club that abuts the community, the limited number of available condominiums and co-operatives in the region, and the amenity of the secured entrance.

Retirement is a complex stage of life, and gated communities have been popular with the over-fifty-five residents since the early 1960s. Retirees are particularly vulnerable to fluctuations in home values and services because most are living on fixed incomes—even these moderately well-to-do retirees. Retirees also worry about their physical safety and security and view the gates as a way to protect themselves. Like my grandparents in the Westminister mobile home park, they are sensitive to changes in the surrounding neighborhood. And with baby-boomers entering their retirement years,[6] the demand for gated communities will consequently grow. Retirees' uneasiness with neighborhood changes, and their desire for security and a controlled, well-kept environment, are not unique, though. Indeed, these are the basic inducements for all gated community residents, regardless of age.

CHAPTER 11

Don't Fence Me In

Anna, Alexandra, and I are packing to spend a long weekend at a dude ranch in Bandera, Texas. We pile extra pillows, blankets, snacks, Alex's disc player and my writing notebook in the back of the Saab. After whizzing along a seventy-mile-per-hour highway singing to Madonna, we climb into "hill country," the homeland of cowboys and endless dusty horse trails, juniper trees, and cedar fever. Bluebonnets dot crude swales cut along the roads. I read out loud from a guide-book—entertaining Anna and boring Alex—about how the end of a tectonic plate creates the irregular copses of oak trees, stony hillsides, and layers of sedimentary rocks perfect for fossil hunting.

Alexandra looks just like her mother, with her long-legged jeans, cowboy boots, and dark hair pulled back in a hair band. Now as tall as I am, she still can act like a kid, and as soon as we arrive she runs off to find her friends while we bring the bags and bedding into the rustic cabin and survey the room. The walls are yellow pine, bare and utili-tarian; a small table and chairs next to the window, miniature refriger-ator in one corner, and two double beds complete the furnishings.

"I want the one farthest from the door," I say, putting my jacket and duffle bag on the bed.

"You always get the best bed," Anna complains, testing the one by the door.

"Only because I'm older and deserve respect." I jump on her bed so hard the boards under the mattress buckle. "Also, I am faster," I tease. "Race you to the car."

Once the car is unpacked, I look for Alex and find her playing pool with her friends.

"Let's go for a walk," I say. Alex resists, saying she would rather stay with her friends.

"We can look for fossils," I entreat.

Alexandra follows me out the door, and then tugs at my hand as we walk down the dirt path at the edge of the ranch.

"Will you interview me again?" she asks. "I wanna be interviewed again." Thinking that this might be a good way to spend time with her, we find a bench overlooking a pasture cropped short by hungry cattle. I get out my notebook and wrap my coat around me to keep out early-spring chill.

"Okay, so do you want to tell me about your ideal home again?"

"Yes," she looks down at her blue nail polish and blurts out, "a little cottage on a hill, two stories with ivy on the outside. Only loved ones and friends nearby." She speaks in a rush without taking a breath, afraid I will stop her.

"Will there be a gate?"

"Only a small alarm and a guard dog. I want to be at least two miles from anything." She takes a breath. "Do you want to know more? When you walk into the room there's a small den with a large-screen TV and radio. On the right side of the bottom floor there'll be a kitchen, and bathroom with a fountain sink." She goes on to describe the house. "Upstairs is a kid's room, a dining room, and a flat TV on top of the bed for my husband and me—oh, and a dressing room. We'll share the dressing room. The only thing we can hear is the birds."

"So how far away is everything?"

"The grocery store is two miles away, and school is three miles away."

"And what will you be doing?" I ask.

"Writing a book about a neo-Nazi girl, and my husband will be a doctor and tennis player like my father wants. We're both very busy and don't see each other a lot, but it's quality time spent sitting by the fire sipping wine or at a nearby restaurant." At least she has gotten away from higher walls and security guards. Now she just wants open space between her home and town.

She adds a few details. "Birds will be rare, and maybe extinct. The ozone layer will be in worse shape, and you won't be able to drink milk, as the cows are all sick." What a grim view of the future she has. Where does it come from? Her parents, school, television? Again I wonder about the impact of media attention to global warming. I guess that is one way to encourage the younger generation to become environmentally concerned. But at what price? I wonder about the consequences of this new fear—not gates but a decontamination zone.

She fidgets and stands up. "Let's go," she says, pulling me up from the bench. "We will be late for dinner."

"Dinner isn't for another hour," I say as I stand and begin to walk back to the main house.

The road cuts through an ancient gorge lined with sedimentary rocks. I slow down, looking to see if there are any exposed fossils.

Alex laughs. "You're crazy," she says. "You have to dig to find fossils. You should know that, you're the archaeologist!"

I smile, happy that she has fallen into my trap. "Let's see what we find," I say, and scramble up the escarpment to where the layers of rock are more distinct.

"You need a digging tool," Alex says, and goes looking for a stick. I pick at the soft stone, and it crumbles in my hand. I do not see any fossils, just layers of soil topped by scraggly juniper bushes struggling to survive in dry, ferrous soil.

Alex returns with a pointed twig from a cottonwood, and begins to scrape at the face of the cliff. The afternoon wind blows the dirt in every direction, coating us with fine red dust. Her mother is going to be furious, I think to myself, and we are both going to have to shower again before dinner. Alex works happily, humming softly to herself.

"We're looking for the past, uncovering our ancestors," I say, partly to myself.

"Don't be silly," she says. "We're just looking for fossils that were in the ocean. They weren't our ancestors. We came from the apes." She holds up her first find, a scarab-shaped lump of dirt with fine lines defining a small sea creature. "A fossil," she says, triumphant.

"A fossil," I agree. "You found the first one. Congratulations."

Later, Alexandra regales her mother with the story of her find: her expert twig sharpening, her strategic choice of digging location, and dexterity at excavating the fossil all in one piece. She is proud of her work, and her earlier disappointment of having to leave her friends has faded away in the face of her newest achievement.

The next morning is spent horseback riding and hiking scenic trails. In the afternoon, Alex joins a nature walk, and Anna and I decide to make a soda run to town. Anna takes a deep breath as we gaze through the windshield at the open landscape.

"Isn't it lovely," she sighs. "I love being out here where it is still wild and free." She reaches into her purse for a cigarette, then, remembering that she stopped smoking years ago, turns to me. "And wait until you see town. There are bars for two-stepping on Saturday night and a cool coffee shop." Ten miles later we walk into the local Safeway and buy a six-pack of diet Dr. Pepper for a caffeine fix, and diet A&W root beer for Alex. Anna takes a long sip.

"I feel better already," she says. "Let's walk around town."

Bandera is exactly as I imagined it—a scenic frontier crossroads with wooden shotgun houses fronted by flat facades and small two-story buildings constructed of hand-cut sandstone boulders. Shops featuring western wear and Native American jewelry line the streets. It is so amazing how cowboy style permeates U.S. culture, I note to myself. Silver belt buckles, Tony Lama boots, and Wrangler jeans that protect cowhands on long rides become symbols of the wild, wild west in the city. Urban badlands are conquered with clothing.

Anna and I decide to go shopping. She is quickly bored, concerned about Alex and getting back in time for dinner. I, on the other hand, buy a snap-button shirt, two Brighton cowboy belts, and Ariat mules that I will never wear riding. Anna watches in amazement, wondering what I am going to do with all these clothes back in New York, but I reassure her that I frequent the Wild Rose, a roadhouse where western wear is in. She finally hauls me back into the car and returns to the ranch.

Dinner is an informal affair signaled by the clanging of a cowbell. Long tables with red-and-white-checkered tablecloths and folding chairs line the wood-paneled hall. Jean-clad visitors serve themselves chicken-fried steak, mashed potatoes, cornbread, and butter. Children run everywhere as their parents beg them to sit down and eat. Wranglers, distinguished by their saddle swagger and rakishly tied handkerchiefs, fill their plates to overflowing, and the children calm down with the appearance of an ice cream bar replete with hot choco-late and caramel sauce.

After dinner, Alex joins the other kids at the pool table. Anna and I sit with the German owners of the ranch, who insist we stay to hear the local entertainer they have scheduled. We are too embarrassed to leave, though the rest of the guests flow onto the porch to watch the flaming red and orange sunset fade into inky darkness. The remain-ing group sits around the fireplace waiting as the cowboy, "Makin' Dust," begins his show.

"Is there anyone here not from Texas?" My sister pokes me. I raise my hand. "And where are you from?" He whistles as I answer. The crowd laughs. "You are a long way from home," he quips and picks up his guitar.

He begins by teaching us the response to the song "Don't Fence Me In." Anna and I exchange a desperate look. I wiggle in my chair. I hate to sing in public, and she knows it. Anna looks straight ahead at the cowboy, trying not to show how she feels. Embarrassed, I suspect, and maybe sorry that she got us into this.

"Oh, give me land, lots of land, under starry skies above," sings Makin' Dust.

"Don't fence me in," I sing haltingly. My sister watches me.

"Let me ride through the wide open country that I love."

"Don't fence me in," she joins me.

Anna and I look at each other, smiling, as we sing about evening breezes under cottonwood trees and nights spent alone under the stars.

"Last verse," Makin' shouts. "C'mon, make it good."

I glance at Anna. "Can you stand it?" I ask. She nods her head. We raise our voices above the other guests, laugh and then pretend to be cowboys losing our senses by looking at hovels and fences.

"All together now," Makin' cries.

"Don't fence me in," I sing, my eyes brimming with tears for no apparent reason.

"No. Poppa, don't you fence me in."

Looking at Anna, I wonder if she hears the irony in those words. In the metaphors of wild open spaces and secure corrals are tracings of our relationship. We yearn for both, to resolve the conflict between the two images—one of freedom and the other of security, but each of us has selected a different life, one that questions the other.

I think we have come to some kind of resolution. For us the threat is internal, produced by our past. Inarticulate longings to be close and to heal old wounds bring us together, time and time again. But the external threats of crime and violence, kidnapping and strangers, that worry Anna also reflect internal fears.

As we sing, I understand the contradiction of Anna's love of the open Texas landscape and her equally powerful desire to protect her child and provide a safe and secure home for her family. In this sense, Anna is like other residents of gated communities struggling with conflicting desires. The gates represent a compromise, even a defense, between the way things are and the way they would like them to be. Gated communities are an attempt to recapture an ideal world in the face of contemporary realities.

What is my resolution of this contradiction? I also want to feel safe and secure, but insist on traveling all over the globe, searching for answers to my questions. Is the gated community that provides security for some inside of me? A gating that I cannot see, one built from being an academic? I don't know, but Anna is my mirror image, and as I begin to understand her, I will understand myself.

BRINGING IT ALL TOGETHER

Every time I sit down to read the newspaper, it seems there is an article about gating and its consequences. News stories as disparate as a federal lawsuit charging racial exclusion in a gated park in New York City, the fencing off of open space in Southampton, the deterioration of downtown areas and rapid growth of gated communities in Las Vegas, and the development of "fake" gated communities in California, all highlight the societal implications and negative repercussions of gating.

Gramercy Park—Gating and Exclusion

Gramercy Park is an East Side Manhattan neighborhood named for a two-acre private park located in a nineteenth-century square. The original homeowners bought the land collectively with deeded rights to the park now accessible only to bordering property owners. Wrought-iron gates and an ornate fence protect this idyllic English garden with gravel walkways, parterre planting beds, and shade trees and restrict its use to the key-carrying residents and others invited to use the park at specific times of day. It is one of only a few locked and gated parks in New York City.

Over the years there have been numerous disputes about park rules, maintenance, and governance. More recently, a group of children, parents, teachers, and one of the property owners contend that the park's administrative body tried to bar invited schoolchildren because of their race.[1] Two groups of minority schoolchildren were ordered to leave by the chairwoman of the Gramercy Park Trust, a property-owners association that manages the collectively owned park. The suit alleges that teachers and students heard her say, "The park is not for these kind [*sic*] of kids,"[2] and is part of an ongoing dispute between a disgruntled property owner and the Gramercy Park Trust.

Whether or not the chairwoman's motivation was racial bias, the incident is symptomatic of problems that arise with gating. Perceived exclusion—whether because of race, gender, class, or activity—is as socially significant as the physical barrier. In the public domain, exclusionary practices are illegal, regardless of whether the issue is access to public space like a park or beach or access to housing. In the realm of private communities and private parks, these rules do not apply. That is why so many gated communities in the news are char-

acterized as exclusive, fortresslike, racist, or elitist. In a heterogeneous, democratic society ostensibly struggling to eliminate inequality, symbols of exclusion carry inordinate emotional and political
weight.

Another consequence of gating that emerges in the Gramercy Park
debate is the problem of collective ownership, and in particular disagreements about the use and care of the collectively owned property.
This aspect of gating exists whenever there is restrictive deeding or
covenants that control how a place is governed and is not necessarily
related to fences or gates. It doesn't matter whether it's the Gramercy
Park Trust or a homeowners association; disagreements arise that rup-
ture the fragile bonds that hold a community together. Not all gated
communities have experienced such divisiveness, but conflicts could
erupt at any time.

Southampton, New York—Limited Access and Social Segregation

"Keep-out! When Gorgeous Open Space in the Hamptons Is So
Expensive They Fence It Off" reads the headline.[3] Southampton, New
York, a historic town on the eastern end of Long Island, has been a
beach resort for families from New York City since before railroads
and automobiles. Like Newport, Rhode Island, and the Gold Coast of
Long Island, wealthy families took horse and buggies to the town to
enjoy the cool weather and ocean breezes at the shore. East Hampton,
further east, became an artists' colony, where cheap rentals available
in the "Springs" created a mecca for experimental modern architecture and abstract expressionism. For generations, "summer people"
and "locals" lived side by side, with the understanding that when
summer was over the summer people would leave.

During the winter, local children went "tubing" on inflated tires
tied behind pickups pulled through the snow on the streets of the private Georgica Association. Fishermen drove on the beach to Georgica
Pond, and hunters stalked pheasants on private cornfields. After the
bull market of the late 1980s and early 1990s, however, fields and
farmlands turned into housing developments. Fences now enclose
once open fields, and guards driving black Jeep Cherokees patrol the

grounds of large estates that were once protected by only white wooden gates.[4]

In response, land preservation became a high priority, and a 2 percent real estate transfer tax was voted on and approved in 1999. The tax money is being used to purchase land and development rights on private land and to create conservation easements.

Conservation easements and the purchase of development rights, however, do not confer public access. An easement simply excludes certain activities from happening on private land. So public money being spent to conserve land may not in fact increase residents' access. And if the local government does not negotiate access at acquisition, the property, although preserved, remains privately owned. Thus, concludes Simms's article, the Hamptons are becoming one big gated community; there are no formal gates, but because of the restrictions on the use of land, and fences and guards, access is no longer possible.

The Hamptons situation represents a different kind of "gating" problem, deriving from the distinction between preservation of and access to public open space. For instance, fishermen are no longer welcome on Georgica Pond, where they have fished for generations. The owners of the surrounding houses have paid so much money for their homes that they feel entitled to their privacy.[5] In the summer, a guard is posted on the one entrance to the development that borders the pond, and as far as I know, no one is allowed through without proper clearance. Georgica Pond is public, but in name only. Access to it has become private, except for the small portion that borders the ocean beach.

Many gated communities function in a similar way. Because access to the community is restricted, public open space within the development cannot be used by nonresidents. Typically, such restrictions elicit negative publicity from local residents who live nearby. They feel that this form of "gating"—that is, restricted access—is a form of social and economic segregation. In the gated communities I studied, social and economic segregation, through the price of the housing, the CC&Rs, and location, is just as visible.

Las Vegas, Nevada—Loss of Community and Urban Deterioration

"Look at all those gated communities, those big beautiful houses where people don't know their neighbors and never talk to anyone," quips the mayor of Las Vegas, Nevada.[6] He presides over one of the fastest-growing metropolitan regions in the United States, yet is facing a deteriorated downtown, a diminished water supply, bad air, and choked traffic.[7]

Many new residents are early retirees who come to Las Vegas to get away from the congestion, pollution, and high cost of living in California. Others are young immigrant families who find jobs in the booming service and construction economy and can afford homes on the suburban fringe. What both groups want is an affordable home in one of the expanding gated suburbs of Las Vegas, or Henderson (an even faster-growing city, ten miles away, expected to have 560,000 inhabitants in ten years). There are so many new gated communities under construction in Henderson, developers have run out of evocative Spanish and Italian place names and have started to use names from California.[8]

One of the consequences of the increased development of gated communities is the loss of a liveable urban center. New residents are not attracted to the "squalid" downtown of Las Vegas, with its small-scale casinos and run-down infrastructure. The mayor wants to encourage a mix of services downtown, including cultural attractions and low-cost housing; without a dense, vibrant center, he thinks, "it is only inviting the kinds of urban ills that have plagued older cities."[9]

The astronomical growth of gated communities surrounding the deteriorating and underutilized city of Las Vegas is prophetic of the future. Abandoned cities will be encircled by suburban rings of gated residential communities, many of them privately controlled and governed by homeowners associations. Many critics agree with the mayor that these new suburbs are places where people don't know their neighbors or participate in community life. And the strained relationship of gated communities to the larger metropolitan region presages a host of other problems.

Newport Beach and Simi Valley, California—Faking Security and Exclusion

The article "Communities Say Keep Out—by Bluffing" reports on the latest trend in gated communities: faux fortresses, called "neighborhood entry identities," that offer all the visible signs of gating but no guards. Since functional gates come with problems, such as the maintenance of private streets and the hiring of internal police, management staff, and landscaping and trash services, these new residential developments are designed to look like a gated community but in fact are not. For many residents, the walls, unlocked gates, and guardhouse are enough to provide the sense of feeling special, exclusive, and secure. The unmanned guardhouse implies that it is a private community, but anyone is free to enter. These pseudo-gated communities provide the same housing and amenities without the additional costs, and eliminate fights with city officials and urban planners, who often oppose real gates. "Many who want to live in a modern-day fortress find the fake model just as good as the real thing."[10]

What is ironic, of course, is that for the fake to provide a sense of security and privacy, the real gated private communities must exist. The symbolic references to guardhouses, walls, and iron fencing evoke these associated meanings and are marketable because gating is so popular. The recent trend in California of building fake gated communities for the upper-middle and middle classes dramatizes the point that "gates" are about deeper psychological and social concerns. They do not reduce crime or keep "others" out, but offer the illusion of physical safety and security, an illusion that does not require the "hardware" of guards and real locks. The illusion is important for homeowners because it enables them to feel better about their social status and place in the world in a period of social and economic transition. This evolution of fake gating from the "real" thing substantiates how profoundly gating permeates American culture, replacing and reconstructing notions of "community" "security" and "the American dream."

Futurists argue that the concept of "community" changed with the advent of the Internet and the World Wide Web. Chat rooms replaced neighborhoods, workplaces, and town centers as locations to meet friends and form new relationships.[11] Civic engagement and social connectedness also declined over the last thirty years; Americans are now less trustful and more isolated.[12] Gated communities are not the cause or even indirectly the result of these societal changes, but they amplify these tendencies, further reducing the possibilities of social interaction between people, and the symbiosis between city and suburb.

Gated communities—in California, as well as in San Antonio, and Long Island—participate in this transformation by redefining the meaning of "community" to include protective physical boundaries that determine who is inside and who is outside. In the 1940s and 1950s, "community" referred to groups of people defined geographically, by where they live and work. But during the 1960s and 1970s, these place-based definitions broke down as social groups—associations, ethnic or religious affiliations, race, and gender—increasingly became the basis of social and cultural identification and urban neighborhoods became more heterogeneous. A location-based definition, one that includes walls and gates, but also the desire for the social homogeneity of an earlier era, is reemerging.

Gated community residents are interested in "community," but a specific kind of community that includes protecting children and keeping out crime and others while at the same time controlling the environment and the quality of services. The "community" they are searching for is one imagined from childhood or some idealized past. In a variety of ways, these residents are all searching for their version of the perfect community, one where there is no fear, no crime, no kidnapping, no "other" people, where there is a reassuringly consistent architectural and physical landscape, amenities and services that work, and great neighbors who want exactly the same things.

Gated community residents use gates to create the community they are searching for. But their personal housing decisions have had unintended societal consequences. Most important, they are disruptive of other people's ability to experience "community": community in the sense of an integration of the suburb and the city, community in terms of access to public open space, and community within the American tradition of racial and ethnic integration and social justice.

Architecture and the layout of towns and suburbs provide con-crete, anchoring points of people's everyday life. These anchoring points reinforce our ideas about society at large. Gated communities and the social segregation and exclusion they materially represent make sense of and even rationalize problems Americans have with race, class, and gender inequality and social discrimination. The gated community contributes to a geography of social relations that produces fear and anxiety simply by locating a person's home and place identity in a secured enclave, gated, guarded, and locked.[13]

One of the striking features of the world today is that large num-bers of people feel increasingly insecure. Whether attributed to glob-alization and economic restructuring, or the breakdown of the tradi-tional insitutions of social control, it has become imperative that governments and neighborhoods respond.[14] The threat of terrorism in the United States following the attack on the World Trade Center deepened Americans' fears. Yet to date the only solutions offered are increased policing in the public sector, and walling and gating, sur-veillance technologies, and armed guards in the private. These are inadequate solutions for what is actually a complex set of issues rang-ing from profound concerns about one's continued existence and emotional stability to everyday problems with economic survival and maintaining a particular way of life. Gated community residents then, like many Americans, are also searching for security.

The reasons people give for their decision to move to a gated com-munity vary widely, and the closer you get to the person and his or her individual psychology, the more complex the answer. At a socie-tal level, people say they move because of their fear of crime and oth-ers. They move to secure a neighborhood that is stable and a home that will retain its resale value. They move in order to have control of their environment and of the environment of those who live nearby. Residents in rapidly growing areas want to live in a private commu-nity for the services. And retirees particularly want the low mainte-nance and lack of responsibility that come with living in a private condominium development.

At a personal level, though, residents are searching for the sense of security and safety that they associate with their childhood. When

THESIS

they talk about their concern with "others," they are splitting—socially and psychologically—the good and bad aspects of (and good and bad people in) American society. The gates are used symbolically to ward off many of life's unknowns, including unemployment, loss of loved ones, and downward mobility. Of course, gates cannot deliver all that is promised, but they are one attempt to resurrect aspects of the American dream that many people feel they have lost.

My sister and her family are visiting us as I complete this book. Anna complains about the length of time it takes her to drive out of her gated community in the morning to take Alexandra to high school. Dust, ditches, and a never-ending string of angry drivers snake slowly past the main artery outside their gate. All other available routes also detour around impassable gates and feed onto this single road that is limited to two lanes by endless construction projects. She has to wait for a stranger to wave and let her into the line of traffic.

"The irony is that we are trapped behind our own gates," Anna says, "unable to exit. Instead of keeping people out, we have shut ourselves in."

Methods

Field methods included participant observation within and around each community, open-ended interviews with residents, interviews with key informants such as the developers, architects, and real estate agents of the subdivisions, behavioral mapping, and the collection of marketing, sales, and advertising documents. An interview guide was developed to elicit residents' decision-making processes concerning their move to the gated community.[1] The research team collected field notes and interviews in the New York area and Mexico City,[2] while I worked alone in San Antonio. The interviews lasted one to three hours, depending on whether the interviewer was taken on a tour of the house. We did not ask to be taken on a tour, but many times interviewees offered, and we used the tour to learn more about the person's tastes, interests, and preferences.

It was difficult to obtain entry into these communities and to contact residents. A sales manager in the upper-income gated community on Long Island helped by contacting two residents she thought would be willing to speak with us. We then used introductions either from the sales manager or from other interviewees to complete the interviews. In the second Long Island community, a real estate agent helped us meet respondents. In Queens, San Antonio, and Mexico City a local resident provided entrée; those residents referred others, and we met interviewees strolling on the roadways or on jogging paths on the weekends.

PARTICIPANT OBSERVATION

Participant observation included talking with people while they were exercising or walking their dogs, attending homeowners association and club meetings, and participating in neighborhood celebrations. I lived in two gated communities—one in San Antonio and one in Los Angeles—for various periods of time, usually during summer or winter break, throughout the eight years. These fieldwork visits allowed me to attend social events and engage in more informal discussions at the clubhouse, on the walkways, or at the swimming pool or tennis club. In Mexico City, the interviewer lived nearby and was able collect ethnographic data on Mexican class structure and social values. Considerable time was also spent in the local commercial areas— shopping, going to restaurants, and visiting real estate agents—providing other contexts for learning about everyday life.

OPEN-ENDED INTERVIEWS

Open-ended, unstructured interviews were conducted in the home with the wife, husband, or husband and wife together, and in one case the oldest daughter, over an eight-year period from 1994 to 2002. Only three single women—one widowed, one divorced, and one never married—were interviewed.

In the United States the majority of the interviewees were white, European Americans, and native born; however, there was some cultural diversity in the households: one interviewee and one spouse identified as Hispanic and were born in Latin America, one interviewee was born in Southeast Asia, one interviewee was born in Africa and identified as black, and one interviewee's spouse was born in the Middle East and grew up in Europe. Interviewees were twenty-seven through eighty years old; all the men were either professionals such as doctors or lawyers, businessmen, or retired from these same pursuits; the three single, widowed, and divorced women worked in clerical or social service jobs. In the majority of families, however, the wives remained at home, while the husbands commuted to work.

In Mexico City all residents were born in Mexico City except for two, who were from small towns four to five hours away. The Mexican interviewees were nineteen through sixty-seven years of age.

A total of fifty in-depth interviews from eighteen men and thirty-two women were collected in these households to supplement the participation observation data: twenty-five in the New York area (thirteen in an upper-middle- to middle-class community, seven in a middle-class townhouse community, and five in a middle-class and working class condominium apartment community); thirteen in San Antonio (ten in the upper-middle- to middle-class community, two in a middle-class community, and one in an upper-class community); and twelve in an upper-middle- to middle-class community in Mexico City. Interviews focused on the upper-middle- to middle-class gated communities where the majority of gated community residents live.

CONTENT ANALYSIS

The ethnographic analysis of participant observation field notes focused on identifying empirical evidence of changes in the local environment. Further, it produced data on casual conversations and everyday observations that naturally occurred and provided a test of ecological validity for data collected through the interviews. Field notes were coded by the themes that emerged during the research process.

A thematic content analysis of the interviews and documents collected from the media, marketing, and sales materials provided both a qualitative and quantitative understanding of the range of discourse available. The interviews were coded based on themes identified in the interviews and in the ethnographic fieldwork. The list of themes provided a qualitative presentation of the data. Depending on the number and specificity of the themes, they were consolidated to allow for a quantitative (ranking, numbering, calculation of percentages) of the expression of those themes.

CRITICAL DISCOURSE ANALYSIS

A critical discourse analysis identified residents' concerns. All the interviews were transcribed in full. Next, I read through the interview transcripts and systematically noted all instances in which concerns were discussed or alluded to. This process produced the body of the data set. In the final stage, I identified different strategies used to talk about living in a gated community. The details of the linguistic constructions with their immediate functions produced an outline of the structure of the conversation. The goal was not to quantify the occurrence of particular themes or rhetorical strategies, but, more important, to illustrate their situated effects.[3]

For example, Colette Daiute uses five strategies to interrogate a narrative: (1) as reporting an event; (2) as evaluating the event; (3) as constructing the meaning of the event; (4) as a critique of the event; and (5) as socially positioning the speaker.[4] I have found her method helpful in identifying otherwise unarticulated discursive goals of the interviewees. One illustration is Cynthia, who reports that there were more than forty-eight robberies in her neighborhood in Queens last year. She then evaluates those robberies by pointing out that they were of homes with security and dogs, but not gated. She then uses the logic of these two statements to construct the meaning of her move to a gated community. Finally, she critiques her own understanding—"so I'm saying to myself, all this in my mind, and I'm saying. . . . I can get robbed"—and positions herself with people inside the gated community (the smart ones) rather than with those living outside (those who are vulnerable to robberies).

The use of ethnographic, content, and discourse analyses produced an extensive as well as intensive textual analysis and interpretation of the interviews and field notes. The conclusions presented in this book are based on a synthesis of the analyses discussed and my own observations and reflections, as well as on insights emerging from data that are currently being collected and transcribed.[5]

Residential History Interview Schedule

Introduction

1. Establish rapport.

2. Brief statement of introduction of the interviewer.

3. Explanation of interview—to understand what life is like in the community.

4. Explain confidentiality issues—establish code name, guarantee confidentiality.

5. Request permission to tape interview; explain significance of taping for research purposes; offer to provide a transcript of the interview.

6. Present informed consent form; explain and have signed before continuing.

Residential History

Questions are only a guide to an open-ended conversation.

1. How long have you been living here at [community name]? (Probe for differences in move-in date and purchase date.)

2. Who lives in the house? What are ages, sex, and occupations of all household members including those not present at the interview? If there are children: How old are your children, grandchildren? Tell me a bit about them.

3. What line of work are you [and your husband, wife] in? (Probe to have a sense of the kind of occupation and amount of time spent working. Identify if the household member works at home or in an office. Locate the office.)

4. Where did you live before moving here? (Probe where they were born and the number of moves to get a general idea of the pattern and then work backward, asking each question for each move):
   - Where did you live prior to moving here?
   - How long did you live there?
   - What was it like living there?
   - Can you describe the house? The neighborhood? The region?
   - Why did you move? (Possible probes: Why did you leave the house, neighborhood, and/or region?)
   - How does your current residence compare to where you lived before?
   - How does your current neighborhood/community compare to where you lived before? (Probe: Can you describe community life before and now in your new home?)
   - Is there anything you particularly liked or disliked about your old community?
   - Is there anything you particularly like or dislike about your present community?

5. Who lives here in this community?

6. How many of the neighbors do you know? Do you visit them? Do they visit you? How often?

7. How is the new community similar or different from your former community? (Probe: Do you see your gated development as more of a community than the one you lived in before?)

8. What do you know about the design and development of your community?

9. What concerns did you discuss with the person who built the house? (Probe: Or who sold you the lot and/or house?)

10. Did the designer have a local or national reputation?

11. Did you look at other similar places before moving here? (Probe: Where did you look?)

12. Why did you choose this community rather than the other places that you looked at? Had you lived in a gated community before? Did you specifically set out to live in a gated community or did you find gated communities as you looked for a new home?

13. How does where you live now compare to the rest of the city/suburbs? (Probe their knowledge of the surrounding area and city, such as who lives there. Do you have friends there? Do you visit that part of town often?)

14. Do you have friends in your gated community? Why did they move to your development? [Probe for reasons given for different friends.]

15. Imagine that you might move again. Why would you move? What would you look for in your house and community?

16. What is a typical day here in your new residence? (Probe: Get as detailed a description as possible and use probe questions as issues emerge. Use probes such as: Why is that? How so? What do you mean? Could you tell me a little more?)

15. Tour of the house, if offered.

Notes

Prologue

1. Davis 1990.
2. A computer game that allows the players to create simulated houses, neighborhoods, and cities.

Chapter 1

1. Hayden 2003.
2. Atlas 1999.
3. Frantz 2000–2001.
4. Barnett 1986.
5. John Van Sickle, professor of classics at Brooklyn College, kindly explained the importance of walls in ancient Rome. This paragraph is based on his personal communication on this subject. Also, Zucker 1959 (46) discusses the *castrum* but emphasizes the grid plan of the form as I do in Low 2000.
6. Barnett 1986.
7. Saalman 1968.
8. Mumford 1961.
9. Ibid.
10. Turner 1999; Lis and Soly 1979; L. Wilson, personal communication.
11. King 1990; Anthony King, personal communication.
12. Hayden 2003.
13. Beito et. al. 2002.

14. Blakely and Synder 1997; Fischler 1998; Guterson 1992; Donahue 1993, Hannigan 1998.

15. Gary McDonogh, personal communication.

16. Dillon 1994, Fischler 1998, Benson 1998.

17. Sanchez and Lang, 2002. My sincere thanks to Haya El Massar who alerted me to the release of these figures and to Robert Lang and Tom Sanchez for allowing me to use their census note for this book.

18. Sanchez and Lang, 2002, based on their text and Table 2. On the top 10 metropolitan regions.

19. Blakely and Synder 1997 for original estimate and Sanchez and Lang 2002 for census totals.

20. Carvalho, George, and Anthony 1997; Dixon and Reicher 1997; Jaillet 1999; Paquot 2000; Caldeira 2000; Frantz 2000–2001; Connell 1999; Burke 2001; Wehrheim 2001; Lentz and Lindner 2002; Glasze and Alkhayyal 2002; Janoschka 2002; Landman 2002; Jürgens 2002; Stoyanov 2002; Wehrhahn, 2002; Kuppinger 2002; Dixon et. al. 2002; Webster 2002; Giroir 2002; Webster, Glasze, and Frantz 2002;Waldrop 2002; also see Cabrales Barajas 2002 for the recent Latin American work.

21. McKenzie 2002; Judd 2002.

22. Low 1997; Harvey 1990; Smith 1984.

23. Phillips 1991, Mollenkopf and Castells 1991.

24. Devine 1996, 1996; Foucault 1975; Schlosser 1998; Susser 1996.

25. Davis 1990, 1992

26. Foucault 1984; Merry 2001; Foucault 1978.

27. Low 2001.

28. Massey and Denton 1988; Bullard and Lee 1994; Denton 1994; South and Crowder 1997; Skogan 1995 (66).

29. Fine 1990, 2000.

30. Merry 1993 (87).

31. Langdon 1994; Jackson 1985; Skogan 1995; Sibley 1995; Angotti 1997; Baxandall and Ewan 2000; Kenny 2000 (6–7).

32. Judd 1995 (155).

33. McKenzie 1994.

34. Bourdieu 1984; Duncan and Duncan 1997; Flusty 2000.

35. McKenzie 1994.

36. Judd 1995 (160).

37. Ross, Smith, and Pritt 1996; Angotti 1997.

38. Webster 2001 (160).

39. McKenzie 1998, 2002.

40. Marcuse 1997.

41. Sennett 1970; Frug 1999 (120); Flusty 1997.

42. Newman 1993, Ortner 1998.

43. Flusty 1997; Stone 1996; Colvard 1997; Brennan and Zelinka 1997.

44. Jacobs 1961; Newman 1972, 1980; Crowe 1991; Atlas 1999.

45. Blakely and Synder 1997. Their work was based on a survey of Community Association Institute (CAI) member associations (19 percent of the responses were from gated communities) and interviews with residents and key informants such as real estate developers and public officials as well as citizens' groups and national associations. Focus group sessions and interviews with residents were conducted in six metropolitan areas with high concentrations of gating, including the San Francisco Bay Area, Los Angeles, Riverside–Palm Springs, and Orange County, California; Dallas, Texas; and Miami, Florida.

46. Blakely and Synder 1997, esp. chapters 2, 3, 4, 5.

47. Blakely and Synder 1997. These categories and associated social values were based on extensive questionnaires and focus group discussions, and became blurred when I was able to spend more time in each community. The gated communities discussed in this book encompass elements of each, including the golf course and fitness club amenities of lifestyle communities, the house style, prestige, and location of elite communities, and the guarded and patrolled aspects of the security zones, and do not conform to these ideal types. Sanchez and Lang 2002, however, also confirm that there is a demographic division between status (white affluent homeowners) and security (minority renter communities.

48. The Phoenix, Arizona study found half of the developments consist of fewer than 100 housing units, 19.3 percent with guarded gates, and 11. 9 percent retirement communities. Frantz 2000–2001 (113).

49. Blakely and Synder 1997 cover this issue; also see Le Goix 2002 for a geographic survey of variations in the maintenance of house value in the southern California region.

50. Wilson-Doenges 2000 discusses the cases of four communities in Orange County and Los Angeles discussed in chapter 3.

51. Wilson-Doenges 2000; Atlas 1999; Frazier 2002; Le Goix 2002.

52. This book is an experiment in the scholarly use of creative nonfiction techniques. I employ the first person to narrate the entire book, reporting incidents and conversations from my point of view. Quotations from interviews reflect what the interviewee said, reported as accurately as possible, based on transcriptions of tape-recorded interviews. Some quotes are taken from field notes and in a few cases from my memory of a particular occasion. Vignettes (personal stories and recountings of interviews) are set off from the main text by a different typeface.

Chapter 2

1. These estates would become incorporated villages, with populations as small as fifty people, to allow the wealthy estate owners to control their own

taxes and decisions about land use. Baxandall and Ewen 2000 suggest that these "private" villages are the beginning of a land use pattern that would lead to exclusive suburbs, and, I would argue, gated communities.

2. Like most towns on Long Island, there is a zoning review board that controls development in the village and the township.

3. Frantz 2000–2001.

4. Ibid.

5. Ibid.

6. Ibid.

7. Sanjek, 1998; Gregory 1998.

8. Brozan 2001.

9. McCall 2000.

10. Plöger 2002a & b.

11. Kirby 2001 personal communication.

12. From a series of interviews by Jörg Plöger completed in 2001.

13. These prices are for 1995–96. In 2001 it was reported by Jörg Plöger that a house sold for as high as $1.8 million.

14. MacCormack 2000.

15. Budd 1996; Graham 1999.

16. Muller 1996.

17. Firestone 2001.

18. Ibid. (A16).

19. Wolfe 1999.

CHAPTER 3

1. Paddison 2001.

2. Wilson-Doenges 2000.

3. Markoff 2000.

4. Marshall 2000 (193).

5. Archer 1996.

6. Tessler and Reyes 1999, p. A1.

7. Blakely and Synder 1997 (29).

8. Wilson-Doenges 2000.

9. This is their term to describe themselves, not mine.

10. Perin 1977.

11. Ibid. (125–17).

12. Sennett 1977.

13. Ibid. (301).

14. Myers and Bridges 1995.

15. Wilson-Doenges 2000, Blakely and Snyder, Lang and Danielson 1997.

CHAPTER 4

1. Ladd 1977; Riley 1979, Chawla 1992.
2. Marcus 1976, 1992, 1997.
3. Jorgensen and Stedman 2001.
4. Altman and Low 1992; Low 1992, Dixon and Burrheim 2000.
5. Marcus 1976, 1992, 1997.
6. Carvalho, George, and Anthony 1997.
7. Sheinberg and Fraenkel 2001.
8. Discussions about what should be done following the World Trade Center bombings illustrate how hard it is to find neutral ground between the conflicting goals of providing a sense of security for New Yorkers and avoiding measures that curtail individual freedom and expression.

CHAPTER 5

1. Owen 1998.
2. Ibid. Factor 1 (personal threat and injury) is the most prominent factor explaining the highest amount of variance (18.6) in these children's reported fears.
3. Owen 1998 defines low SES as children who qualify for the school's free lunch program.
4. Owen 1998 (491).
5. Glassner 1999 (61).
6. Ibid.
7. Williams, Singh, and Singh 1994.
8. Merry 1982.
9. News notes, *San Antonio Express-News*, August 6–25, 1990.
10. Pisano 1995.
11. Devine 1996.
12. Egan 2001a.
13. Colloff 1999; Baldauf 1999.
14. Durington 1999.
15. Durington 1999 (8).
16. Durington 1999.
17. William Cross suggested this idea when discussing this work.
18. Katz 1995, 2001.
19. Ibid.

CHAPTER 6

1. Sanjuán 2002.
2. Caldeira 1996; Carvalho, George, and Anthony 1997; Rotker 2002.

3. See Kalousek 2000 for a firsthand account of the "rape gate" that guards the entrance to the bedroom within the house.

4. Colvard 1997; Brennan and Zelinka 1997; Butterfield 2001.

5. *New York Times* 1997.

6. National Archive of Criminal Justice Data 1997.

7. Judd 1995; Stone 1996.

8. Glassner 1999, Williams and Dickinson 1993.

9. Heath and Gilbert 1996 (382–83) for a review of this literature.

10. Jackson 1985; Warner 1968.

11. Tuan 1979; Higley 1995; McKenzie 1994; Flusty 1997; Lofland 1998.

12. Farnham 1992.

13. See Adams and Serpe 2000 for extensive review.

14. Merry 1982; Anderson 1990; Bourgois 1995.

15. Skogan 1987; Roundtree 1998.

16. Roundtree 1998; Adams and Serpe 2000.

17. Roundtree 1998; Hagan 1992; Adams and Serpe 2000.

18. Hagan 1992 (137).

19. The poor section of San Antonio; also more dominated by Spanish-speaking populations.

20. There has been considerable debate concerning whether gating improves or maintains housing values in all settings. Although Atlas 1999 found that gates were effective in increasing house values in south Florida, the same results have not been found in parts of southern California and Texas.

21. Helsley and Strange 1999.

22. Adams and Serpe 2000.

23. Rotker 2002.

24. Caldeira 2000 (296). A study of closed condominiums in Alphaville, one of the world's largest gated communities, with 25,000 inhabitants, located outside of São Paulo, reports how the first suburban gated communities appeared in the 1970s as part of the middle- and upper-income exodus to outlying residential areas where lower-income people had been settling since the 1940s. Because there was no longer a physical separation of the social classes, gated and walled developments started to be built there as well. See Carvalho, George, and Anthony 1997.

25. Rivera-Bonilla 1999.

26. Sosa Elízaga 2002. Mexico is an extreme case of the Latin American pattern in which government abandons the well-being of the populace for its economic elites, instituting neoliberal policies such as financial deregulation and the privatization of governmental enterprises. The government has been more concerned with growth, lowering the national debt, and keeping inflation under control than with providing adequate social services. Further, the misappropriation of resources and other abuses of the system within the government and

embezzlement within the banking industry have reached an all-time high, yet there has been little to no prosecution.

27. Dillion 1998; Smith 1999.

28. Cabrales Barajas and Canosa Zamora 2001; Janoschka 2002b.

29. Thompson 2002.

CHAPTER 7

1. From Franz Kafka's story "The Great Wall of China," in which he asserts through the voice of a Chinese narrator that the real purpose of the wall was not to serve as protection from ravaging hordes but to give people a sense of unity in their separate and isolated villages.

2. See T. C. Boyle, *The Tortilla Curtain* (New York: Viking, 1995), 100–3.

3. Klein 1963; Silver 2002.

4. Burke 2001 (147).

5. Baumgartner 1988 (103).

6. Baumgartner 1988.

7. Sibley 1995 (86).

8. Sibley 1995.

9. Ngin 1993.

10. Ray, Halseth, and Johnson 1997.

11. This type of analysis is considered "discourse analysis" and is discussed in the methods appendix.

12. Billig 1997. Using research on intergroup contact and desegregation in the new South Africa I found that my interviews elicited narratives about maintaining, justifying or challenging racist (or elitist) practices. In South Africa, a number of "disclaiming statements" were elicited by asking respondents about their new black neighbors in a legalized squatter settlement. In the gated communities, I asked similar questions about "Mexican laborers" in San Antonio or "recent immigrants" in New York, which produced disclaiming statements as well as a better understanding of the social categories used by residents.

13. Modan 2000; also personal communication.

14. Kevin Birth also suggests that age may play a role in structuring these communities, especially the age of those who are feared. Personal communication.

CHAPTER 8

1. Baumgartner 1988, Fishman 1987.

2. Perkins and Taylor 1996; Taylor and Covington 1993.

3. Government by the nice 1992; Robinson 2002.

4. McKenzie 1995; Archer 1996.

5. Flusty 2000. The concept of "nice" is used in a variety of ways. For example, when describing how the beautification of neighborhoods in Los Angeles, California, entailed the eviction of established residential populations, a bystander interjected how similar efforts were under way in her hometown. She enthusiastically exclaimed that decaying neighborhoods were being made "nice, so nice people can move in."

6. Page 1998 (64–65).

7. Atlas 1999; Newman 1980.

8. McKenzie 1994; Judd 1995.

9. Ross, Smith, and Pritt 1996.

10. Ibid.

11. Higley 1995; Duncan and Duncan 1997.

12. Brodkin 2000; Fine 2000.

13. Kenny 2000; Bourdieu 1984.

14. Newman 1993; Zukin 1991.

CHAPTER 9

1. Tocqueville 1945 (1835), as quoted in Kennedy 1995.

2. See chapter 11 for a discussion of Gramercy Park. McKenzie 1994.

3. Howard 1902.

4. Blakely and Snyder 1997 (20).

5. Richard Briffault, vice-dean and Joseph P. Chamberlain, professor of legislation at Columbia Law School, personal communication. Briffault points out that "there is one very famous Supreme Court case from the 1950s, *Shelley* v. *Kraemer*, which held that judicial enforcement of racially restrictive covenants is unconstitutional state action. So, private covenants are not entirely sacrosanct. There are also a very tiny number of lower court cases applying constitutional norms to CC&Rs. One involved a federal district court in Florida that invalidated a covenant that banned flying the U.S. flag. (The Florida legislature subquently prohibited such covenants.)" For the complete story of the origin of restrictive covenants, see McKenzie 1994.

6. Nelson 1999a & b; (i); Kennedy 1995. Evan McKenzie puts this figure at one-eighth of all housing.

7. Webster 2001; Nelson 1999; Ellickson 1998.

8. Evan McKenzie, professor of political science, University of Illinois, Chicago, personal communication.

9. Nelson 1999a & b.

10. Richard Briffault points out in personal communication "that in some condo communities, the condo has by covenant the power to veto sales. In these situations, though, the condo may have to buy the property at a market price. In other words, they may be able to control entry into the community,

but they cannot place the financial burden on the owner." Also see McDowell 2002.

11. Romano 2002. Co-op boards are even considering rejecting prospective buyers if they are not U.S. citizens in light of fear of foreign terrorists after the World Trade Center attack, a new form of social exclusion that would not be possible in the condominium situation.

12. Baumgartner 1988 (10).

13. Ibid. (127).

14. Evan McKenzie in personal communication points out that the variation in kinds of suburbanites makes it difficult to make Baumgartner's claims for all residents. Lang and Danielson 1997 mention the quest for intermediary institutions.

15. Plöger 2002.

16. Ibid.

17. Ibid.

18. Ibid.

19. Webster 2001, 2002.

20. Beito, Gordon, and Tabarrok 2002; Foldvary 2002.

21. Webster 2002b.

22. Webster 2001.

23. Ibid. (163).

24. Ibid. (164).

25. Annexation is a process by which a town, county, or other governmental unit becomes part of the city, in this case the metropolitan region of San Antonio.

26. The second largest increase in revenue from annexation and population growth of Sunbelt cities with a population over 500,000.

27. Kantor 1995 (179).

28. Richard Briffault, personal communication.

29. Stark 1998.

30. Ibid.

31. Homeowner-Taxpayer Association (www.htasa.org) 2002.

32. The translation of this interview was completed by Lymari Benitez, a bilingual graduate student in environmental psychology born in Puerto Rico.

33. Nieves 2002; Mansnerus 2002.

34. McKenzie 1998.

35. At a conference held at the Institute of Geography at Johannes Gutenberg University in Mainz, I was able to talk with many of my European colleagues, who were surprised at how little attention was being paid to private governance in the United States by social scientists.

36. Briffault 1999.

37. McKenzie 1998.

CHAPTER 10

1. This kind of age discrimination has been challenged in California courts and may no longer be enforced.

2. Most Chinese and Asian traditional foods do not include dairy products.

3. Findlay 1992; Blakely and Snyder 1997.

4. Findlay 1992; Blakely and Snyder, 1997 (49–50).

5. From the point of view of a New Yorker, $80 per square foot is very reasonable. However, construction in Texas does not require the same kind of insulation and windows that are necessary in a region with cold winters. In Texas, $80 per square foot was considered expensive.

6. A point also made by Haya El Nasser of *USA Today*.

CHAPTER 11

1. Kleinfield 2001.

2. Ibid (B1).

3. Simms 2001 (19).

4. Ibid.

5. Ibid. One of the best-known celebrities who lives in the Georgica Association is Steven Spielberg.

6. Egan 2001b (A1).

7. According to the 2000 census reported in Egan 2001, Las Vegas is adding 70,000 people a year to a population of 1.4 million.

8. Egan 2001b (A13).

9. Ibid.

10. Halper 2002 (B14).

11. Markoff 2000, Low 1996.

12. Putnam 2000.

13. Massey 1994; Fine 2000; Martin and Talpade 1986.

14. Tulchin and Golding forthcoming.

APPENDIX 1

1. The residential history interview schedule is included in appendix 2.

2. Elena Danaila, Andrew Kirby, and Suzanne Scheld worked on this project in New York. Mariana Diaz-Wionczek and Lymari Benitez worked on the Mexico City part of the project.

3. Elder 1998; Low 2001; Wetherell and Potter 1992.

4. Daiute forthcoming; Fairclough 1995; Bertram, Hall, Fine, and Weir 2000.

5. In order to protect the identity of interviewees I have changed their names, physical descriptions, and where they live. I have not changed what was said or any relevant contextual details.

BIBLIOGRAPHY

Adams, Richard E., and Richard T. Serpe. 2000. Social integration, fear of crime, and life satisfaction. *Sociological Perspectives* 43(4): 605–27.

Altman, Irwin, and Setha Low. 1992. *Place attachment.* New York: Plenum.

Anderson, Elijah. 1990. *Streetwise: Race, class and change in an urban community.* Chicago: Chicago University Press.

Angotti, Thomas. 1997. A metropolis of enclaves: Image and reality in North America. *Urbana* 22: 13–24.

Archer, Matthew. 1996. Strategies of exclusion: Gated communities and the prefabrication of place. Paper presented at the American Anthropological Association. Chicago.

Atlas, Randy. 1999. Designing safe communities and neighborhood. Proceedings of the American Planning Association.

Baldauf, Scott. 1999. When heroin touches an entire town. *Christian Science Monitor.* October 5, 1.

Barnett, Jonathan. 1986. *The elusive city.* New York: Harper and Row.

Baumgartner, M. P. 1988. *The moral order of the suburb.* New York: Oxford University Press.

Baxandall, Roslyn, and Elizabeth Ewan. 2000. *Picture windows: How the suburbs happened.* New York: Basic Books.

Beito, David T. 2002. The private places of St. Louis: Urban infrastructure through private planning. In *The voluntary city: Choice, community, and civil society*, ed. D. T. Beito, P. Gordon, and A. Tabarrok, pp. 47–75. Ann Arbor: University of Michigan Press.

Beito, David T., Peter Gordon, and Alexander Tabarrok, eds. 2002. *The volun-tary city: Choice, community, and civil society*. Ann Arbor: University of Michigan Press.

Benson, Bruce. 1998. *To serve and protect*. New York: New York University Press.

Bertram, Corrine, Julia Hall, Michelle Fine, and Lois Weis. 2000. Where the girls (and women) are. *American Journal of Community Psychology* 28(2): 731–55.

Billig, Michael. 1997. The dialogic unconscious. *British Journal of Social Psychology* 36: 139–59.

Blakely, Edward J., and Mary Gail Snyder. 1997 *Fortress America: Gated com-munities in the United States*. Washington, D.C.: Brookings Institute.

Bogdan, Albert A. 1995. Reinventing urban neighborhoods: Making older urban neighborhoods more competitive with the modern suburbs. *Planning and Zoning News* 5: 5–12.

Bourdieu, Pierre. 1984. *Distinction*. London: Routledge and Kegan Paul.

Bourgois, Philippe. 1995. *In search of respect*. New York: Cambridge University Press.

Brennan, D., and A. Zelinka. 1997. Safe and sound. *Planning* (August): 4–10.

Briffault, Richard. 1999. A government for our time? Business improvement dis-tricts and urban governance. *Columbia Law Review* 99: 365–477.

Brodkin, Karen. 2000. *How Jews became white folks and what that says about race in America*. New Brunswick: Rutgers University Press.

Brozan, Nadine. 2001. Two-family homes to rise near hospital in Queens. *New York Times*, January 5, B8.

Budd, Kenneth. 1996. Gated communities: Do they really stop crime? *Common Ground* (September/October): 1–8.

Bullard, R., and C. Lee. 1994. Racism and American apartheid. In *Residential apartheid*, ed. R. D. Bullard, J. E. Grigsby III, and C. Lee, pp. 1–16. Los Angeles: Center of Afro-American Studies.

Burke, Matthew. 2001. The pedestrian behavior of residents in gated communi-ties. Paper presented at Walking the 21st Century. Perth, Western Australia, February 20–22.

Butterfield, Fox. 2001. Killings increase in many big cities. *New York Times*, December 21, A1.

Cabrales Baragas, Luis Felipe. 2002. Latinamérica: Paises abiertos, ciudades cer-radas. Coloquio. Guadalajara, Jalisco, Mexico, July 17–20.

Cabrales Baragas, Luis Felipe and Elia Canosa Zamora. 2001. Segregación resi-dencial y fragmentacíon urbana. *Espiral, Estudios sobre Estado y Sociedad* 7 (20): 223–53.

Caldeira, Teresa P. R. 1996. Fortified enclaves: The new urban segregation. *Public Culture* 8: 303–28.

———. 2000. *City of walls: Crime, segregation, and citizenship in São Paulo*. Berkeley: University of California Press.

Carvalho, M., R. V. George, and K. H. Anthony. 1997. Residential satisfaction in *condominios exclusivos* in Brazil. *Environment and Behavior* 29(6): 734–68.

Chawla, Louise. 1992. Childhood place attachments. In *Place attachment*, ed. I. Altman and Setha Low, pp. 63–86. New York: Plenum.

Colloff, Pamela. 1999. Teenage wasteland. *Texas Monthly* 27(1): 102–13.

Colvard, Karen. 1997. Crime is down? Don't confuse us with the facts. *HFG Review* 2(1): 19–26.

Connell, J. 1999. Beyond manilla: Walls, malls, and private spaces. *Environment and Planning A* 31: 417–39.

Crowe, Timothy. 1991. *Crime prevention through environmental design.* Stoneham, Mass.: Butterworth-Heinemann.

Daiute, Collette. Forthcoming. Individual's transformation of society. In *Narrative analysis*, ed. C. Daiute and C. Lightfoot. Thousand Oaks, Calif.: Sage.

Davis, Mike. 1990. *City of quartz: Excavating the future in Los Angeles.* London: Verso.

———. 1992. Fortress Los Angeles: The militarization of urban space. In *Variations on a theme park*, ed. M. Sorkin, pp. 154–80. New York: Noonday.

Denton, Nancy. 1994. Are African-Americans still hypersegregated? In *Residential apartheid*, ed. R. B. Bullard, J. E. Grigsby III, and C. Lee, pp. 49–81. Los Angeles: Center for Afro-American Studies.

Devine, John. 1996. *Maximum security.* Chicago: University of Chicago Press.

Dillon, David. 1994. Fortress America: More and more of us are living behind locked gates. *Planning.* June 60 (6): 8–13.

Dillion, Sam. 1998. Mexico can't fathom its rising crime. *New York Times*, June 28, iv: 1, 5.

Dixon, Jenny, Ann Dupuis, Penny Lysnar, and Clare Mouat. 2002. Body corporate: Prospects for private urban governance in New Zealand. Paper presented at the International Conference on Private Urban Governance. Institute of Geography, Johannes Gutenberg Universität, Mainz, June 5–9.

Dixon, J., and K. Durrheim. 2000. Displacing place-identity. *British Journal of Social Psychology* 39: 27–44.

Dixon, J. A., and S. Reicher. 1997. Intergroup contact and desegregation in the new South Africa. *British Journal of Social Psychology* 36: 361–81.

Donahue, Phil. 1993. Town builds fence to keep people out. Transcript of television show aired December 2.

Duncan, Nancy, and James Duncan. 1997. Deep suburban irony. In *Visions of Suburbia*, ed. R. Silverstone, pp. 161–79. London: Routledge.

Durington, Matthew. 1999. Unpredictable spaces: The discourses of drugs in suburban Dallas. Paper presented at the American Anthropology Association, Chicago.

Egan, Timothy. 2001a. Santee is latest to blow the myth of suburbia's safer schools. *New York Times*, March 9, A1.

———. 2001b. Las Vegas bet on growth but doesn't love payoff. *New York Times*, January 26, A1, A13.

Elder, Glen S. 1998. The South African body politic: Space, race, and heterosexuality. In *Places through the body*, ed. H. J. Nast and S. Pile, pp. 153–64. London: Routledge.

Ellickson, Robert C. 1998. New institutions for old neighborhoods. *Duke Law Journal* 48(1): 75–110.

Fairclough, N. 1995 *Critical discourse analysis*. London: Longman.

Farnham, Alan. 1992. U.S. suburbs are under siege. *Fortune*, December 28, 42–45.

Findlay, John M. 1992. *Magic lands: Western cityscapes and American culture after 1940*. Berkeley: University of California Press.

Fine, Michelle. 1990. "The public" in public schools: The social construction/constriction of moral communities. *Journal of Social Issues* 46(1): 107–19.

———. 2000. "Whiting out" social justice. In *Addressing cultural issues in organizations*, ed. R. T. Carter, pp. 35–50. Thousand Oaks, Calif.: Sage.

Firestone, David. 2001. 90's suburbs in West and South: Denser in one, sprawling in other. *New York Times*, April 17, A1.

Fischler, M S. 1998. Security the draw at gated communities. *New York Times*, August 16, 14LI: 6.

Fishman, Robert. 1987. *Bourgeois utopias: The rise and fall of suburbia*. New York: Basic Books.

Flusty, S. 1997. Building paranoia. In *Architecture of fear*, ed. N. Ellin, 47–60. New York: Princeton Architectural Press.

———. 2000. Banality of interdiction: Surveillance, control, and the displacement of diversity. *International Journal of Urban and Regional Planning* 25(3): 658–664.

Foldvary, Fred. 2002. Private governance as explicit contracts among legal equals. Paper presented at the International Conference on Private Urban Governance. Institute of Geography, Johannes Gutenberg Universität, Mainz, June 5–9.

Foucault, Michel. 1975 (1977). *Discipline and punish. The birth of the prison*. Trans. Alan Sheridan. New York: Random House.

———. 1978. Governmentality. *Aut Aut* 167–68. September–December. P. Pasquino, trans. and editor.

———. 1984. Des espaces autres. *Architecture, Movement, Continuité*. Octobre: 46–49.

Frantz, Klaus. 2000–2001. Gated communities in the USA: A new trend in urban development. *Espace, Populations, Societes* 101–13.

Frazier, Tom. 2002. Citadel of sovereignty: The territorial administration and defense of a private residential gated community. Paper presented at the International Conference on Private Urban Governance. Institute of Geography, Johannes Gutenberg Universität, Mainz, June 5–9.

Frug, Gerald E. C. 1999. *City making: Building communities without building walls.* Princeton, N. J.: Princeton University Press.

Giroir, Guillaume. 2002. The purple Jade Villas (Beijing): A golden ghetto in Red China. Paper presented at the International Conference on Private Urban Governance. Institute of Geography, Johannes Gutenberg Universität, Mainz, June 5–9.

Glassner, Barry. 1999. *The culture of fear.* New York: Basic Books.

Glasze, Georg, and Abdallah Alkhayyal. 2002. Gated housing estates in the Arab world: Case studies in Lebanon and Riyadh, Saudi Arabia. *Environment and Planning B: Planning and Design* 29: 321–36.

Government by the nice, for the nice. 1992. *Economist* 324(7769): 25–26.

Graham, Lee. 1999. Straddling the fence. *Dallas Morning News.* August 7, 1.

Gregory, Steve. 1998. *Black Corona.* Princeton, N. J.: Princeton University Press.

Guterson, D. 1992. No place like home. *Harper's Magazine*, November, 35–64.

Hagan, John. 1992. Class fortification against crime in Canada. *Canadian Review of Sociology and Anthropology* 29(2): 126–39.

Halper, Evan. 2002. Communities say keep out—by bluffing. *Los Angeles Times*, May 28, B1.

Hannigan, John. 1998. *Fantasy city.* New York: Routledge.

Harvey, David. 1990. *The condition of postmodernity.* New York: Blackwell.

Hayden, Dolores. 2003. Building American suburbia: Green fields and urban growth, 1820–2000. New York: Pantheon Books.

Heath, Linda, and Kevin Gilbert. 1996. Mass media and fear of crime. *American Behavioral Scientist* 39(4): 378–86.

Helsley, Robert W., and William C. Strange. 1999. Gated communities and the economic geography of crime. *Journal of Urban Economics* 46: 80–105.

Higley, S. R. 1995. *Privilege, power, and place.* London: Rowman and Littlefield.

Howard, Ebenezer. 1902. *Garden cities of tomorrow*, 2nd ed. London: S. Sonnenschein.

Jackson, Kenneth. T. 1985. *Crabgrass frontier.* Oxford: Oxford University Press.

Jaillet, Marie-Christine. 1999. Peut-on parler de sécession urbaine à propos des villes européenes? *Revue Esprit* 258: 145–67.

Jacobs, Jane. 1961. *The death and life of great American cities.* New York: Random House.

Janoschka, Michael. 2002a. Nordelta: A private new town in competition with local authorities. Paper presented at the International Conference on Private Urban Governance. Institute of Geography, Johannes Gutenberg Universität, Mainz, June 5–9.

———. 2002b. Latinoamérica: Paises abiertos, ciudades cerradas. Paper presented at Urbanizaciones Privadas in Buenos Aires. Hacia un nuevo modelo de la ciudad latinamericana? Guadalajara, Jalisco, July 17–20.

Jorgensen, B. S., and R. C. Stedman. 2001. Measuring sense of place: Lakeshore property owners' attitudes toward their properties. *Journal of Environmental Psychology* 21(3): 233–248.

Jorgensen, Paul E. 1995. Socioeconomic analysis of gated communities. M. S. thesis, University of Nevada, Reno.

Judd, Dennis. 1995. The rise of new walled cities. In *Spatial practices*, ed. H. Ligget and D. C. Perry, pp. 144–45. Thousand Oaks, Calif.: Sage.

———. 2002. Policy communities and the reconstruction of the local state. Paper presented at the International Conference on Private Urban Governance. Institute of Geography, Johannes Gutenberg Universität, Mainz, June 5–9.

Jürgens, Ulrich. 2002. Gated communities in the Johannesburg area: Experiences from South Africa. Paper presented at the International Conference on Private Urban Governance. Institute of Geography, Johannes Gutenberg Universität, Mainz, June 5–9.

Kalousek, Selma. 2000. In harm's way: I never wanted to admit how defenseless we were. Now I must. *New York Times Magazine*, December 31, 58.

Kantor, Paul. 1995. *The dependent city revisited: The political economy of urban development and social policy*. Boulder, Colo.: Westview.

Katz, Cindi. 1995. Power, space, and terror. Paper presented at Landscape Architecture, Social Ideology, and the Politics of Place Conference, Harvard University, March 17–18.

———. 2001. The state goes home: Local hypervigilance of children and the global retreat from social reproduction. *Social Justice* 28(3) 47–56.

Kennedy, David. 1995. Residential associations as state actors: Regulating the impact of gated communities on non-members. *Yale Law Journal* 105: 761–803.

Kenny, Lorraine Delia. 2000. *Daughters of suburbia*. New Brunswick, N.J.: Rutgers University Press.

King, Anthony. 1990. *Urbanism, colonialism, and the world economy*. New York: Routledge.

Klein, Melanie. 1975. On the sense of loneliness. In *Envy and Gratitude and Other Works, 1946–1963*, pp. 300–13. New York: Delta, 1975.

Kleinfield, N. R. 2001. Federal lawsuit charges racial exclusion at gated Gramercy Park. *New York Times*, January 18, B1, B13.

Kuppinger, Petra. 2002. Exclusive greenry: New gated communities in Cairo. Paper presented at the American Anthropological Association Annual Meeting, New Orleans, November 20–24.

Ladd, Florence. 1977. Residential history: You can go home again. *Landscape* 21(2): 15–20.

Landman, Karina. 2002. Gated communities: Building or barriers? Paper presented at the International Conference on Private Urban Governance. Institute of Geography, Johannes Gutenberg Universität, Mainz, June 5–9.

Lang, R. E., and K. A. Danielson. 1997. Gated communities in America. *Housing Policy Debate* 8(4): 867–99.

Langdon, Philip. 1994. *A better place to live*. Amherst: University of Massachuetts Press.

Le Goix, Renaud. 2002. Gated communities in southern California: Assessing the geographical aspects of urban secession. Paper presented at the International Conference on Private Urban Governance. Institute of Geography, Johannes Gutenberg Universität, Mainz, June 5–9.

Lentz, Sebastian, and Peter Lindner. 2002. Social differentiation and privatization of space in post-socialist Moscow. Paper presented at the International Conference on Private Urban Governance. Institute of Geography, Johannes Gutenberg Universität, Mainz, June 5–9.

Lis, Catherine, and Hogo Soly. 1979. *Poverty and capitalism in pre-industrial Europe*. New York: Humanities Press.

Lofland, Lynn. 1998. *The public realm*. New York: Aldine de Gruyter.

Low, Setha M. 1992. Symbolic ties that bind. In *Place attachment*, ed. I. Altman and S. Low, pp. 165–84. New York: Plenum.

———. 1996. A response to Castells: An anthropology of the city. *Critique of Anthropology* 16: 57–62.

———. 1997. Urban fear: Building fortress America. *City and Society* (Annual Review): 52–72.

———. 2000. *On the plaza: The politics of public space and culture*. Austin: University of Texas Press.

———. 2001. The edge and the center: Gated communities and the discourse of urban fear. *American Anthropologist* 103(1): 45–58.

MacCormack, John. 2000. District 6 faces its own great divide. *San Antonio Express-News*, May 22, 1–11.

Mansnerus, Laura. 2002. Lawsuit tests power of homeowner associations. *New York Times*, August 13, B1.

Marcuse, Peter. 1997. The enclave, the citadel, and the ghetto. *Urban Affairs Review* 33(2): 228–64.

Marcus, Clare Cooper. 1976. The house as symbol of self. In *Environmental Psychology*, ed. H. Proshansky, W. H. Ittelson, and L. G. Rivlin, pp. 435–448. New York: Holt, Rinehart, and Winston.

———. 1992. Environmental memories. In *Place attachment*, ed. I. Altman and S. Low, pp. 87–112. New York: Plenum.

———. 1997. *House as a mirror of self: Exploring the deeper meaning of home*. New York: Conari Press.

Markoff, John. 2000. A newer, lonelier crown emerges in Internet study. *New York Times*, February 16, A1, A13.

Marshall, Alex. 2000. *How cities work: Suburbs, sprawl, and the roads not taken*. Austin: University of Texas Press.

Martin, Biddy, and Chandra Talpade. 1986. Feminist politics: What's home got to do with it? In *Feminist studies/critical studies*, ed. T. de Lauretis, pp. 191–212. Bloomington: Indiana University Press.

Massey, Doreen. 1994. *Space, place, and gender.* Minneapolis: University of Minnesota Press.

Massey, D. S., and Nancy Denton. 1988. Suburbanization and segregation. *American Journal of Sociology* 94(3): 592–626.

McCall, C. 2000. *Queens: An economic review.* New York: Office of the State Deputy Comptroller.

McDowell, Edwin. 2002. At small cooperative, the name is apt. *New York Times,* July 21, (Long Island), 1, 4, 5.

McKenzie, Evan. 1994. *Privatopia.* New Haven, Conn.: Yale University Press.

———. 1998. Homeowner associations and California politics. *Urban Affairs Review* 34(1): 52–75.

———. 2002. Private residential governance in the U.S. Paper presented at the International Conference on Private Urban Governance. Institute of Geography, Johannes Gutenberg Universität, Mainz, June 5–9.

Merry, Sally. 1982. *Urban danger.* Philadelphia: Temple University Press.

———. 1993. Mending walls and building fences: Constructing the private neighborhood. *Journal of Legal Pluralism* 33: 71–90.

———. 2001. Spatial governmentality and the new urban social order: Controlling gender violence through law. *American Anthropologist* 103(1): 36–45.

Modan, Gabriella. 2000. The struggle for neighborhood identity. Discursive constructions of community and place in a U.S. multi-ethnic neighborhood. Ph.D. diss., Georgetown University, Washington, D.C.

Mollenkopf, John, and Manuel Castells. 1991. *The dual city.* New York: Russell Sage.

Muller, Peter O. 1996. The evolution of American suburbs: A geographical interpretation. In *Urbanization and the growth of cities,* ed. N. L. Shumsky, pp. 395–404. New York: Garland.

Mumford, Lewis. 1961. *The city in history.* New York: Harcourt, Brace, and World.

Myers, Joanne, and Suzanne Bridges. 1995. Public discourse: Property rights, public good, and NIMBY. In *Contested terrain: Power, politics, and participation in suburbia.* M. L. Silver and M. Melkonian, pp. 133–48. Westport, Conn.: Greenwood.

National Academy of Sciences. 1995. *Mexico's city water supply.* Washington, D.C.: National Academy of Sciences.

National Archive of Criminal Justice Data. 1997. *Crime statistics.* Ann Arbor: University of Michigan Press.

Nelson, Robert H. 1999a. Privatizing the neighborhood: A proposal to replace zoning with private collective property rights to existing neighborhoods. *George Mason Law Review* 7(4): 827–80.

———. 1999b. Zoning by private contract. In *The fall and rise of freedom of contract,* ed. E. H. Buckley, pp. 157–76. Durham, N.C.: Duke University Press.

Newman, Katherine S. 1993. *Declining fortunes: The withering of the American dream.* New York: Basic Books.

Newman, Oscar. 1972. *Defensible space.* New York: Macmillian.

———. 1980. *Community of interest.* Garden City, N.Y.: Anchor Press.

Ngin, ChorSwang. 1993. A new look at the old "race" language. *Explorations in Ethnic Studies* 16(1): 5–18.

New York Times. 1997. Portrait of crime. February 17, B4.

Nieves, Evelyn. 2002. A yellow house? Well, we can't have that. *New York Times,* Wednesday, July 24. A10

Ortner, Sherry. 1998. Generation X: Anthropology in a media-saturated world. *Cultural Anthropology* 13(3): 414–40.

Owen, Patricia R. 1998. Fears of Hispanic and Anglo children: Real-world fears in the 1990's. *Hispanic Journal of Behavioral Sciences* 20(4): 483–92.

Paddison, Ronan. 2001. Communities in the city. In *Handbook of Urban Studies.* ed. R. Paddison, pp. 184–205. London: Sage Publications.

Paquot, Thierry. 2000. Villes privées. *Urbanisme* (May/June) 312: 60–85.

Perin, Constance. 1977. *Everything in its place: Social order and land use in America.* Princeton, N.J.: Princeton University Press.

———. 1988. *Belonging in America: Reading between the lines.* Madison: University of Wisconsin Press.

Perkins, Douglas, and Ralph Taylor. 1996. Ecological assessments of community disorder. *American Journal of Community Psychology* 24(1): 63–107.

Phillips, Kevin. 1991. *The politics of rich and poor.* New York: HarperCollins.

Pisano, Marina. 1995. A wound not healed: Abduction anniversary painful for girl's parents. *San Antonio Express-News,* August 5, 11.

Plöger, Jörg. 2002a. Analysis of the causes that lead to a concentration of gated communities in North Hills. Rights to the city conference. Rome, May 29–June 1.

———. 2002b. Gated communities in North Hills. Diplomarbeit im Studiengang Diplom-Geographie. Universität Hamburg. Institut für Geographie.

Prohansky, H., A. K. Fabian, and R. Kaminoff. 1983. Place-identity: Physical world socialization of the self. *Journal of Environmental Psychology* 3: 57–83.

Putnam, Robert D. 2000. *Bowling alone: The collapse and revival of American community.* New York: Simon and Schuster.

Ray, Brian K., Greg Halseth, and Benjamin Johnson. 1997. The changing "face" of the suburbs. *International Journal of Urban and Regional Research* 21(1): 75–99.

Riley, Robert. 1979. Reflection on the landscapes of memory. *Landscape* 23: 11–18.

Rivera-Bonilla, Ivelisse. 1999. Building "community" through gating: The case of gated communities in San Juan. Paper presented at the American Anthropological Association annual meeting, Chicago, November 19.

Robinson, P. Stuart. 2002. The privatization and fortification of public space.

Paper presented at the International Conference on Private Urban Governance. Institute of Geography, Johannes Gutenberg Universität, Mainz, June 5–9.

Romano, Jay. 2002. Can a co-op exclude noncitizens? *New York Times*, Sunday, July 21, P1 RE. 5.

Ross, Mary Massaron, Larry J. Smith, and Robert D. Pritt. 1996. The zoning process: Private land-use controls and gated communities. *Urban Lawyer* 28(4): 801–7.

Rotker, Susana. 2002. *Citizens of fear: Urban violence in Latin America.* New Brunswick, N. J.: Rutgers University Press.

Roundtree, Pamela Wilcox. 1998. A reexamination of the crime-fear linkage. *Journal of Research in Crime and Delinquency* 35(3): 341–74.

Saalman, Howard. 1968. *Medieval cities.* New York: George Braziller.

Sanchez, Tom, and Robert L. Lang. 2002. Security versus status. The two worlds of gated communities. *Census Note* 02: 02. Alexandria, Va.: Metropolitan Institute at Virginia Tech.

Sanjek, Roger. 1998. *The future of us all.* Ithaca: Cornell University Press.

Sanjuán, Ana María. 2002. Democracy, citizenship, and violence in Venezuela. In *Citizens of fear.* ed. S. Rotker, pp. 87–101. New Brunswick N.J.: Rutgers University Press.

Schlosser, Eric. 1998. The prison-industrial complex. *Atlantic Monthly.* December, 51–77.

Schriffrin, Deborah. 1994. *Approaches to discourse analysis.* Cambridge, Mass.: Blackwell.

Sennett, Richard. 1970. *The uses of disorder.* Harmondsworth: Penguin.

———. 1977. *The fall of public man.* New York: Knopf.

Sheinberg, M., and P. Fraenkel. 2001. *The relational trauma of incest: A family-based approach to treatment.* New York: Guilford.

Sibley, D. 1995. *Geographies of exclusion.* London: Routledge.

Silver, Catherine. 2002. Construction et deconstruction des identités de genre. *Cahier du Genre* 31: 185–201. (Paris: Caisse National d'Assurance Vieillesse).

Simms, Susan. 2001. Keep out! When gorgeous open space in the Hamptons is so expensive they fence it off. *Dan's Paper.* January 26, 19–20.

Skogan, Wesley G. 1987. The impact of victimization of fear. *Crime and Delinquency* 33: 135–54.

———. 1995. Crime and the racial fears of white Americans. *Annals of the American Academy of Political and Social Science* 539(1): 59–72.

Smith, James F. 1999. Shootings renew focus on violent crime in Mexico. *New York Times*, August 20, A5.

Smith, Neil. 1984. *Uneven development.* Oxford: Basil Blackwell.

Sosa Elízaga, Raquel. 2002. Terror and violence in Mexican political culture at the end of the twentieth century. In *Citizens of fear,* ed. S. Rotker, pp. 72–86 New Brunswick, N. J.: Rutgers University Press.

South, S., and K. D. Crowder. 1997. Residential mobility between cities and suburbs: Race, suburbanization, and back-to-the-city moves. *Demography* 34(4): 525–38.

Sparks, Alister. 1990. *The mind of South Africa.* New York: Knopf.

Stark, Andrew. 1998. America, the gated? *Wilson Quarterly* 22(1): 58–80.

———. 1999. Arresting developments: When police power goes private. *American Prospect* 42: 1–14.

Stephenson, Neal. 2000. *Snow Crash.* New York: Bantam Doubleday Dell.

Stewart, Jill. 1996. The next Eden: The movement into gated communities is not about escape: It's about building neighborhoods. *California Lawyer* 16(11): 39–83.

Stone, C. 1996. Crime and the city. In *Breaking away: The future of cities*, pp. 98–103. New York: Twentieth Century Fund Press.

Stoyanov, Petar. 2002. Gated communities in Bulgaria: A new trend in the post-communist urban development. Paper presented at the International Conference on Private Urban Governance. Institute of Geography, Johannes Gutenberg Universität, Mainz, June 5–9.

Susser, Ida. 1996. The construction of poverty and homelessness in U.S. cities. *Annual Review of Anthropology*: 411–35.

Taylor, Ralph B., and Jeanette Covington. 1993. Community structural change and fear of crime. *Social Problems* 40(3): 374–95.

Tessler, Ray, and David Reyes. 1999. Gated communities are latest to seek city-hood. *Los Angeles Times*, January 25, p. IA.

Thompson, Ginger. 2002. Files bare dark secrets of Mexico's dirty war. *New York Times*, July 6.

Tocqueville, Alexis de. 1945. (1835). *Democracy in America.* New York: A. A. Knopf.

Tuan, Y. 1979. *Landscapes of fear.* New York: Pantheon.

Tulchin, Joseph S., and Heather A. Golding. forthcoming. Citizen security in global perspective. In *Crime and violence in Latin America.* ed. H. F. Ehrlich and Joseph S. Tulchin. Washington, D.C.: Woodrow Wilson Center.

Turner, E. S. 1999. Gilded drainpipes. *London Review of Books*, June 10, 31–32.

United States Department of Justice. 1995. *Uniform crime reports.* Washington, D.C.

Warner, Sam Bass. 1968. *The private city.* Philadelphia: University of Pennsylvania Press.

Waldrop, Anne. 2002. Fortification and class relations: The case of a New Delhi colony. Paper presented at the American Anthropological Association Annual Meeting, New Orleans, November 20–24.

Webster, Chris. 2001. Gated cities of tomorrow. *Town Planning Review* 72(2): 149–70.

———. 2002a. Private communities and China's dual land market. Paper presented at the International Conference on Private Urban Governance.

Institute of Geography, Johannes Gutenberg Universität, Mainz, June 5–9.
——. 2002b. Property rights and the public realm: Gates, green-belts, and gemeinshaft. *Environment and Planning B: Planning and Design* 29(3): 397–412.

Webster, Chris, Georg Glasze, and Klaus Frantz. 2002. Guest editorial. *Environment and Planning B: Planning and Design* 29: 315–20.

Wehrhahn, Rainer. 2002. Gated communities in Madrid: Origins and causes of the actual expression. Paper presented at the International Conference on Private Urban Governance. Institute of Geography, Johannes Gutenberg Universität, Mainz, June 5–9.

Wehrheim, Jan. 2001. Surveillance and spatial exclusion in German cities. Paper presented at the American Anthropological Association annual meeting, Washington D.C., November 28–December 2.

Weisman, Steven. 2002. Walls throughout history: Built for security but often victims of strategy. *New York Times*, May 28, A16.

Western, J. 1981. *Outcast Cape Town*. Minneapolis: University of Minnesota Press.

Wetherell, Margaret, and Jonathan Potter. 1992. *Mapping the language of racism*. New York: Columbia University Press.

Williams, Paul, and Julie Dickinson. 1993. Fear of crime: Read all about it? The relationship between newspaper crime reporting and fear of crime. *British Journal of Criminology* 33: 33–56.

Williams, Sherwood, B. Krishna Singh, and Betsy Singh. 1994. Urban youth, fear of crime, and resulting defensive actions. *Adolescence* 29(114): 323–31.

Wilson-Doenges, Georgeanna. 2000. An exploration of sense of community and fear of crime in gated communities. *Environment and Behavior* 32(5): 597–611.

Wolfe, Peter. 1999. *Hot towns*. New Brunswick, N. J.: Rutgers University Press.

Zucker, Paul. 1959. *Town and square: From agora to the village green*. Cambridge, Mass.: MIT Press.

Zukin, Sharon. 1991. *Landscapes of power*. Berkeley: University of California Press.

INDEX